Future of the
OLYMPIC GAMES

John A. Lucas, PhD
The Pennsylvania State University
University Park, PA

Human Kinetics Books
Champaign, Illinois

Library of Congress Cataloging-in-Publication Data

Lucas, John A. (John Apostal), 1927-
    Future of the Olympic Games / John A. Lucas.
      p.   cm.
    Includes index.
    ISBN 0-87322-357-8
    1. Olympics--Philosophy. 2. Olympics--Social aspects.   I. Title.
  GV721.6.L83   1992
   796.48--dc20   91-46818
                                           CIP

71776

ISBN: 0-87322-357-8

Developmental Editor: Mary E. Fowler
Assistant Editors: Elizabeth Bridgett and Julie Swadener
Copyeditor: Dianna M. Matlosz
Proofreader: Pam Johnson
Indexer: Theresa Schaeffer
Production Director: Ernie Noa
Art Director and Text Design: Keith Blomberg
Typesetter and Text Layout: Angela K. Snyder
Cover Design: Jack Davis
Cover Photo: Dave Black
Printer: Edwards

Printed in the United States of America

10 9 8 7 6 5 4 3 2 1

Human Kinetics Books
A Division of Human Kinetics Publishers, Inc.
Box 5076, Champaign, IL 61825-5076
1-800-747-4457

Canada Office:
Human Kinetics Publishers, Inc.
P.O. Box 2503, Windsor, ON N8Y 4S2
1-800-465-7301 (in Canada only)

Europe Office:
Human Kinetics Publishers (Europe) Ltd.
P.O. Box IW14
Leeds LS16 6TR
England
0532-781708

To J. Kenneth Doherty, PhD, athlete, Olympian, teacher—coach-mentor, and one of the kindest men in the world

To Those Amateurs who run

Primarily because

To run is

Natural,

Fun,

and Worthwhile

For its own sake;

Who honor the principle

That amateur sports must be

Avocational,

And act

Within the limitations of

Material reward

and

Time for preparation

Which it requires;

And yet,

Who,

Within those limitations,

Strive to their utmost

To run

Ever farther and faster,

And more enjoyably.

Ken Doherty

Note. From *Modern Training for Running* by J. Kenneth Doherty by permission. Copyright 1964 by Prentice Hall, Inc.

Contents

Foreword

As the Olympic centenary and the end of the 20th century approach, the Olympic Movement is enjoying enormous prestige and plays an essential role in the peaceful development of human society and education. However, the scale and importance of this prestige and social role create within our Movement and sport in general a certain vulnerability. Our supporters must protect Olympism against this by taking a stance with regard to the future of this philosophy of life and social phenomenon and by devoting serious study to the way they should like sport to develop. This is precisely what John Lucas has done in *The Future of the Olympic Games*.

The strength of this book lies in the fact that the author wrote it from several perspectives. First, John Lucas is an Olympic fan of unique experience; he has attended all the Olympic Summer Games since Rome in 1960 and was an official observer of the International Olympic Committee at the Games of the XXIV Olympiad in Seoul in 1988. Second, Lucas is recognized as one of the world's leading scholars of Olympic history, having written two books and many seriously researched articles on the subject. Third, Lucas has had a long and active association with both the United States Olympic Academy and the International Olympic Academy, helping to organize sessions and delivering a number of well-received lectures. Based on this substantial background and experience, together with his use of countless interviews with members of the International Olympic Committee, National Olympic Committees the world over, and international sport federations, as well as Olympic athletes themselves, Lucas offers his readers a unique insight into the anxieties of those responsible for addressing the major problems facing the Olympic Movement today and in the nearest future and for bringing about their satisfactory solution.

As John Lucas says, the future of the Olympic Games, as with all sports, depends on the purity of the various skills involved, plus the integrity of everyone involved in the enterprise.

The readers of this book will find a great deal of information on the Olympic Movement and its philosophy, Olympism. I am convinced it will help to promote the Olympic ideal and I hope sports enthusiasts throughout the world will enjoy it.

Juan Antonio Samaranch
Lausanne, November 1991

Preface

In the libraries of the world are hundreds of books on the history of the modern Olympic Games, but not a single text on the future of the world's largest peaceful gathering of humanity. Every discipline, whether medicine, metaphysics, engineering, or education, has divided into subdisciplines. History is no different, and specialists abound in this ancient scholarship.

Even within a subdiscipline, further focusing becomes necessary. In sport history, a small cadre of Olympic scholars has arisen. Only a few have written on contemporary Olympic history, and none have addressed the implications of today's political and sporting events on the future of the Olympic Games. In taking on this challenge, I'm not abandoning my role as historian; rather, because history is an unending continuum, I'm extending my historical concern for the past into the present and on to the remaining years of the 20th century—the future.

Futurism is not a science, and this is especially true when one projects more than a few years. It may be that historians are among the people better prepared to make cautious predictions and modest suggestions. I have done just that regarding the continuation of the undergirding Olympic philosophy, the century-old struggle against uncontrolled patriotism, and the crises of the Olympic program of sports, disciplines, and events. I have tried to speak insightfully to the "agony and ecstasy" that befall Olympic athletes.

The future is now, and so this book is about contemporary issues and challenges that call for solutions. It is a book for those inside the vast international Olympic family, and at the same time for those not connected with the Olympic Movement, but who, nevertheless, love this most exciting of all international athletic competitions and who see in them, as I do, the need to secure and share the overarching Olympic ideal of universal brotherhood and sisterhood through sport.

University scholars, sport historians around the world, and the 30,000 Olympic administrators in 168 nations will find this book helpful, because it provides factual information coupled with seriously formed ideas about where the gigantic Olympic engine seems to be headed. University students at the graduate level in sport science, history, political science, and international relations will find it of more than passing interest. The unorganized but devoted international audience of the Olympic Games will find the book challenging and instructive.

Chapters 1 and 2 outline the dual history and background of the modern Olympic Games, the symbiotic integration of ancient Greek athletics and Pierre de Coubertin's highly personalized view of humanity. The world has changed greatly since Coubertin, but the official Olympic Charter still retains the essence of his philosophy and dream. Chapter 3 shows how this dream continues to be a powerful force in promoting greater international goodwill.

Chapter 4 on nationalism is important because nationalism has been an integral component of all modern Olympic Games. Although there seems to have been a lessening of Olympic nationalism recently, the fires of excessive patriotism on the playing field can become supercharged. Chapters 5 and 6 deal with the key actors on the Olympic stage—the athletes—and remind us that the giant engines of both the Olympic Games and the Olympic Movement should work primarily for them.

Chapters 7 and 8 discuss Olympic money-making and how several billion dollars of income are spent. Chapter 9, Olympic Games Overkill, deals with possible dilemmas of the recent decision to hold the Games every 2 years instead of 4. *Citius, Altius, Fortius* and Drugs (chapter 10) are inextricably linked, for the Olympic motto means to strive for greater and greater speed, agility, and strength. For some, this suggests that any and all means are justified in the effort to win.

Success and mounting criticism seem to go hand in hand, and chapter 11 discusses some possible responses.

Chapter 12 addresses the contributions of women to the Games and the need for their larger representation in the future. Three-quarters of a century of discrimination by the Olympic "fathers" resulted in a radical disproportion of female athletes as competitors. Though redress began in the last decade of the 20th century, women in the Olympic Movement is a constant topic of discussion at the Olympics' highest level.

Chapters 15, 16, and 17 deal with the extraordinary breadth of projects and enterprises, almost unknown to the public, that consume the time and resources of Olympic leaders. The implications for the future of the Games, should any of these projects fail, are presented in these three chapters. The last chapter is an effort to sum up my concerns for the future of the Games, one of this century's most interesting public culture and sporting experiments.

These 18 chapters present an accurate picture of the problems facing Olympic Games organizers. Failing their solution, the Olympic Movement cannot survive into the 21st century. Its leaders are aware of this, and their frequent national and international meetings, independent of the quadrennial winter and summer Games, deal entirely with problem solving and future Games. In this book, I offer my own suggestions for modification and change, the result of input from more than 100 Olympic Games leaders, from scores of Olympic athletes, and from my reading of most of the pertinent literature.

This book is an effort to see the immediate future of the Olympic Games and of the larger, international sport structure—the Olympic Movement. Much of this future will be fortuitous; some will be downright dangerous. I have tried to outline both possibilities and, as a historian-turned-futurist, hope that these images and predictions will better inform and therefore better protect all participants—organizers *and* athletes.

The great French writer Emile Zola, in the introduction of his 1885 tragedy *Germinal*, wrote that "a work of art must have some fundamental human truth." I agree and add that a work of art—including a serious book—must have the capacity for individual spiritual enrichment, which is my primary reason for writing this book.

Acknowledgments

I'm deeply grateful to my colleagues at The Pennsylvania State University's College of Health and Human Development and its Department of Exercise and Sport Science; to Debbie Lalli and Louise McQuillan; to the Pattee Library staff in documents, interlibrary loan, periodicals, and microfilm departments; to President Samaranch and the International Olympic Committee members, especially the staff at the Château de Vidy; to Olympic House administrative and technical staff of the United States Olympic Committee; to close friends around the world who rendered invaluable assistance; to Dick Cecil and Clyde Partin in Atlanta, GA; and to Katie, Pam, Mark, and especially, Joyce.

C·H·A·P·T·E·R·1

Ancient Hellas and the Ether of Pierre de Coubertin

It was to religion that the athletics and Greek athletic festivals owed their vitality.

Edward Norman Gardiner, *historian*

The one constant of all historical research is revision, whereas the greatest inconstancy is the public's willingness to accept new interpretations of events. For example, "the truth" about the bombing of Pearl Harbor on 7 December 1941, has repeatedly been altered. Some historians claim that the American political and military leadership were completely surprised when Japanese planes bombed the harbor. Other historians, equally reputable, offer "proof" that the American leadership knew days and even weeks in advance of an imminent attack. In another case, initial media reports blamed the 1989 Alaskan Exxon oil spill tragedy on a single shipmaster, whom it labeled alcoholic. But by late 1990, investigators laid the blame on several individuals and at least three organizations.

Historical exactitude is probably not achievable. Just how the ancient Greeks, for example, thought and then behaved is difficult to determine. Historians of the late 18th and 19th centuries in Europe and North America, influenced by their Romantic Age, read the available literature on ancient Greece and made interpretations. So have late-20th-century experts on Hellenic culture and on the ancient Olympic Games, the other great Greek athletic festivals, and Hellenic physical training and competitions. But some of these later scholars, reading essentially the same body of factual data, come to different conclusions, finding earlier scholars' viewpoints unacceptable, unrealistic, and almost Pollyannaish. Both groups sought truth, but both visions are colored by the times and by the "ether" that all must breathe.

Baron Pierre de Coubertin (1863-1937), founder of the modern Olympic Games (begun in 1896), counted history as one of many areas of deep interest. He knew contemporary French history extremely well, had a good grasp of the sweep of European history, was an ardent dilettante (like so many well-educated Europeans) of world history, and was an earnest amateur historian of ancient Greek culture. He read much of the available 19th-century literature of professional historians' facts and interpretations of Hellenic life. To a large degree, Coubertin, affected by the prevailing values of his age, idealized ancient Greek culture and Greek athletes. His ideology infused every aspect of his new creation, the Olympic Games, including the confused and unscientific but prevailing attitude that all women were unsuited physiologically and psychologically for the stresses of elite international athletic competitions.

All of these factors—the older historians' views, the prevailing theories of contemporary historians, and Coubertin's view of the importance of athletic contests in ancient Greece—are germane to today's Olympic Games and have implications for the remaining 1990s, and probably beyond.

A Traditional View of the Ancient Olympic Games

The principle outcome of the four Greek festivals, especially the festival at Olympia, was the observance by all Greeks of their already ancient customs, especially the worship of their gods. For more than a thousand years, their delight in highly competitive athletics was inextricably bound to their living religion. Olympic athletes were motivated more by religious rapture than by secular or material motives. Love of their city-states, a lifelong narcissistic emphasis on developing a beautiful physical body, and a lust for money all motivated the best athletes, but less powerfully than did their consecration to the anthropomorphic national religion. During the second great Greek revival, 18th- and 19th-century scholars saw what they wished to see regarding life in ancient Hellas, including the life of the Olympic competitor. That life, seen through the filter of nearly 15 centuries, was frequently described in terms of honor, patriotism, altruism, noncommercial amateur motive, and above all fervent religious belief. Complex motives urged athlete and spectator to converge on the village of Elis and these ancient Olympic Games, but none were so universal as prayers to Zeus for protection and triumph.

Nineteenth-century historians who studied Hellenic culture, sport, and the Olympic Games were no less educated than today's specialists, but earlier scholars were influenced by a romanticism that espoused the natural goodness of humankind and produced an intellectual and popular literature emphasizing individualism, social democracy, hero worship, and "the romantic use of an imaginative or idealized past."[1] Frequently these attitudes were grafted onto historical analyses of the much earlier Greek civilization, which did not need them, for all acknowledged the greatness of much of that ancient society.

Historians and writers passionately believed that the foundation and sustaining ethos of the ancient Olympic Games were *la religion, la patrie, et l'art* (religion, country [i.e., city-state], and art), that, for the Greeks, these games were the embodiment of all that was noblest and fairest of their ideals and aspirations, a veritable consecration to their national religion.[2] These games, "the noble emulation of the Greeks," were performed, not just for the great gathering of spectators, but "as an act of worship, to honour and appease" the gods and their own departed heroes.[3]

The influence of these sage 19th-century classicists and their credible and mesmeric message continued into the early 20th century. Edward Norman Gardiner's 1925 *Olympia* talks about the glory of Greece, the magnetism of the religious celebration at sacred Olympia (although Gardiner was convinced that the athletic contests were secular in origin), and the kingly treatment accorded Olympic winners. His equally famous *Athletics of the Ancient World* is a classic hymn of praise for the so-called nonprofessional athlete, of antipathy for the ill-named professional, and of the purity of the Greek athletic ideal, observing that "it was to religion that Greek athletics and Greek athletic festivals owed their vitality."[4]

Historians ascribed many benefits to these ancient Greek games— increased commerce, intercommunication of ideas and sentiments within the Hellenic world, "racial unity and intensified . . . creative genius in the fields of art and intelligence."[5] Raymond Block applauded the domination of "religious sentiments,"[6] and the modern archaeologist-historian, Nicolaos Yalouris, a modern Greek with old-fashioned ideas, emphasized the insoluble link of worship to games. There was no festival or sanctuary in Greece, concluded Yalouris, "that did not link worship of the gods with the holding of the games."[7]

George A. Christopoulos, a contributor to Yalouris's book, believed that religion gave the Greek sporting ideal "an established position in the great panhellenic sanctuaries" and that the sacred nature of these games brought "a man into contact with the gods" in a very real way. Greek historians looking at their own heritage were convinced that religious worship by the athletes elevated these human competitions ''into the sphere of the gods and gave them dimensions of an ideal''—a religious ideal. For holding these ancient Olympic Games was ''not a commitment to athletics in a religious setting. It was a commitment to religion which had athletics as one of its most important modes of expression.''[8]

Coubertin's Vision and Ideology

To understand the ideological and philosophical beliefs that have sustained the Olympic movement for most of its 100-year history, we must try to grasp the mind-set of a visionary educator, Pierre de Coubertin. During the years 1890 to 1915, he was wholly responsible for the Olympic rules of eligibility, and his ''strict amateur code'' was eloquent and idealistic, though a less than historically correct amalgam of ancient Greek athletic philosophy and the so-called British cult of male muscular Christianity. His views persisted within the framework of the Olympic world through its first 75 years. Though his rules were modified in the 1970s (and changed radically in the 1980s and 1990s), the core of Coubertin's vision is still a part of Olympic ideology and will probably persist for many years.[9] He consistently wrote that high-minded international sport, especially his Olympic Games, could foster individual and collective goodwill, and even contribute to world peace. So frustrating was his habit of asking so very much of sport, an understandable sin in one steeped in romantic literature and constitutionally a visionary mystic,[10] that F.M. Messerli was convinced that Coubertin created the Games primarily to foster ''the courteous spirit of fair play thus avoiding the display of chauvinism.''[11] The words are from Messerli, the Olympic historiographer, but the spirit is Victorian and vintage Coubertin. Anyone in today's late 20th century who believes that this kind of thinking has been purged from the minds of people connected with the worldwide Olympic Movement is very much mistaken.

Dr. Juan Antonio Samaranch was president of the International Olympic Committee (IOC) through the 1980s into the 1990s. He was the *summum bonum* of Olympic business manager-politicians, the eternal diplomat, the disciplined workaholic. Yet, in his more pensive moments, Samaranch, too, was a Coubertin disciple, having told the world that ''our philosophy proceeds from the belief that sport is an inalienable part of the educational process and a factor for promoting peace, friendship, cooperation and understanding among peoples.''[12] In Coubertin's time the Olympic Games rationale was viewed through a romantic haze and, remarkably, 100 years later (in what seems to be a most unromantic era), the dream of Olympic fraternity, mutual respect among competitors, and balanced patriotism among the media, athletes, and spectators still exists.

The Olympics' Struggle to the Bimillennial Year

Probably the most widely read and persistent critic of the validity of the Greek origins of Olympic amateurism is the classicist David C. Young. He and several other scholars maintain that the British aristocracy of the 18th and 19th centuries—not the ancient Greeks—invented the concept of athletic amateurism, that they fabricated the moral superiority of the amateur over the professional, and that the phrase "amateur athlete" does not even exist in ancient Greek language.[13] Yet Young states without risk of contradicting himself, "I happen personally to support the Modern Olympic Movement without a qualm. I view it as one of the world's greatest institutions—potentially, perhaps, its greatest hope."[14] Said differently but with the same intent, the restrictive concept of "pure athletic amateurism" is infinitely less important than the possibility that Olympic athletes might not only break world records, they might contribute collectively to the uplifting of humanity and move us a little bit more in the direction of mutual trust, understanding, and peace. This is exactly what Coubertin meant by his often-used and poorly understood concept of "the Olympic idea." During his long adult life, he was never enthusiastic about insisting that every Olympic athlete be a "simon-pure" amateur. That passion was left to those who succeeded him in the 1920s and 1930s.

Throughout the 100-year history of the modern Olympic Games, the institution has been in jeopardy, attacked by ignorance, avarice, threats of violence, and violence itself. So, too, have all larger societies, all civilizations, for fifty times the life of these Games. Rumors of the demise of either are exaggerated. The Coubertin legacy—the Olympic legacy of honor and international fraternity, of fair play in the midst of athletic struggle—is wounded, but not dead. There are forces at work pumping a healing elixir into the Olympic circulatory system, and the most important of these is the integral honor of the overwhelming majority of athletes from 168 participating nations. The Olympic Charter begins with a prayer for peace, an affirmation of fair play always, and a warning against blinding nationalism. International Fair Play societies, the philosophical Pierre de Coubertin Society, and the quietly persistent efforts of the United Nations and the United Nations Educational, Scientific, and Cultural Organization (UNESCO) continue to foster what prominent medical doctor and historian Ernst Jokl called "the strongest remaining link between man and nature."[15] Over the past 30 years, the International Olympic Academy (IOA) and 54 national Olympic academies have graduated 15,000 young men and women, all of them educated in Coubertinian ethics, all of them familiar with the very much more difficult challenge of teaching athletes to be fierce and clever, to shed no blood, to strive unremittingly for excellence, and to never cheat. All Olympic committees and all international sport federations have codes of conduct and cardinal points of civility. Olympic judges and athletes must, in full public view, pledge allegiance to disinterestedness and sportsmanship. There is hope, but much more needs to be done for the double legacy of these modern Olympic Games—Coubertin's blend of the pure, controlled passion of the ancient Greek athlete and the French-English medieval code of chivalry—to live on.

The Olympic legacy, sometimes called *Olympism* (a Coubertin coinage), remains ambivalent in these last years of this century, in the same way that courtesy, on and off the athletic field, has been found wanting. But it can be reclaimed, cry voices from Czechoslovakia, France, the United States, Germany, and Switzerland. Four-time gold medal winner Emil Zatopek of Czechoslovakia insisted that the high-principled Olympic code of sportsmanship is more important than the gold: "The world cannot live only from technology, commerce and politics." Olympic historian Jean-François Brisson noted that fair play and the Olympic Games could somehow exist independently of one another, but only precariously. He wrote, "Il faut sauver l'olympisme avec les Jeux, par les jeux (To save Olympism, we must have Olympic Games)." Gold or failure are not the only two options open to us, said America's most successful cross-country skier, Bill Koch, a silver medalist in 1976. Honor and "striving for your own excellence" are more important. German intellectual Ommo Grupe believed that ideally "sport differentiates men [and women] according to their achievements but unites them at the same time in spite of different religions, ideology and origin." After half a century in the Olympic business, IOC emeritus member from Switzerland, Raymond Gafner, reminded readers that 90% of all IOC money is spent on the athletes and, therefore, "serves humanity."[16]

The future of the Olympic Games (and all sport, professional and nonprofessional) depends on the excellence of execution of the skills required—both administrative and athletic—and the integrity of everyone involved. When excellence and integrity run high, the Games can surmount racism, presenting a new effort at bridging the gap between peoples of diverse backgrounds and interests. Music, dance, and art can do the same. Almost everyone in the world can understand what David Young called "that quest for distinction through excellence"[17] (and it was not confined to ancient Greeks alone); thus the universal interest in and importance of art and sport. "Sport requires constant care and attention to keep it from dishonor and corruption," observed Coubertin at the Closing Ceremony of the first Winter Olympic Games in Chamonix, France, in February 1924.[18] He could just as well have included all human institutions. The Olympic Games of the 1990s and beyond will falter if they are not monitored by wise, noble, and pragmatic leaders. The sacred and aesthetic must somehow mingle with the technological and human.

The Olympic Games will be 100 years old in 1996, and preparations for the Summer Games of 2000 are receiving global attention. Both are like black holes in sporting history, where "any occurrence, activity, or idea which reaches the perimeter . . . will then be drawn into the maelstrom of meanings that it finally comprises."[19] Symbolically, that summer's Olympic Games will take on a special burden, a unique role in the history of the Olympic Movement, for they will be even more so under the universal microscope and thus will presage the success or failure of the Movement to a greater degree than have any other Olympic Games.

Those who honor Pierre de Coubertin, not as the perfect person, but as the main architect of an inspirational idea—a world sport festival called by its ancient name, the Olympic Games—must see both the man and the Games as imperfect, and because we can do nothing about the former, we must consecrate our energies to improving the latter. The Olympic Games of the future, if they are organized expertly in every way, have the capacity to "become the symbolic expression of the common culture of [all] peoples."[20] Almost nothing in the world that emanates from human hands is common to all peoples everywhere. The visible and invisible Olympic Games, like some soothing, uplifting ether, might some day fill this role, if only in the most modest way.

The world Olympic bureaucracy is enormous. More than 165 nations, 40-plus international sport federations, and 95 IOC members from all 6 continents belong to the "family Tripartite." Some members, with little provocation, will invoke the name Pierre de Coubertin when discussing the subtle and overt differences between the Olympic Games and an athletic world championship. Among the top intellectuals of the IOC is Germany's Willi Daume, who in a brilliant speech titled "Do the Olympic Games and the Olympic Idea Have a Future?" answered a tentative "yes." Survival is possible only if today's leadership "fully comprehend and put into coordinated action the Coubertin balance of idealism and realism, the perfect effort at intermingling new and old, of traditional and ultra-progressive ideas."[21] This Coubertin-Daume concept is bold only in its time-honored common sense, that is, to save the precious Olympic institution by preserving only the very best of the past and melding it wherever possible to the cutting-edge ideas of the present. The future of the Olympic Games in the 21st century, said former Tunisian prime minister and IOC member, Mohamed Mzali, is "to find enlightened leadership that combines the strongest and wisest personal qualities of Baron de Coubertin, Avery Brundage, and Mr. Samaranch."[22] Because these three IOC presidents embodied both similar and quite different strengths and personal expertise, Mzali and Daume were talking about the same thing—balance. The philosopher, the power personality, the most adroit diplomat-business person-administrator would be, in the mind of these two longtime IOC members, the ideal "dream-leader" of the Olympic future. He or she would be capable of the steadfast leadership that would prevent the Olympic ship from foundering in excess and vulgarity.

Coubertin is one of the keys to understanding the Olympic Games dilemma, whether one is talking about the 1890s or the 1990s. The man died in 1937, and, as the premier Coubertin scholar, Yves Pierre Boulongne, said sardonically, "The neo-Marxists killed him a second time" during the 1970s and 1980s, this time with a stream of invective criticizing the ability of international sport to engender peaceful coexistence. But Coubertin is hugely relevant today, in the single most important area—the athletes in the arena. "Coubertin's humanism comes through today in recognition and respect of the dignity of the athlete," wrote Boulongne.[23] Olympic medal winner and French minister of sport, Roger Bombuck, on the 50th anniversary of Coubertin's death, believed strongly that the baron "seems . . . more alive than ever. He places us before our responsibilities."[24]

Coubertin was one of the first to recognize at the close of the 19th century that honest sport, enriched with style, ritual, and symbolism, could act for millions of people as a distinct set of beliefs, a kind of secular religion. A recognized expert in this area, John J. MacAloon insists that this is exactly what Coubertin did.[25] This second president of the IOC (1896-1925)[26], a man of unchallenged earnestness, is still incompletely understood. To unravel some of his more serious ideas is to better understand how to steady the whole undergirding of the worldwide Olympic Movement in these last days of the 20th century. I said just that in a 1988 essay, "From Coubertin to Samaranch: The Unsettling Transformation of the Olympic Ideology of Athletic Amateurism."[27]

The world of Pierre de Coubertin is gone—but the timeless attributes of honesty and fairness mean as much today as they did 100 years ago. Still, greater change has taken place within the Olympic Movement during the tenures of Presidents Lord Killanin (1972-1980) and Samaranch (1980-1993) than in all the preceding 78 years. "It seems to me," wrote International Baseball Federation president, Robert E. Smith, "that the Olympic Movement needs to slow down a bit and really weigh all the issues of the changes that are occurring and bring into the discussion more than just . . . the IOC."[28] Ethics and temperance, always in short supply, must continue to grow within the everexpanding Olympic engine. In his own convoluted way, Coubertin said exactly this many times in his 50 years of nonstop writing. The very best, the most highly idealized view of ancient Greek life and athletics must be grafted onto these new Olympic Games, he said. Even more frequently, he stressed that all that was noble and good about 19th-century athletics in France, America, and especially England must become part of the Olympic ideology. Without these two legacies intact, understood by all, and set in motion by the athletes themselves, his "new invention" would degenerate into a kind of vulgar, gladiatorial display.

Coubertin needs no apologists. What he meant was that the highest kind of morality common to human creatures everywhere (not just English, French, American, or Athenian) must make up the foundation on which 20th-century Olympic Games are built, else they will be too feeble to survive the next century. Historian Thomas Woody believed that one can learn from the past, that history holds up a mirror to life in which "one may see what came to pass; and, if we are willing to accept a bit of Thucydidean philosophy of history, we can see what will come again."[29] I read Coubertin similarly. What some claim as wholly extraneous to these late 20th-century Winter and Summer Olympic Games (i.e., the oaths of honesty, the flags, the ceremony; "doves of peace," parades, music, and pageantry; the drug and sex testing, judges, and juries of appeal; and more) may have been Coubertin's way (and that of today's organizers) of partially warding off incipient evil. Certainly the organizers of the Games of the Xth Olympiad had no qualms in adding to the moral "baggage" of their participants when they invited Dr. Robert Gordon Sproul, president of the University of California, to open the games.

On 30 July 1932, in full view of 100,000 Californians, Sproul said that the Games must try to emulate the ancient contests when they were at their very best—ancient international gatherings involving "the totality of human activity, physical, mental and spiritual." He talked about high-minded, competitive international contests capable of social and intellectual good, of energizing every constructive element of modern life.

May these games help humanity to all higher metaphysical values, the basis for the good life, he intoned:

> With one heart and one voice we who are here assembled, spectators and competitors alike, dedicate these games to the high purpose in which the original Olympiad was conceived and to which it ideally ministered—to clean sport and fair play, to the development of sound minds in sound bodies, to the loyalties of the team leading to the loyalties of life, to respect for opponents, win or lose, to the brotherhood of mankind. We ask for the Xth Olympiad, conceived in this spirit, the blessing of the Most High as an instrument in His awful hand for the peace of the world, for the good will of peoples, for the building of His kingdom upon the earth.[30]

Sproul probably talked too fast for those present as he went on, weaving a tapestry of ideas which included balance, harmony, beauty of spirit, sacrifice, and prayer. Probably not everyone in the Olympic Coliseum was listening. No wire services or newspapers reproduced the whole of Sproul's speech. But I believe that had the physically fragile Coubertin been inside the stadium on that sunny afternoon, he would have nodded in approval, for the Olympic Movement and its most visible manifestation, the Games, must go beyond mere facts, statistics, and physical superlatives—beyond what Sir Kenneth Clark called "heroic materialism." Future Olympic Games must incorporate all of this, for these segments are not intrinsically evil, and embrace something of the wonder and mystery that is the collective humankind. The Olympic Games, at their best, can do all of this for us.

Notes

1. John Wilson Bowyer, Ed., *The Victorian Age—Prose, Poetry, and Drama* (New York: Crofts, 1938), 21.

2. M.E. Audouin, *Olympie et Les Jeux Olympiques* (Paris: Audiu et Cie, 1896), 15; William Andrew Robinson, "The Olympian Games at Athens," *The Bachelor of Arts, 2* April 1896, 583; Edward Norman

Gardiner, *Greek Athletic Sports and Festivals* (London: Macmillan, 1910), 3-4.

3. F.M. Cornford, "The Origin of the Olympic Games," in Jane Ellen Harrison, ed., *Themis* (Cambridge University Press, 1912), 213.

4. Edward Norman Gardiner, *Olympia* (London: Oxford University Press, 1925), 65-68; Gardiner, *Athletics of the Ancient World* (London: Oxford University Press, 1930), 33.

5. George Willis Botsford, *Hellenic History* (New York: Macmillan, 1950), 91.

6. Raymond Block, "Sports in the Ancient World," *Diogenes, 94* (Summer 1976), 58.

7. Nicolaos Yalouris, Ed., *The Olympic Games Through the Ages* (Athens: Ekdotike Atheon S.A., 1976), 5 by the publisher, George A. Christopoulos; M. Andronicos, 9; J. Sakellarakis, 35; Yalouris, 77.

8. Earl R. Anderson, "Athletic Mysticism in the Olympics," *The Gamut* (Cleveland State University), 2, Winter 1981, 85.

9. Coubertin's ideology is discussed by scores of authors, among them Marie-Thérèse Eyquem, *Pierre de Coubertin—L' Épopée Olympique* (Paris: Calmann-Lévy, 1966); Yves Pierre Boulongne, *La vie et l' oeuvre pédagogique de Pierre de Coubertin 1863-1937* (Ottawa: Leméac, 1975); John J. MacAloon, *This Great Symbol: Pierre de Coubertin and the Origins of the Modern Olympic Games* (Chicago: University of Chicago Press, 1981); Louis Callebat, *Pierre de Coubertin* (Paris: Fayard, 1988).

10. I discussed this tendency in chapter 5, "The Olympic Idea in an Age of Rising Expectations," *The Modern Olympic Games* (New York: Barnes, 1980).

11. F.M. Messerli, "Impressions and What We Learned From Them," *Bulletin du CIO, 36*, 15 November 1952, 15.

12. J.A. Samaranch, "Setting Our Sights on the 21st Century," *Olympic Panorama, 1*, 1989, 12.

13. David C. Young, *The Olympic Myth of Greek Amateur Athletics* (Chicago: Ares, 1984).

14. Ibid., ix.

15. Ernst Jokl, "Sport and Culture," *Proceedings* of doping seminar, Brussels, May 1964, 22.

16. Emil Zatopek, quoted in *Track and Field News*, July 1984, 76; Jean-François Brisson, quoted in *L'Enjeu Olympique* (Paris: Marcel Valtat, 1982), 10; Bill Koch, quoted in *Sports Illustrated, 60*, 6 February 1984, 48; Ommo Grupe, quoted in *International Journal of Physical Education, 4*, 1985, 10; Raymond Gafner, quoted in *Olympic Message, 24*, July 1989, 5.

17. Young, *The Olympic Myth of Greek Amateur Athletics* (Chicago: Ares, 1984), 176.

18. Coubertin, quoted in *LeTemps* (Paris), 7 February 1924, 5.

19. Bernard Joerges, "'Global 2000': Social Science Ecology and the Bimillenium," *Futures, 22*, January-February, 1990, 6.

20. H.E. Wirth, *Minutes of the Olympic Congress of Berlin 1930* (Berlin: Julius Sittenfeld, 1930), 5.

21. Willi Daume, "Haben die Olympischen Spiele und die Olympische Idee (noch) eine Zukunft?" A speech delivered in Frankfurt, 14 September 1989. Published in *Kulturgut oder Körperkult? Sport und Sportwissenschaft in Wandel*, Ommo Grupe, ed., (Attemptoverlag Tübingen 1990), 273-288.

22. Mohamed Mzali, interview with author, Olympia, Greece, 23 June 1990.

23. Yves Pierre Boulongne, "For Coubertin," *Olympic Review, 210*, April 1985, 237.

24. Roger Bombuck, in *Proceedings*, Comité International de Pierre de Coubertin, 10 February 1989, 2.

25. Read MacAloon's entire essay, "Olympic Games and the Theory of Spectacle in Modern Societies," in his edited *Rite, Drama, Festival, Spectacle* (Philadelphia: Institute for the Study of Human Issues, 1984).

26. Coubertin appointed Greek scholar Dimitrius Vikelas as the first IOC president from 1894 to 1896.

27. *Stadion, 14* (1) 1988, 65-84.

28. Robert E. Smith, letter to author, 17 August 1990.

29. Thomas Woody, "Professionalism and the Decay of Greek Athletics," *School and Society, 47*, 23 April 1938, 528.

30. Robert G. Sproul, quoted in *Riverside* [California] *Press-Enterprise*, 1 August 1932.

C·H·A·P·T·E·R·2

Olympic Games Ideology Defined and Redefined

Olympics have more to offer than medals.

Los Angeles Times

By a ghastly coincidence, only shortly before IOC member from Kuwait, Sheikh Fahad al-Ahmad al-Sabah, was killed by the gunfire of soldiers invading his country on 2 August 1990, that day he had written in a letter that "the Olympic Movement is much stronger than ever and is able to play its role as a master factor in world peace."[1] Though they might state it a little differently, many members of the international Olympic Tripartite, the consortium of the IOC, the national Olympic committees (NOCs), and the international sport federations (ISFs), believe like he did that the Olympic ideology is still viable.

Although it is not among the "top three," this vague idealism is one of the reasons why cities all over the world compete so vigorously to host an Olympic Games. It is frequently expressed in less saccharine terms than those of the good Pierre de Coubertin or the sentiments of Sheikh Fahad.

Olympic steeplechase champion and veteran journalist for the *London Sunday Observer*, Christopher Brasher, wrote that staging an Olympic Games can bring in big money for a community and, short of war itself, ''can stretch a community to show to the world what they can do, and life is dull if you are not stretched to the limit of your capabilities.''[2] This is the Olympic dream—redefined.

Seeking a Modern-Day Philosophy

Sir Denis Follows of the British Olympic Association defined *Olympic Movement* as the actions of international organizations attempting to fulfill ''the purpose for and aims of our endeavours,'' and they work continuously.[3] There is no modern-day consensus on an Olympic philosophy, though there may have been before the First World War. The ''Wise One'' of today's IOC, Willi Daume, is a veteran ideologue and constantly iterates the idealistic-realistic tone of certain intellectual members of the Olympic family. Above all, he said, we must ''overcome the East-West and North-South differences.''[4] The Olympic confraternity, at the risk of perceived contradiction, must graft old ideas onto new and emerge with a set of guidelines that are significantly more democratic and international than they were previously. Once again, Willi Daume observed that former IOC president Avery Brundage would probably ''whirl in his grave'' if he knew what was going on inside the 1990 Olympic Movement. But Brundage would be wrong, according to Daume who said that every effort possible is being made to retain the very best from an illustrious but narrow past and make the new thinking work for everybody in the world.[5]

There can be no consensus about these Olympic principles, because, as German historian Manfred Lämmers commented, ''there is nowhere a binding definition of what is to be understood by the Olympic Idea.''[6] Olympic decision makers no longer invoke the phrase *athletic amateurism*; they talk about *eligibility*. Subject to the scrutiny of domestic and international sport federations—not that of the IOC—almost every top-level athlete is eligible for Olympic competition, excluding professional boxers, baseball players in the professional leagues inside the United States, and the small cadre of the world's best soccer players. Even some of these restrictions may change by century's end. Educator-historian (and staunch pacifist) Peter McIntosh wrote that adaptability must be an IOC trait or the Olympic Games will perish,[7] and the IOC today is just that—adaptable.

The new ideology is active and quintessentially pragmatic rather than contemplative. During Samaranch's tenure, Olympic canons have attempted to compromise and adapt without losing precious principles. There are signs that this is working. For example, in 1920 (the year Samaranch was born), the nations of the world were not all represented at the Antwerp Olympic Games, because of the devastation of World War I; many more of the athletes who did attend were from middle and upper-middle economic classes than from the poor. This is no longer true in the Games of the 1990s.

The rules have changed. The Olympic Games are not looking for amateurs, but for those possessing the elusive "amateur spirit," a certain mind-set wherein the profit motive does not dominate all other motives, a thought process in which the individual perceives himself or herself as being more in love with the enterprise for its own sake than for the money involved. Because there is no way to read minds, to tell one kind of athlete from the other, past IOC president Lord Killanin and now Samaranch have invited them *all* into the Olympic arena: An amateur athlete is anyone who honestly considers himself or herself to be one. Such easy access to and from the amateur and professional realms is the new Olympic *laissez-passer* and despite its near universal acceptance will continue to be a source of irritation for some.

Blending the Old and the New

There must be some areas of personal concern where compromise is absolutely unacceptable, but any attempt at an exposition of Olympic principles for the late 1990s and the 21st century must settle on some noncontradictory compromise of old and new ideas. There is nothing at all naive or inappropriate in the new age Olympian's acceptance of Coubertin's 1906 homily—that all of us who love mankind must work toward making the Olympic Games "more peaceful, more cultural, and above all an educational and moral tool."[8] Can we not also accept in the same intellectual-emotional moment the sentiments of Richard Pound, the IOC's vice president from Canada, who outlined a modern scenario of Olympic business dealing with television contracts, reports of "doping" investigations, multimillion-dollar commercial negotiations, endless technical reports, serious international political crises, and "all of this with the athlete foremost in mind, amidst an atmosphere of civility and scrupulous honesty"?[9] There is a difference between Coubertin and Pound, but the two of them, taken together, could readily redefine a fundamental ethos for a very modern Olympic ideology. Even in the glare of the Olympic world, there is a way of melding high idealism with practical diplomacy and hard-headed, honest business negotiations with many of the world's biggest corporations. Alone, Baron de Coubertin would be lost in this kind of world, but no more than Samaranch and Pound would be at one of the baron's Olympic seances in Paris 90 years ago.

Raoul Mollet, Belgian's venerable Olympic athlete and administrator, has written many essays arguing that not only can idealism and pragmatism live together in today's Olympic world, they must do so if the Movement is to "offer the politicians another vision of the world."[10] Most thoughtful IOC members are concerned about this meld. For example, Francisco J. Elizalde of the Philippines wrote that the Olympic Movement must take advantage of "commercial opportunities without the sacrifice of intrinsic principles, that is, the exploitation of commercialization for the [Olympic] common good."[11] There are many ways of saying the same thing about the changing sentiment within the Olympic Tripartite consortium of IOC, national Olympic committees, and sport federations from that of earnest, well-educated European gentlemen with almost no knowledge of sport administration to that of technocrats and business people. The latter group have succeeded in creating the most stunning and spectacular sport festivals in all of human history, the Olympic Games of the 1980s and 1990s. Philosopher Hans Lenk has no quarrel with this, but he warns that beneath the glittering surface there exists a malaise, an even greater danger: "Without the infusion of more true intellectuals, men and women of a lofty pedagogical bent," today's monstrously large Olympic Games may have to give way to alternate games that are "smaller, more beautiful, more intimate, more participatory, more humane."[12] This scenario may not develop, but no one can say that we have not been warned against mindless materialism. Some kind of modern Golden Mean, some theoretical balance of body, mind, and morality must be impressed upon every aspect of the Olympic Games and its larger component, the Olympic Movement—and it must be now.

Jean-Louis Meuret worked for many years inside the IOC's Château de Vidy and later as editor of the General Association of International Sports Federations (GAISF) *Newsletter*. The gold must never dominate the spirit of the Games. Balance is everything, as Meuret wrote, "balance between the show and the deeper meaning of the movement."[13] The Olympic Games is a unique world showcase for the exaltation of the human species. It is more than that, too, but no other combination of characteristics—commercial, combative, or egocentric—can surpass this primary stamp.

Naturally, all of these characteristics have been part of both the ancient and modern Olympic Games. The problem has been in achieving balance. But the essential question need not be, Shall the Olympic Games be marketplace or temple? A better question would be, Can the Olympic Games survive an imbalance between the marketplace and the temple? To the second, better-formed inquiry the answer is an emphatic No.

Few journalists feel compelled to talk or write about this dilemma of the Olympic Movement, but Randy Harvey of the *Los Angeles Times* is a rare species—a legitimate media expert on the Olympic Games whose essential message was summarized in a sports page headline: "Olympics have more to offer than medals." He wrote that we do wrong when we urge our athletes to "go for the gold." Victory is legitimate, but so are "beauty, justice, boldness, honor, joy, imagination, progress, and peace."[14] In the same article, anthropologist-historian John J. MacAloon said that "the Olympic Games are a means to an end rather than an end in themselves."[15] The Games are not gladiatorial, medal-hunting contests, nor are they the temples of a new theology. Ideally and necessarily they are part reality and part play. A competitively sane viewpoint is needed—and one is supplied by the brilliant Olympic silver medalists, Peter and Kitty Carruthers, who discovered that "you can't just say you're going to win and then win. Kitty and I didn't come here to win a medal. We came to do the best we could."[16]

Samaranch: The Start of a New Ideology

Ideology may be defined in many ways; for example, it is "an interrelated set of convictions or assumptions that reduces the complexities of a particular slice of reality to more comprehensible terms and suggests appropriate ways of dealing with that reality."[17] And make no mistake, the relationship of personality to ideology is powerful and direct. Avery Brundage led the Olympic Movement for 20 years (1952-1972) and during that time far outdid the milder-mannered Pierre de Coubertin by his fierce and narrow protection of the so-called pure amateur athletic concept. Lord Killanin's tenure (1972-1980) was marked first by ambivalence and then by significant change; the genial Irishman looked backwards with fondness on the world of honorable amateurism yet was fully aware that change was long overdue.

With only momentary glances over his shoulder, Samaranch has spent his years in office (1980-1993) maintaining a steady, eyes-forward advance resulting in an Olympic policy that is a mirror-image of the man. Samaranch's ideological twig consistently bends away from the saccharine, soaring idealism of his predecessors. His imprint is everywhere in the Olympic world of the 1980s and 1990s, and in every case, his voice has been sincere, artful—an unmistakable blend of traditional Olympic views and new ideas, new directions. His is the new Olympic ideology redefined.

Political analyst George Will called diplomacy "the art of splitting differences."[18] Samaranch is the Olympic movement's ultimate diplomat, forever trying to see and frequently empathizing with conflicting views, "splitting" his intellect and emotion in order to see merit, if any exists, in the blizzard of images that come to him from governments, sport federations, national Olympic committees, his own IOC, and Olympians male and female. The new Olympic family had joined the real world, rather than remain aloof, and Samaranch was largely the architect for this redefinition. One exception to his usual capacity to "split the difference" and see both sides was his confrontation in 1985 with longtime IOC director, Monique Berlioux.

Monique Berlioux was born in Metz, France, in 1925, loved all sports as a child, especially swimming, and advanced to the London Olympic Games swimming semifinals in 1948. She was educated at the Sorbonne and worked as a reporter, columnist, foreign correspondent, producer, and director for French television. From 1960 to 1967, she was in the press department at the Ministry for Youth and Sport. In 1969, she joined the IOC staff as director for press, public relations, and administration and, in 1971, accepted the position of IOC director.[19] During her long tenure with the IOC (1971-1985), she lived apart from her husband, Serge Groussard, a Paris-based journalist. She wrote six books and many essays on politics, sport, women, the Olympic Games, the IOC, and the Tripartite administration.

Berlioux was a powerful person—intellectually, physically, and in the force of her personality—a woman of charm and charisma with innate leadership capabilities that rubbed many people the wrong way. From the Olympic office in Switzerland, she worked magnificently in the names of absentee IOC presidents Brundage, Killanin, and, for several years, Samaranch. Dozens of essays about the Iron Lady, the queen of the Olympic Movement, the brains of the IOC created a legendary air about her, a heady mix of admiration, respect, and sometimes fear. Some IOC members felt a strong but repressed resentment that one of their highest level employees had taken on so much responsibility and power during the perpetual absences of the presidents.

Then in 1983, Samaranch moved from Barcelona to Lausanne, the first president to do so since Coubertin. It soon became evident that the two could not work together, for Samaranch's herculean work schedule seemed to make Berlioux's role not only redundant but antagonistic. In 1985, she resigned amid a flap heard 'round the Olympic world.[20]

The two were of opposite personalities. Berlioux wore her authority on her sleeve, whereas Samaranch was much more guarded in his exercise of authority. He was an IOC member; she was not. Despite her outwardly forceful Gallic personality, Berlioux was conservative about Olympic reform in the two ascendant issues of amateurism and commercialism. She believed passionately that change was necessary but that it must take place with circumspection. The outwardly reserved Samaranch disagreed. The whole future of the Olympic Movement was in immediate jeopardy, he believed, and so with a kind of passionate quietude, he initiated radical reform in these two all-important areas. The great irony was that they loved with equal fervor the Olympic Movement, the Games, and the overarching Olympic idea.

Typically, Samaranch was too busy to comment on Berlioux. Berlioux wrote that "Mr. Samaranch moved too fast and although the present evidence may seem otherwise, he will not have, ultimately, served well the larger and loftier aims of the Olympic movement."[21]

Berlioux tried to guide the Movement along traditional lines and gradually into new vistas. Samaranch sought and found new directions and instigated radical reforms. The two were incompatible in the Olympic world of the 1980s, so they split their considerable talents; she went to Paris as deputy assistant to the mayor, and Samaranch remained in Lausanne to engineer more change in his presidential years than did all previous IOC presidents combined.

Monique Berlioux, in a dozen years of unofficial control, attempted to distill a modern definition of the Olympic idea from the old, whereas the seventh IOC president, J.A. Samaranch, carved out a new, exciting, expansive definition of what it means to be Olympic, and he did it in the same length of time.

Samaranch took great pride in merging the very best traditional Olympic values with his vision of a new Olympics "more embracing, more humane, a sport-for-all through Olympic elite championship concept, a breathtaking new-old idea that embraces Coubertinian vision with the near-realized reality of the Olympic Movement as one of the world's most pervasive peaceful sources for good."[22] Invariably, and possibly unconsciously, Samaranch implored the Olympian "gods" of old, and then quickly moved onto a present-day temporal plane and ended with his vision of the future. He usually took this triple direction.

The harder the Olympic Movement seeks to contribute to world peace, he said in Paris, 2 June 1984, the more a very few, unscrupulous politicians try to sink the Olympic ship. He told the Association of Summer Olympic International Federations (ASOIF), meeting in Monte Carlo on 15 October 1984, that standing still would mean the death of the Olympic Movement.[23] All the world must soon realize the "independence and authority of our movement," he said 4 years later at the 93rd IOC Session in Calgary. "Human brotherhood, understanding and peace are more important to us than anything else."[24]

Speaking like his predecessors, but with a considerably different mindset, Samaranch talked about the "weighty responsibility [and] uplifting mission" taken on by the Olympic Tripartite. Standing as tall as he could on the Athenian Hill of the Pnyx on 21 June 1990, he told a receptive audience that "the Olympic movement is stronger than ever before, in part, thanks to you. The Olympic movement has become a force for good in the world."[25] When he received an honorary doctorate from Laval University in Quebec City on 22 May 1990, Samaranch reminded the audience that the difference between ordinary sport and Olympic sport is that the latter has "culture and a mission."[26]

Untangling and Prioritizing the Olympic Images

In today's disquieting world, the Olympic idea defined and redefined may be thought by many to be irrelevant and antiquarian, and by others to be real but wholly subject to arbitrary interpretation. A few find direction in history, not only for defining this idea, sometimes called Olympism, but for shaping a new definition for the future. (It may be too much to hope that this chapter will shed some light on both.)

The newer Olympic ideology seems to revolve more around fairness than around world peace. Without mutual respect and high-minded (not old-fashioned) individual and collective motives, the Olympic Games are nothing. As Canadian teacher and poet John Powell said in the wake of the 1988 Seoul festival and drug tragedy, "If we don't have ethics we don't have Games; we have performances."[27]

But no specific Olympic code is required, and insistence on such was a fatal flaw of old-line Olympic ideologues. What *is* badly needed in the Olympic world on the brink of a new millennium is an unmaterial attitude about athletic competition and involved individuals who understand, like classicist Bliss Perry, that this clearer vision "ministers to [one's] life."[28] This code or idea need not be a religion nor even a way of life. It should be a dimension adjunct to one's personal set of beliefs—an attitude about how people should be treated and how sport should be contested. A perception of self would be involved, as well as the often ill-defined expression of humankind's hope for something that is not, but ought to be.

For longtime IOC member from Tunisia, Mohamed Mzali, the ideal 21st-century Olympic leadership "should embody the very best qualities of Avery Brundage, Juan Antonio Samaranch, and an essential x factor presidency."[29] The Olympic Movement will be capable of sustaining and even heightening its image and integrity if its leadership, while generating large sums of money and disbursing them appropriately, continues to recruit uncommonly gifted men and women to succeed the old guard. And that leadership must be sustained, at a significantly higher level, by an agreed upon set of fundamental ideas that are universally humane, idealistic, and spiritually enlightened.

Philosophies and ideologies must be constantly studied and discussed. The present Olympic Tripartite hierarchy does too little of this kind of introspection, self-evaluation, and careful study of either the intrinsic purity of its own philosophy or the temporal efficiency of that code. Canadian Olympic high-hurdler and longtime IOC member, James Worrall, at the 1990 Symposium on Coubertin said that "we in the Olympic Movement are still not yet free of demagogues and dummies. They, along with the unethical and those unencumbered by morals, need to invite themselves *out* of our organization."[30]

For 40 years, the French journalist Jean-François Brisson studied every dimension of the Olympic Movement and Games, from Guy Drut's hurdle technique in Montreal to Pierre de Coubertin's integral humanism. He concluded that massive reeducation within the Olympic family is needed, and right now. Similarly, an Olympic education of the greater public is long overdue. Only then, he shared, can the Movement be sustained into the next century.[31]

All the detritus, the debris that accumulates around a structure like the Olympic Tripartite can hide the fact that an energizing idea, understood to varying degrees yet maintained by most, must supersede all else, including technology, spectacle, sport performance, and entrepreneurship. In this the distant voice of Coubertin was correct. Olympic images count for a great deal; they just need to be disentangled and prioritized. What a surprise it was to read former *Sports Illustrated* senior editor Frank Deford's comments about the Olympic Games. They offer the world "an image of peace," he wrote, and added this:

At the risk of sounding like Pollyanna, I submit that the modern Olympics play a greater role for good and peace in the world than the ancient Games ever did. . . . The point is not to take a break from war for the Games. The point is to learn from the Games how to avoid war.[32]

The vice president of the organizing committee for the 1994 Winter Olympic Games in Lillihammer believed that he had covered the essentials when he reported candidly that the Olympic Games of our time are hugely profitable and their philosophical concept "has greater meaning today than at any time." Arne Myhrvold touched on the essence of this chapter, the definition and redefinition of the Olympic idea. If only Myhrvold, in his other role as president of the Norwegian Olympic Committee, had spoken of ideology first rather than opening his remarks saying, "the Olympic Games are one of the most profitable investments we can make."[33]

Moving Into the 21st Century

A hundred years of continual stress and skirmishes have strengthened the Olympic Movement to a degree that has surprised some of its members. It has moved beyond survival into grandiose entertainment and drama with a level of symbolism and ritual rivalling anything else in the world. But it needs to go still further in the closing years of this century. The Movement must make its central sun, the Winter and Summer Olympic Games, better and more representative than they are at present. Only then can the Movement turn its powers to aiding other agencies in strengthening the world by means of universal good health practices, physical education in all schools, a sport-for-all dimension that will include millions of people, and Olympic "Solidarity" monies for emerging athletes in underdeveloped countries. This grand plan cannot unfold the way that it should, warns Portugal's IOC member, Fernando F.L. Bello, "until we purge from our own house the excessive sense of self-satisfaction, even ennui, that continues to inhibit our growth."[34] This imperfect IOC is the key. Four generations ago, the weary Baron de Coubertin admitted that only a small inner core of IOC men, selected by himself, were of any use in running the Movement. This is no longer the case; most men and women associated with the Olympics perform well. But Bello is correct; the world of Olympic sport needs the fuller involvement of every IOC member and the greater participation, integrity, and efficiency of all international sport federations, as well as the more than 160 national Olympic committees. I like the way president of the French Republic, François Mitterrand paraphrased Immanuel Kant's categorical imperative. Kant's three moral laws were erected for universal application, and with no irreverence to Kant (or Mitterrand), I suggest these actions be nailed to the walls of the offices of every member of the Olympic Tripartite.

1. Act as if the maxim of your action were to be erected into a universal law of Nature.

2. Act in such a way that you always treat humanity as an end and never as a means.
3. Act as if your maxim were to serve as a universal law for all reasonable beings.[35]

The idea of well-played sport contributing to fair play, and fairness to justice is a concept powerfully relevant in the closing years of the 20th century. This deeper meaning of the Olympic idea needs broader dissemination through worldwide television and other media, and through the cooperation of schools around the world. The Olympic Games, at their very best, can do this just as well.

Notes

1. Sheikh Fahad al-Ahmad al-Sabah, letter to author, 17 June 1990. Fahad's obituary was written by David Miller in the *London Times*, 4 August 1990, p. 12. Fahad's killers from the north are described in Julie Flint's "The Looting of Kuwait," *London Observer*, 5 August 1990, 13.

2. Christopher Brasher, *London Sunday Observer*, 19 October 1986, 49.

3. Sir Denis Follows, "Future of the Olympic Movement," *Olympic Sport*, 1981 Olympic Congress Special Feature (London: British Olympic Association, 1981), 9.

4. Willi Daume, quoted in *Bulletin 6*, 11ᵉ Còngres Olympique, Baden-Baden, 1981, n.p.

5. Daume, "Brundage wurde sich im grabe umdrehen," *Der Spiegel, 1*, 1986, 133-136.

6. Manfred Lämmers in *Bulletin 6*, 11ᵉ Còngres Olympique, Baden-Baden 1981, 13.

7. Peter McIntosh, ibid, 26.

8. Pierre de Coubertin, "Le Serment des Athlètes," *Revue Olympiques*, July 1906, 108.

9. Richard Pound, letter to author, 7 July 1989.

10. Raoul Mollet, "Les grands courants du Movement Olympique," *Olympic Magazine Tribune ACNO, 1*, May 1990, 37. Colonel Mollet competed in Berlin (1936) and London (1948) in the Olympic military pentathlon; he is president of Belgium's NOC and president of Conseit International du Sport Militaire (CISM).

11. Francisco J. Elizalde, letter to author, 24 May 1990.

12. Hans Lenk, letter to author, 9 August 1989.

13. Jean-Louis Meuret, letter to author, 28 November 1989.

14. Randy Harvey, *Los Angeles Times*, 22 February 1989; Part 3, 7.

15. John J. MacAloon, quoted in Harvey, ibid.

16. "An Olympic Lesson: Just Enjoy It," *New York Times*, 19 February 1984, 25.

17. See the illuminating essay "Ideology," by Michael H. Hunt, *Journal of American History, 77*, June 1990, 108.

18. George Will, on ABC-TV's "This Week With David Brinkley," 2 September 1990.

19. *Olympic Biographies 1978*, pp. 180-183. Several longer Berlioux sketches can be found in *Sports Illustrated, 54*, 13 April 1981, 69-73; *Ms.*, 12 November 1983, 121-125; *Los Angeles Times*, 24 July 1983, Home section, 20-21, 36; *London Times*, 2 December 1984, Magazine section, 49-50; *New Yorker, 60*, 19 March 1984, 104-115; *London Times*, 13 May 1986, 28.

20. The European sport press was filled with news of Berlioux's departure. Several English language announcements can be found in the *Washington Post*, 3 June 1985, D2; *Los Angeles Times*, 3 June 1985, Part 3, 3; *London Times*, 5 June 1985, 23; *Washington Post*, 6 June 1985, D2 and 7 June 1985, E1, E4. Also Berlioux, "I Have a Dream for the Olympic Movement," *London Times*, 13 May 1986, 28.

21. Monique Berlioux, letter to author, 23 September 1989.

22. J.A. Samaranch, interview with author, in Lausanne, 26 February 1990.

23. *Olympic Review, 200*, June 1984, 433; *Olympic Review, 205*, November 1984, 873.

24. Samaranch, in *Olympic Review, 245*, March 1988, 84.

25. Samaranch, in *Olympic Message, 26*, April 1990, 8; and his opening address at the 30th session of the International Olympic Academy (IOA), Athens, Greece, 21 June 1990.

26. *Olympic Review, 273*, July 1990, 311.

27. John Powell, quoted in Bruce La Plaunte, "Effect on Youth Saddest Part of Case," *Guelph* [Ontario] *Mercury*, 27 September 1988, n.p.

28. Bliss Perry, "The Amateur Spirit," a 1901 speech reproduced in *Phi Beta Kappa Orations* (Boston: Houghton Mifflin, 1915), 264.

29. Mohamed Mzali, interview at Olympia, Greece, 23 June 1990. Enlightened leadership within the Movement and an Olympic education for the world's children are the themes of Mzali's 1984 book *L'Olympisme Aujourd'hui* (Paris: Les Editions Jeune Afrique). Mzali's *x* factor is a 21st-century technological capability possessed by neither Brundage nor Samaranch.

30. James Worrall, interview with author, in Quebec City, Canada, 23 May 1990.

31. Jean-François Brisson, letter to author, 12 October 1989. Brisson elaborates on these themes in his important book, *L'Enjeu Olympique* (Paris: Editions Marcel Valtat, 1981), especially in the preface to Part 2, "Une Réforme par Olympise Ressuscité." He was eloquent in an essay titled "Can the Media Come to the Rescue of Olympism?" *Olympic Review, 184-185*, February-March 1983, 126-129.

32. Frank Deford, in *Sports Illustrated, 69*, 26 September 1988, 114.

33. Arne Myhrvold, "The World Needs the Olympic Games," *Newsflash* (XVIIth Olympic Winter Games), *2*, June 1990, 2.

34. Fernando F. L. Bello, interview with author at the International Olympic Academy, Olympia, Greece, 24 June 1990.

35. See Mitterrand (and Kant) in the *UNESCO Courier, 42*, June 1989, 7.

C·H·A·P·T·E·R·3

The Olympic Games as Metaphor: IOC Meeting, Tokyo 1990

The 'movement' is paramount, the concept of 'family' is the symbol we wish to project.

Juan Antonio Samaranch

At the 1984 Olympic Games in Los Angeles, 100,000 people saw a tiny woman "fly with wings" over the 400-meter hurdles to win a gold medal. Nawal El Moutawakie from Casablanca, Morocco, was the first Islamic woman to win an Olympic medal. Olympic champion and *London Observer* journalist, Chris Brasher, never sure of his feelings about the Olympic Games, wrote me that "the Olympic movement is too far down the 'slippery slope' which is 'greased with money.'"[1] The device of metaphor, giving one thing the characteristics of another, is used frequently in discussing the Olympic Games. Brasher mixed metaphor with hyperbole when he wrote about Barcelona's successful bid for the Summer Olympic Games, "The prize was the greatest bargain available in the world today—the license to stage the Olympic Games of 1992.''[2]

From 12 to 21 September 1990, the IOC and its Tripartite family met in Tokyo's Takanawa Hotels to discuss complex sporting and business matters and to select one city from among six to stage the 100th-anniversary celebration of the modern Olympic Games in the summer of 1996. Before the final selection of Atlanta over Athens, Melbourne, Toronto, Manchester, and Belgrade, the meeting halls were filled with pathos and hyperbole, enlivened with allegory and analogy, inundated with allusion and exaggeration, and overwhelmed with a mix of metaphor, flowery rhetoric, and a Niagara of factual data. The announcement of the winning city, televised to two billion people worldwide, left the winning delegation ''wild with ecstasy'' and the disconsolate losers ''weeping in the aisles.'' All life is metaphor, and few aspects of human existence lend themselves more to figurative language than do the Olympic Games. Only war surpasses these quadrennial festivals in pathos, passion, and persistence. But wars kill the young, whereas the Games, with one horrible exception being Munich in 1972, do not.

A hundred journalists mingled with 87 IOC members and several hundred men and women from national Olympic committees and all 44 sport federations. Prime ministers, heads of state, governors, Olympic champions, movie stars, and famous entertainers mixed with corporate heads and television bosses. The Emperor and Empress of Japan were the guests of President Samaranch at the opening ceremonies of this 96th annual meeting of the International Olympic Committee. A tiny group of Japanese and Canadian Anti-Olympic Games Coalition adherents tried to make more noise than their numbers warranted as they wandered through the hotel lobby in search of allies. What the *Japan Times* called the ''Tokyo meeting to guide modern Games into its second century'' was about to begin. Samaranch warmed up to his task by accepting still another honorary doctorate, a law degree from Nihon University.[3]

The opening ceremonies in Tokyo's vast NKH Hall on 16 September, 1990, were a window into the future of the Olympic Movement. President of the Japanese Olympic Committee and former world champion sprint swimmer, Hironoshin Furuhashi, gave the welcoming address, ending his brief remarks with the prediction that the Olympic Movement in these last years of the 20th century will be a force of even greater ''international goodwill'' and might very well be one of the ''noblest and [most] valuable endeavors in the world today.''

Next, IOC president Juan Antonio Samaranch talked about the future, after first acknowledging the death of his comrade, Sheikh Fahad, murdered in a street of Kuwait City by an invading army. Then, apartheid must fall, Samaranch insisted, his voice rising just a little. The use of illegal drugs in the Olympic arena, ''this poisoned thorn in our Olympic flesh,'' must cease. In the immediate future, he concluded, the 1998 Olympic Games will be selected in Manchester (1991); the Albertville and Barcelona Games will take place (1992); the new Olympic museum in Lausanne will open its doors (1993); the IOC will celebrate its first century in its Paris birthplace (1994); and the Centennial Olympic Games will take place (1996) in one of six cities. "Our revenues continue to increase," he concluded, adding that the IOC was now in a position to aid "the entire world Olympic Family." One city would win the 1996 bid; five would be disappointed. But all will share the "Olympic peace," and in the Movement's second century, all of us can come together

> beneath the symbol of the five interlinked rings to make a reality of those values, ceaselessly proclaimed but ceaselessly called into question, namely freedom, the greater welfare of all, solidarity and peace.[4]

Reports on the 1992, 1994, and 1998 Organizing Committees

Most of the Château de Vidy staff were in Tokyo for this important meeting and all nine departments of the IOC sent their top people (NOCs; sport federations; Solidarity; finances; legal affairs; information; internal management; marketing; and the Olympic museum). These 80 people work closely, and without their collective skill and loyalty, the Olympic Movement would be impossible, wrote IOC director general, François Carrard.[5] The whole staff was needed to coordinate the Olympic octopus, beginning with reports from the Albertville Winter and the Barcelona Summer Olympic Games committees.

Albertville organizers Jean-Claude Killy and M. Michel Barnier reported that their Comité d'Organisation des XVIᵉ Jeux Olympiques (COJO) was working well, and that state-of-the-art facilities were completed and ready "from winter 1990/1991 onwards."[6] The master plan of the Comité d'Organisation de Barcelona (COOB) was working just fine despite delays and some Olympian boondoggle, reported co-organizers, Mayor Pasqual Maragall and Jordi Pujol.[7] Because COJO and COOB had submitted detailed reports at the 19 June 1990 meeting in Barcelona of the Association of National Olympic Committees (ANOC), the Olympic Tripartite moved forward rapidly. They needed no lengthy interrogation of delegates from the Norwegian town of Lillehammer, already selected as the site of the 1994 Winter Olympics. Instead, the LOOC committee chairman, Gerhard Heiberg, working with a billion-dollar budget, submitted his *Status Report* and, pleased by its approval, "welcomed the world to Lillehammer in 1994."[8]

A blizzard of news bites flew from the press booths of Tass, UPI, AFP, Reuters, AP, Kyodo News, and JIJI Press. Only the World Cup soccer tournament came close to the intensity of media coverage demanded by Olympic Winter Games aficionados who had read only preliminary reports from the resort cities of Aosta, Italy; Jaca, Spain; Nagano, Japan; Ostersund, Sweden; Salt Lake City, USA; and Sochi in the Soviet Union. The IOC devoted all of September 15th to exhaustive interrogation of these six city delegations, the winter federation experts, and certain NOC members, even though the site would not be selected until the IOC's 97th annual meeting in Birmingham, England, in June 1991.[9]

High Drama: Selecting the Centennial City

The new and old Prince Takanawa Hotels, separated by exquisite Japanese gardens, are among the world's largest hotels. Several thousand rooms, 10 restaurants, a shopping center, scores of cavernous meeting halls (one as large as a football field), and the Pamir Congress Centre catered to the IOC's every need—business, dining, and cultural. Banquets every night for a week preoccupied many delegates—occasions hosted by the Japanese government, the Japanese education department, the host nation's Olympic committee, the "winning" 1996 city, Atlanta, and finally, a special affair hosted by Samaranch and the IOC.

Anticipating the inevitable keen loss felt by the five cities passed over for the Centennial Games, Larry Siddons wrote that "cities gain even when they don't get Olympics." After all, said eyewitness Siddons, these are the top six cities in the world—the Olympic world. Making a bid for the Games is a great catalyst for future development of a city, and even a losing bid leaves a community with fond memories and other "intangibles such as [improved] tourism and business awareness."[10] Samaranch said much the same thing using his own favorite images. At a September 17th press conference, he repeated his theme that the Games are only an instrument for a universal dedication to all youth, everywhere. "The 'movement' is paramount, the concept of 'family' is the symbol we wish to project."

On the eve of the all-important IOC vote for a 1996 Olympic Games site, the metaphoric game continued as two tiny anti-Olympic coalitions flew banners and passed out literature saying, "Bread not Circuses"—save the environment and use government monies for the poor, not the Olympics. They had very little impact in Tokyo, though other coalitions in the century's last decade might generate a more widespread outrage. The editor of the *London Times* probably disagreed with these splinter dissidents, for he wrote on the eve of the election,

> Even if its bid fails, Manchester will have reminded the world of its existence and given itself a salutary kickstart in[to] the next century. Win or lose, the 3 million pounds investment in Manchester's morale was a canny one. The good the Olympics have done Manchester has been not in winning but in playing the game.[11]

Less experienced photographers and journalists invited into the grand hall during the early hours of September 18th may have missed the importance of 87 IOC members flanked by members of advisory but nonvoting national Olympic committees and international sport federations. It was an historic family gathering, unheard of during the tenures of the six preceding IOC presidents.

With the full cooperation and expertise of NOC and sport federation experts, the IOC began the candidate-city interviews. For 10 hours the Tripartite questioned the representatives of the bidding cities—first, Atlanta; then, through the long day and evening, Athens, Toronto, Belgrade, Melbourne, and Manchester. After each city's presentation, at a press conference directed by the IOC's spokesperson, Michèle Verdier, the city's organizers summarized what had taken place behind the closed doors.

At about 7 p.m., the NOC and federation personnel were asked to leave and the 86 IOC members began voting in secret. (Samaranch, who had abstained in Lausanne in 1986, once again decided not to vote.) Nearly 2 hours later, before some 3,000 people, many of them wildly anticipatory, President Samaranch opened the letter, the contents of which were known only to "les scrutateurs"—IOC members Mark Hodler (Switzerland) and Zhenliang He (People's Republic of China), and Judge Kéba Mbaye from the International Court of Justice in The Hague. Without expression (although it seemed common knowledge that he favored Athens), Samaranch announced that "the International Olympic Committee has selected as the site of the 1996 Olympic Games . . . the city of Atlanta." Figure 3.1 provides election results.

The Future Is Now: The IOC's Message to All Olympic Cities

The merits—and weaknesses—of Atlanta, Georgia, as host city for the 1996 Summer Olympic Games (and critiques of Athens, Melbourne, Toronto, Manchester, and Belgrade) took up significant space in scores of North American and European newspapers—in editorials, in home sections, in columns devoted to politics, on financial pages, in advertising, and under major by-lines on sporting pages.[12] It was the perfect encapsulation of what the Olympic Games is all about.

The Games and their overarching Movement comprise the largest sporting and cultural happening in history. But they definitely are not, as some say, a wolf in sheep's clothing, nor are they the savior of humankind.

Like everything else in the human world, the IOC's selection process is imperfect. "We are always open to trying a new system of elections, if there is a better one," said the ever astute, polite Samaranch.[13] Yet only an hour after the secret balloting, IOC member Mary Alison Glen-Haig, a worried look on her face, said,

> We do good work, but not good enough. Several members of my IOC are guilty of factionalism, geographic provincialism, and these same

ELECTION DE LA VILLE HOTE DES JEUX DE LA XXVIE OLYMPIADE EN 1996
Procès-verbal des résultats définitifs

Scrutins	1	2	3	4	5	6	7	8	9
Bulletins distribués	86	86	86	86	86				
Bulletins reçus	86	86	86	86	86				
Bulletins blancs	0	0	0	0	0				
Suffrages exprimés	86	86	86	86	86				
Majorité absolue	44	44	44	44	44				
Bulletins nuls	0	0	0	0	0				
Abstentions	0	0	0	0	0				
Athenes	23	23	26	30	35				
Atlanta	19	20	26	34	51				
Belgrade	7	—							
Manchester	17	5	—						
Melbourne	12	21	16	—					
Toronto	14	17	18	22	—				

Belgrade   Manchester   Melbourne   Toronto   Atlanta

Candidature éliminée: _____

ATLANTA EST ELUE

Observations: _____

_____

_____

Fait à Tokyo, le 18 septembre 1990

Les scrutateurs:

Noms: Kéba MBAYE   Zhenliang HE   Marc HODLER

Signatures: _____

Figure 3.1 Eighty-six men and women voted. An absolute majority of 44 was needed for a city to claim victory. On a ballot numbers 1 through 4, none of the six cities was able to get 44 or more votes. On the fifth ballot, all IOC members swung to either Atlanta (51 votes) or Athens (35 votes). Ballot courtesy of the IOC.

people are either unsympathetic to or unfamiliar with the classic, open democratic process. I'm almost, but not quite, desirous of an 'open' IOC selection process for future Olympic Games cities.[14]

Once again the IOC had brought down alternating fury and praise on older heads. A thoughtful Walther Tröger looked beyond the vote for Atlanta, which he considered, on balance, a wise decision on the part of the IOC. To him, the city seemed to exude a warm, Southern tradition—a kind of American Olympism melded to 21st-century technology. At a private, post-election interview, Tröger said that his concern was with the future of the whole, overarching Olympic Movement of which Atlanta is now a part—and suggested that the destiny of the Movement is directly proportional to the quality of its leadership and the degree of intelligence and morality of the IOC membership. Warming to his subject, Tröger volunteered that in the Olympic world

gigantism, drugs, the threat of excessive commercialism are critical challenges, but they can be solved by men and women of intelligence, possessing a high degree of morality, and imbued with a Kantian sense of 'categorical imperative,' a kind of moral urgency to always do what is right, to act rationally, to do that which is absolutely good, and, in layman's terms, to make the very best of things as a result of conscience.

I had the feeling as Dr. Tröger left that his vote for 1996 Olympic Games city had been the result of factual input, moral urgency, and a kind of personal earnestness that is all too rare. His last comment, an equally insightful declaration, was that not only did the Olympic world owe Samaranch a great deal, but that he, Samaranch, must be in debt to his own Movement "for providing so many extraordinary challenges, the only way that the hidden and latent organizational genius that was Samaranch could have emerged full-blown."[15]

Old and new China seemed to blend into a single wisdom during my interview with retired IOC member Henry Hsu and the much younger Dr. Ching-kuo Wu. They expressed themselves differently, but they agreed that

1. yesterday's vote for Atlanta was done with a high degree of disinterestedness.
2. commercialism and Olympic entrepreneurship are a reality for good but must be monitored with the greatest care in order that the world does not perceive the Olympic 'ship' as mere international commerce.
3. although worlds apart in style, Brundage and Samaranch had, in carbon-copy ways, an abiding belief in the power of the Olympic Movement as altruistic potential education of inestimable proportions and the essential business of the Olympic Movement.
4. Samaranch has, for the first time in Olympic history, infused the concept of 'family' into the thinking of most Tripartite members.

> ·Such a mind-set must soon bring tangible benefit to untold numbers
> of youth, especially in the less privileged areas of the world.
> 5. the Olympic world must rid itself of demagogues, power-hungry
> and selfish sport leaders. Until that happens, the Movement is
> handicapped in its fight to expunge apartheid from the larger world
> and to curb internally those that would deviate from that enlightened
> document, the Olympic Charter.[16]

By definition, Olympic committee meetings are efforts for orderly future
growth. One extraordinary outcome has been the combined efforts of the
IOC, NOCs, and international sport federations to enhance, if not guarantee,
the Movement's financial strength.

In 1981, the IOC created a commission to seek new sources of money
other than television. The International Olympic Marketing program in 1985
appointed the International Sport Leisure (ISL) as its exclusive, worldwide
consultant and The Olympic Programme (TOP) as marketing agent for the
proper sale of the Olympic emblem to business corporations. The TOP-ISL
consortium (the creation of the late German shoe manufacturer, Horst Dassler,
and IOC president Samaranch) accepts only a select clientele—those who
receive IOC approval and can afford the multimillion dollars to join. So far,
in its very short history, the consortium has generated several billion dollars.[17]

Though not exactly its motto, the IOC has been driven by its determination
to be financially secure for the first time in its 100 years of existence. The
more money we can make, the more we can distribute around the world,
especially to the national Olympic committees of less developed countries,
is the explanation frequently given by Tripartite representatives in defending
their new concern (critics call it "excessive preoccupation") with money
and profit.

There was nothing secret about the billion-dollar contracts signed with
numerous television companies around the world and with some of the
biggest national and international corporations. At the Tokyo meeting,
members of the press were invited almost daily to IOC discussions about
such contracts and the monies involved. Agreements for the Albertville
Winter and Barcelona Summer Olympic Games, both in 1992, plus the
television rights for the 1994 Winter Games in Lillehammer, Norway, have
a potential income of $944 million.[18] United Press International projects an
estimated $1-billion price tag for the Olympic Games in Atlanta in 1996.[19]

The Tokyo meeting of the IOC proudly presented three more partners in
the new Olympic cartel. Brother Industries, Ltd., of Nagoya, Japan, was
granted exclusive sponsorship rights in the typewriter category for the IOC,
COOB, COJO, and all 166 NOCs. It was a multimillion-dollar arrangement,
and in gratitude, Brother agreed to provide "2,473 typewriters for use at the
Games in Barcelona and Albertville . . . plus a million-dollar donation to the
new Olympic museum in Lausanne."[20] Larger still and running into several
hundred million dollars was the IOC contract with the Japanese RICOH

Company, Ltd., which would supply facsimile (fax) machines to 134 national Olympic committees, to the Sapporo winter Asian Games (held in March 1990), and fax machines for both Olympic Games of 1992. "I believe we are the most appropriate company to undertake the establishment of a facsimile network connecting Olympic Family members throughout the world," said RICOH's company president, Hiroshi Hamada. This Olympic fax network will connect IOC headquarters with almost all NOCs and, hopefully, "will dramatically enhance the speed and precision of messages sent."[21]

The grandiose plan for a centennial commemorative coin program promises another financial bonanza. The IOC, in cooperation with the national mints of Australia, Austria, Canada, France, and Greece, agreed to strike one gold coin and two silver coins from 1992 to 1996. This is the first time that the IOC has initiated an international issue of legal tender, commemorative coins, a celebration of family and history, because each nation has a very special Olympic Games heritage. "We are honoured," said Samaranch, "that these legal tender coins will pay tribute to the first successful 100 years of Olympism and express optimism toward the future." IOC vice president Richard Pound estimated that possibly 5 million coins will be sold and expressed the feeling that "an unprecedented, generous 3% of sales to the IOC would generate a great deal of money for them . . . and for us."[22]

The Double Message of Success

In the back of the room during these billion-dollar negotiations stood the tall, dignified, elder statesman and two-time Olympian from Belgium, Colonel Raoul Mollet. After 55 years in the Olympic Movement, he thought he had heard and seen everything; but, half smiling, he said,

> I'm so pleased with the progress that the Olympic Movement has made, not the least of which are financial arrangements such as we have just seen with Brother, RICOH, and the five mints. My constant concern, even dread, is that these, my colleagues and friends, may not know when to stop, when to draw a line in the Olympic sand, when to mark a line of demarcation and say, 'This far and no more.'[23]

"Too much money corrupts," growled Romania's Alexandru Siperco, a 36-year member of the IOC. "But thus far, my colleagues have used IOC monies only for good. We must, therefore, be everlastingly vigilant about where our money comes from and on what and whom we spend it."[24] Siperco's more extroverted IOC companion, vice president Richard Pound, reminded the press and anyone else who would listen that such huge sums of money from the private sector do two things: "These monies are turned back to the NOCs to help the athletes, and these same profits tend to lessen our previous total dependence on television income, something that may not always be with us."[25]

The IOC's 96th meeting was an aggressive act of faith, an expression of the abiding belief of its membership (and family) that despite the most horrendously uncertain times in modern history, the Movement is vital. It is capable of serving directly tens of thousands of elite athletes and is positioning itself to aid millions of children and youth in every land in the very near future.

This was the unfulfilled dream of Coubertin, and it has become a realizable, unfolding plan during Samaranch's long and remarkable tenure as president. But nefarious, Caligula-like figures remain fixtures in the Olympic theater and threaten the Movement and the Games. Ambition can be laudable, but selfishness is unpraiseworthy in the Olympic world; theologian William Sloane Coffin said it best: ''There is no smaller package in the world than that of a person all wrapped up in himself.''

When trying to project the future of the Olympic Games, one should observe sociologist Daniel Bell's dictum to avoid the extremes of gloom or glee. ''The key variable is scale,'' or balance, and with it will usually come disciplined rationality, wrote futurist Bell.[26]

It may be that Atlanta's surprising election as host for the 1996 Olympic Games was won by a balanced mix of manners and money, of genuine Southern graciousness and American multibillion-dollar discretionary funds. In any case, 86 voting members of the IOC deemed it superior to Athens's clumsy efforts and more functional than Olympic Games in Melbourne during the southern hemisphere's awkward month of October, when most of the world's greatest athletes are not physically at their best. The cities of Manchester, Toronto, and Belgrade did excellent work and should be encouraged to bid for a 21st-century Olympics. For that matter, so should Athens[27].

Atlanta won the Olympic Games and with them a 6-year-long ''agony and ecstasy.'' In the future, it will take more to host this greatest nonbelligerent happening in human history. It will take powerful technological and pragmatic advantages touched with genuine civility and sympathy for the Olympic hymn, the Olympic code, the Olympic idea. Balance should be the way of the larger world, and it must be the way of the Olympic Movement into the year 2000 and beyond.

An Olympic committee meeting, like any business or collegial assembly, is an act of faith in the immediate future. More than anything else, the momentous Tokyo meeting was about the future. What remains to be seen is whether those gathered were or will yet prove to be men and women of high intelligence, compassion, and vision.

Notes

1. Chris Brasher, letter to author, 30 November 1987.

2. C. Brasher, ''Why Brum Missed Barcelona's Bull,'' *London Observer*, 19 October 1986, 49.

3. *Japan Times*, 13 September 1990, 21; also 14 September 1990, 19.

4. J.A. Samaranch in *Program Cérémonie d'Ouverture de la 96ème Session du CIO*, 16.

5. François Carrard, "IOC Role: Unifying the Movement," *Time*, 17 September 1990, Special Olympic section.

6. *Flash COJO, 34*, 19 July 1990; also *Flash COJO, 35*, 10 September 1990.

7. Dossier de presse COOB (January 1990), *Barcelona Olympic News, 11*, April-May 1990.

8. LOOC's *Newsflash, 1* (April 1990) and *2* (June 1990).

9. *Official Program*, XCVIIth Session of the IOC, Birmingham, England, 1991.

10. Larry Siddons, in the *Mainichi* [Japan] *Daily News*, 14 September 1990, 10.

11. Editorial, *London Times*, 18 September 1990, 19.

12. See the *London Times*, 19 September 1990, 46; the *Japan Times*, 19 September 1990, 6; the *Christian Science Monitor*, 20 September 1990, 7; the *Arab News*, 21 September 1990, 7; the *Atlanta Constitution*, 21 September 1990, A1, A6, F3; the *New York Times*, 23 September 1990, 8C; the *International Herald Tribune*, 19 September 1990, 17, and the *Toronto Globe and Mail*, 21 September 1990, A14.

13. *Montreal Gazette*, 21 September 1990, B7.

14. Mary Alison Glen-Haig, interview with author, Tokyo, 18 September 1990.

15. Walther Tröger, interview with author, Tokyo, 19 September 1990.

16. Henry Hsu and Ching-kuo Wu, interview with author, Tokyo, 19 September 1990.

17. See R.W. Palmer, "Report of the NOCs' Representative on the IOC Commission for New Sources of Finance," 1 May 1990; *TOP—An Opportuniy for Worldwide Sponsorship of the Olympic Movement; Global Sports Marketing ISL; TOP—The Consumer View; TOP Bulletin*. All of these documents and many more are readily available from ISL Marketing in Lucerne, Switzerland. See also Matthias Rauter, "A History of the International Olympic Committee's TOP-ISL Programme," Masters thesis, The Pennsylvania State University, 1991.

18. *New York Times*, 24 August 1989, D24; also 16 September 1990, 32.

19. See note 12.

20. Brother Industries, Ltd., news release, Tokyo, September 1990.

21. RICOH publications 1 (June 1, 1990) and 2 (September 1990); RICOH, news release, September 1990; and remarks of François Carrard, IOC director general, at the 96th IOC Session, Tokyo, 17 September 1990.

22. "IOC Announces Centennial Commemorative Coin Programme," press release, Tokyo, 17 September 1990; also Richard Pound, press interview, 17 September 1990. See also "IOC Strikes Mint of a Deal," *Japan Times*, 18 September 1990, 20.

23. Raoul Mollet, personal discussion with author, Tokyo, 17 September 1990.

24. Alexandru Siperco, interview with author, Tokyo, 18 September 1990; also letter to author, 19 September 1990.

25. Richard Pound, press conference, Tokyo, 17 September 1990.

26. Daniel Bell, "The World and the United States in 2013," *Daedalus, 116*(3), Summer 1987, 26, 31.

27. Consistent with this chapter's title, the journalists in Tokyo during the IOC session were full of metaphorically colorful phrases. Greek movie star and former minister of culture, Melina Mercouri, was quoted to say about Atlanta's successful bid, "Coca-Cola won over the Parthenon" (Randy Harvey, *Los Angeles Times*, 19 September 1990, A16). The name "William Porter Paine" is far too formal and stuffy, said journalist Harvey. Why, this president of the Atlanta bid committee is "just Ol' Billy" and his triple given name "goes with the man no more than a mint julep goes with chateaubriand" (*Los Angeles Times*, 20 September 1990, C11). "Atlanta's victory sent Athens into 'a deep funk'" wrote the *U.S. News and World Report* on 1 October 1990 (14). And when IOC president Samaranch went from Tokyo to Beijing to attend the Asian Games (the day after the IOC meeting ended), he immediately became embroiled in a political cauldron regarding India's two disenfranchised IOC members. David Miller, who accompanied the IOC, wrote, "Juan Antonio Samaranch . . . steers like a white-water canoeist from one set of rapids to the next" (*London Times*, 24 September 1990, 34). The most outrageously angry newspaper tirade must be Simon Barnes's blistering criticism of Atlanta and the IOC, "Money Power Triumphs Over Sentiment." In it, he used a few phrases like "hypocritical clap-trap"; "the street-fighting, brawling aggression of money"; "a Coke bottle belching sacred Olympic flames"; "the harlot of naked commercialism" (*London Times*, 21 September 1990, 36).

C·H·A·P·T·E·R·4

Nationalism and the
Olympic Games

National pride must learn to live easily alongside the ideology
of One-World Olympism.

Richard Pound, *IOC vice president*

As a boy and then a young man during the 1870s, Pierre de Coubertin was
touched by France's national watchword *Revanche,* revenge against the
Germans who had so humiliated his country in the abbreviated Franco-
Prussian War. He was strongly influenced by the ambient nationalism
encouraged by the French leadership and, from 1885 to 1890, did all he
could to strengthen education, physical education, and recreational and elite
sport in his beloved France. He was a good and loyal patriot. Yet, early in
his life, and before the beginning of the 20th century, his thinking had begun
to take on a more international bent.[1]

During Coubertin's adulthood, nationalism was a mass emotion, the most
powerful force in his familiar Europe. He was never able to reconcile the

concept of sane and healthy nationalism with the ever-growing awareness of *inter*nationalism. Neither could anyone else. So, Coubertin built into the Olympic Games, especially in the elaborate opening and closing ceremonies, parallel but separate rituals to embody national patriotism and suprainternationalism. He believed in both, embraced them simultaneously, and included these ostensibly contradictory ideologies in his great quadrennial festival. Despite continued criticism predating World War I, both are still an integral part of the games 100 years after their modern re-creation.

The conundrum remains: How much of Olympic pageantry and displays of individual patriotism is a dangerous form of ultranationalism? How far should Olympic leaders go in removing signs of national affiliation and replacing them with those of one-world internationalism?

In these early years of the 1990s, an overwhelming majority of athletes from underdeveloped and Third World nations strongly desire the display of their country, and flag, and national affiliation inside the Olympic arena. The greater number of all athletes find the use of national flags, uniforms, and anthems inoffensive. Still, the IOC and the organizing committees should seriously consider rearranging the time and place of ceremonies, anthems, and medal-award observances. A protocol that satisfies the taste of all the athletes, officials, and Olympic administrators should be the IOC ideal.

Press and media sensibilities also are important to Olympic administrators but represent an even greater challenge. The media seek news, often in the form of confrontation, conflict, and controversy. All exist at the Olympic Games, as they do everywhere. But media personnel do not always take the time to see thorny issues in the proper perspective. Convincing them that the present system of Olympic Games is a successful blend of cosmopolitan internationalism that can comfortably accommodate expressions of personal and national pride is an ongoing task.

Glib generalities praising or denegrating nationalism are no longer as acceptable as they were two generations ago. Historians, sociologists, political scientists, and other social scientists have become more circumspect, and very few unequivocally condemn nationalism. There are so many shades and nuances, ranging from expressions of playfulness between nations to open hostility. One nationalistic thrust, the use of boycott, widespread from 1976 through 1988 is less a threat in the 1990s. Boycotts proved to be counterproductive, and in the 1990s, the majority of the world's nations strongly desire to participate in the Games, whatever their individual, political reasons.[2]

National Pride Gains Acceptability

For a full week following President Samaranch's announcement that Atlanta had won the privilege of hosting the 1996 Olympic Games, the *Atlanta Constitution* devoted nearly half a million words, mostly euphoric, to the great event. When the Atlanta organizing team returned home from Tokyo, a ticker-tape parade with open-car procession met them, and the *Constitution* headline shouted, "Half a Million Atlantans Dance in the Street." Almost every section of the Sunday issue—sports, home, editorial, Perspective, Art, and Entertainment—was filled with Olympic highlights, most trumpeting civic pride and ever more civic pride. Just what had happened? Was it unabashed boosterism and bragging, a city "awash in optimism" that prompted someone to write that America's "greatest city," the community "too busy to hate," had captured the right to host the Olympic Games?[3] However else we define it, this was no form of dangerously patriotic rhetoric.

In October 1988, the South Korean press echoed the world press, but decibels higher, that the recently completed Olympic Games in Seoul had been the most magnificent in history and signaled what many Koreans envisioned as the arrival of their country as one of the international family of great nations. Exaggeration mixed with nationalism and an innocent exuberance marked the joy of most Koreans. Is expression of national pride permissible for a small country but not for a giant nation like the United States, whose eagle screamed loud and clear in winning most of the gold in Los Angeles '84? How bursting with pride the Soviets were after winning so much gold, silver, and bronze at the 1980 Olympic Games! Do we condemn the tiny South American nation of Suriname for declaring a national holiday when its very own Anthony Nesty came from "nowhere" to beat the world's best in the 100-meter butterfly? Was this any more dangerously nationalistic? What about the reaction of the citizens of Kampala, Uganda, when their great one, John Akii-Bua, won Olympic gold in the 400-meter hurdles in 1972? Ugandans went temporarily insane with joy! Yet in no way could this have been construed as vulgar nationalism.

The U.S., the Soviet Union, East Germany—in fact, most nations—have made nationalistic "hay" out of Olympic victories. Some held forth that Olympic victories were the result of a superior national political system or, possibly, a superior race or ethnicity. But it took no time at all for the world audience to see through such nationalistic claptrap. None of the deluge of propaganda was more than ephemeral. In these last years of the 20th century, there must be no one who believes otherwise.

The International Family Meets Patriotic Reality

Those closest to the hub of the Olympic Movement counter criticisms that nationalism frequently runs amok at the Games by stressing the family concept of member nations, instead of the strident media version of "medal count and conquest." The president of the Association of European National Olympic Committees (ACNOE), Jacques Rogge of Belgium, asked rhetorically, "Where can you find a more absolutely peaceful gathering of men and women from divergent political and geographic areas than we have in ACNOE?"[4]

It would be foolish to trivialize the acts of ultrapatriotism, unsportsmanlike conduct, uncivil behavior on and off the athletic field, and, of course, the violence that have occurred at every Olympic Games from Athens in 1896 through the most recent celebration. They are chronicled in scores of books written in half a dozen languages. Most NOCs take too little time and effort to educate their traveling Olympic teams in international courtesy, whereas the host city's organizing committee must work hard to prepare its whole population on acceptable public conduct, inside and outside the many stadia. In addition to the NOCs and the organizing committee, the IOC, working closely with all the international federations, can insist on irreproachable conduct by every visiting Olympian, a mind-set enveloping both high national pride and sincere respect for others.

The IOC's recent efforts to cultivate a sense of family among the NOCs and the ISFs may have improved communication and, to some degree, international education in this Olympic entity. Richard Pound said as much in a 1990 speech at the University of Rhode Island, when, addressing a group of international journalists, he reminded them of their shared obligation to not incite jingoism or phony patriotism, or pant after gold medals at any cost. The media plays a role, said the peripatetic Pound:

> We all have it in our power to help reduce excessive nationalism and to highlight universalism. The whole Olympic Movement in concert with the media can work toward avoiding the Balkanization of the Olympic Games into 166 factional fighters. National pride must learn to live easily alongside the ideology of One-World Olympism.[5]

Never in the nearly 100-year history of the IOC has that body been so aware of its mission to help heal the twin nightmares of narrow nationalism and racism, said the youthful looking Ching-kuo Wu to a much younger audience at the 1990 United States Olympic Academy on the campus of Emory University. Give the Olympic Games "the chance to work their magic," and the world community can be touched in a small but positive way.[6]

In the most circumspect manner possible, the former president of the Swaziland Olympic Committee (and later, IOC member), David Sikhulimi Sibandze, cautiously pronounced that "the whole Olympic thing has to work nearly perfectly in order to reduce excessive African and world nationalism. But there is a way." Although a successful businessman, Sibandze made a conscious decision to help his people by bringing to them simultaneously a recreational, healthful, sport-for-all reality and elite, Olympic sport opportunities for the gifted; to elevate national pride without sinking into lilliputian nationalism; and "through Olympic education and Olympic Games participation [to] make a contribution to the eventual end of apartheid."[7]

The Olympic Games, heavy with the burden of bringing together in a single arena representatives of every race, color, religion, and political persuasion, are no ordinary human diversion. Veteran Olympics journalist, Jim Murray of the *Los Angeles Times*, put it better when he wrote, "The Olympics is just a track meet. Oh, sure. And Helen of Troy was just a pretty face."[8]

One of the true old-timers of the IOC, the Egyptian scholar of ancient sport, Ahmed Touney, admitted that every evil perpetrated by humans against humans finds its way into the Olympic Village and Olympic stadia. "But we have tools to fight these evils," wrote Touney, a former platform-diving champion. He suggested that "we all put the Olympic Idea to work inside the Olympic vortex. It will work more times than it will fail."[9] Such was the faith of an old man who had seen six decades of Summer Olympic Games, suffered through a cataclysmic world war, and survived many humanly-generated "brush-fires" in his own middle-eastern world.

Of course, some would say that the 83-year-old Touney was an out-of-touch devotee of Baron de Coubertin who said, in another century, that the Olympic Movement has the capacity of engendering, first patriotism, then a noncerebral cosmopolitanism, and eventually, for some, enlightened "intellectual internationalism."[10] Touney did believe in ethereal Coubertinism, and he also subscribed to the convoluted internationalism taught him by the IOC's fifth president, the American engineer Avery Brundage. But it seems a non sequitur to accept the thesis that because the Games have not reached the Olympian heights of intellectual internationalism hoped for by Coubertin, Brundage, and others, they are inherently dangerous, nationalistic enterprises.

Coping With Political Turmoil

The Olympic Games in the last years of the 20th century have moved beyond the threat of classic nationalism. Today's Olympic leaders and Olympic Games organizers wrestle daily with the problems of security against terrorism, the high cost of preparing for the Games, and the tremendous challenge of having every nation in the world represented at the quadrennial celebration without exceeding the host city's capacity. Nationalism, or the excessive zeal of any group for its nation-state, is no longer a serious concern on the Olympic agenda.

Over a period of 10 years, IOC President Samaranch met with the political leaders of 168 Olympic member-nations—an unprecedented odyssey, something unique in politics and in sport. Samaranch was convinced that such meetings were helpful in clarifying issues, reducing tensions, and giving direction to those dealing with unethical and aberrant behavior at the Olympic Games. Sport and politics coexist, and cooperation with governments is a present-day reality for the Olympic Movement. But cooperation does not mean integration. "We must preserve our autonomy and independence," Samaranch avowed in a presentation called "Setting Our Sights on the 21st

Century."[11] Our Olympic family can assist in the reduction of societal ills such as nationalism and racism, Samaranch frequently stated, but only when we have defined and implemented "a sports policy which is adapted to the new political, social, and economic circumstances of our planet."[12] Samaranch, the 95 IOC members, and the dozen men and women who occupy high-level administrative and technical positions inside the Château de Vidy rarely mentioned the word *nationalism*, but they put blatant displays of mindless superpatriotism on the long list of issues to be immediately dealt with at all recognized international competitions, especially the Olympic Games.

When Olympic gold medalists from tiny, less developed nations take a victory lap, some worshipful journalists call it "glorious," yet on the same site only hours later, call similar displays by excited Soviet or American winners "dangerously chauvinistic." The same behavior cannot have two faces and should not be given dissimilar descriptions in the world press or on television. If such displays of spontaneous joy (admittedly, sometimes planned ahead by a superstar's managers) are unauthorized, then Olympic officials on the site must gently restrain anyone so inclined, whether the athlete is from Djibouti or Canada. There needs to be collective joy for all winners—with perhaps, if one wishes, a so slightly louder hurrah for one's own compatriots.

After nearly 35 years of on-site Olympic Games watching, I would change nothing in the daily victory ceremonies, with one exception: the playing of national anthems. National anthems are played 400 times at the Summer Olympic Games, and the audience must stand up and listen to all of these anthems. This underscores, more than anything else, the tension between internationalism and nationalism. Each winning athlete wears his or her nation's uniform, is identified in the official program as a member of that nation's team, and has his or her name and nation announced over the loudspeaker and to 2 billion television viewers. The whole world knows, at the moment of victory, where that gold, silver, or bronze medal-winner is from. Four hundred national anthems are excessive, unnecessary, and overtly negative, especially when 300 of them are for just 12 to 14 nations out of 168. Ninety percent of the world's nations never hear their own anthems played at an Olympics. In a perceptive essay, a *Time* magazine writer pointed out that small nations will never win many medals, but that "the IOC strives to maximize what their systems can support"[13] through Olympic Solidarity monetary contributions to both small and underdeveloped lands.

The IOC continues to emphasize globalism over nationalism. Key figures within the Olympic Movement tend to follow a collective mind-set that perceives nationalism to be not a universally uniform ideology but a particular geographic passion directed inward. The IOC leadership constantly reminds itself that its own Olympic Charter states clearly that all committee members are ambassadors of the IOC to their countries of citizenship, not the other way around. It is an important difference. This is not an effort by Olympic leadership to minimize widespread political dysfunction and unrest, but rather a recognition by them that they must learn to work effectively with small geographic enclaves, as well as with the great nation-states. The fires of nationalism on the eve of the 21st century are neither burned out nor banked; they have been transformed into a hundred dangerous brush-fires. The Olympic Tripartite must deal with them if the Olympic Games are to remain viable and sufficiently important to several billions of people, in order to survive and prosper in the next century. The president of the Olympic Committee of Israel, Isaac Ofek, angry that his nation has consistently been disallowed from competing in the Asian Games, wrote,

> The main ideas and views on the Olympic movement in the 21st century, from the Israeli point of view, are based on the hope that in spite of the political and diplomatic boycott by the Asian countries, that the International Olympic Committee will, nevertheless, find a way to ensure that we are like all countries of the world and able to take part in competitions on the Asian continent, *where we live.*[14]

Retired IOC member, Berthold Beitz of the former German Democratic Republic said that the IOC has much more cause to worry about "small revolutions everywhere" than the possibility of World War III.[15] The IOC and its copartners in the Olympic Games business, the NOCs and the sport federations, must work their own familiar sport territory while keeping a wary eye on the hair-trigger world of local and international politics. By such perseverance and fortitude, Thomas Paine, the 18th-century American patriot, said, "We have the prospect of a glorious issue [or] by cowardice and submission, the sad choice of a variety of evils." He was talking about nationhood, but the perpetuation of the Olympic Movement requires the same kind of vigilance and a consistent, enduring stance on the tenets of the 1991 Olympic Charter.

Mutual trust in the IOC has given rise on the Asian continent to four sovereign Olympic committees: the Korean Committee (1947), the Olympic Committee of the Democratic People's Republic of Korea (1957), the Chinese Taipei Olympic Committee (1960); and most recently, the Chinese Olympic Committee (1979). The South African Olympic Committee was disenfranchised during the tumultuously political 1960s, and yet a quarter-century later, President Samaranch engaged in quiet, intense talks with black and white leaders of that country, which culminated in the momentous reinstatement of South Africa in the Olympic community of nations on 9 July 1991.[16] The number of NOCs has grown rapidly, despite the integration of the two Yemen committees into a single NOC and the swift melding in 1990 of the two German Olympic committees. At the 96th IOC meeting in September 1990, there were 166 Olympic committees represented, with several of the Soviet republics straining to gain admittance. The IOC must be prepared for further realignment in the Olympic structures of these unsettled nations.[17]

Local and regional outbursts of nationalism seemed to occur everywhere in 1990 and 1991, though without the reemergence of old-time large nation-state nationalism. If this is a trend, the Olympic Movement must prepare itself. Nowhere in the Olympic rules is there a discussion of nationalism. But throughout the 60-page Olympic Charter (1990), it is implied that external political influence has no place at Olympic Games. There is to be "no discrimination in them against any country or person on grounds of race, religion or politics." Adding up points and determining a national winner of the Olympic Games is a violation of Principle 9. In Principle 51, "every kind of demonstration or propaganda, whether political, religious or racial, is forbidden."[18] It is manifestly clear that for nearly 100 years, acts of patriotism, superpatriotism, national chauvinism—however one wishes to say it—have occurred inside the stadium. Eliminating the national anthems of victorious athletes throughout the 16 days of Olympic competitions will help reduce unnecessary patriotic drum-beating without reducing in the least the prideful recognition of the countries of origin of medal winners. Nothing more is required to reduce nationalistic excess.

The IOC and the national Olympic committees will be everlastingly challenged by political turmoil and upheavals and social, political, and military events around the world. IOC member Ivan Dibos spoke with fervor about this:

> My father was an IOC member before me, and so for 50 years we have seen narrow politics and unseemly acts of nationalism attempt to wreck the Olympic Games . . . but without success. The collective wisdom of individual Olympic family members, the Olympic Charter, and the integral strength of the Olympic Movement, Olympic Games' athletes, will absolutely not allow it.[19]

Antonio Rodriguez, president of the Comité Olimpico Argentino, wrote that local and international political upheavals and acts of nationalist passion will occur forever. "But the universal perception that the Olympic family, especially the IOC, are apolitical and that the Olympic Charter is an eminently nonpolitical document, helps our cause."[20] The IOC has no police force, nor will it need one so long as it enacts its Charter with fairness and firmness.

The Olympic Charter (1990) states that "there may be a maximum of two IOC members" who are citizens of a single country. The two Germanys became one on 3 October 1990 and instantly Principle 12 was violated because *three* members were German citizens. Willi Daume, Gunther Heinze, and Walther Tröger were the members; Daume's personal choice to succeed himself, Thomas Bach (Olympic gold medalist, 1976), was "waiting in the wing."[21] (This was resolved by allowing the three members to remain on the IOC until there are two as a result of death, retirement, or resignation.) Probably the IOC wished that German reunification had not occurred so swiftly. But they (the IOC) have learned how to deal with politics, at least in a limited sense.

The IOC program committee must deal with another problem, one of many, before the Summer Olympic Games in Barcelona in 1992. The understandable lamentations of the Greek delegation at the 1990 IOC meeting in Tokyo (when Atlanta was chosen the site of the centennial Olympic Games) brought to light a plan in which *Athens*, instead of Atlanta, might have the honor of holding the classic men's marathon race for the 1996 Summer Games. The *New York Times*, in discussing such an unprecedented possibility, used as its sources interviews with President Samaranch, Robert Helmick, and Andrew Young.[22] The union of the two Germanys, a 1996 Olympic marathon race in Athens, and China's aggressive bid to host the Olympic Games in 2000 are all political as well as athletic problems. Fortunately, unlike its 1960s counterpart, today's IOC works skillfully—and politely—with all governments.

Speaking for himself and all his Olympic family, President Samaranch told an editor, "We are not afraid of the year 2000."[23] Samaranch and the IOC are bound to perpetual political diplomacy on the one hand and committed ideologically to an all-world, secular humanism on the other. They are looking to the future with gusto, sure of their cause and certain that they have planned well. Of course, what might happen next in world politics is unknown, but the IOC seems confident that its recent moral and financial commitment to world health and its own 100 years of Olympic management will see the Games through all but the most horrific of political exigencies.

Notes

1. Several score books in French, German, and English deal in their early chapters with the early activities of Coubertin. Among them are his two autobiographies, *Une Campagne de Vingt-et-un ans 1887-1908* (Paris: Librairie de L'Éducation Physique, 1909) and *Mémoires Olympique* (Lausanne: Bureau International de Pedagogie Sportive, 1931); Marie-Thérèse Eyquem, *Pierre de Coubertin—L'Épopée Olympique* (Paris: Calmann-Lévy, 1966); John Lucas, *The Modern Olympic Games* (New York: Barnes, 1980); Yves Pierre Boulongne, *La vie et l'oeuvre pédagogique de Pierre de Coubertin 1863-1937* (Ottawa: Éditions Leméac, 1975); John J. MacAloon, *This Great Symbol: Pierre de Coubertin and the Origins of the Modern Olympic Games* (Chicago: University of Chicago Press, 1981); Klaus Ullrich, *Coubertin Leben, Denken und Schaffen eines Humanisten* (Berlin: Sportverlag, 1982); Geoffroy de Navacelle, *Pierre de Coubertin sa vie par l'image* (Zurich: Weidmann, 1986); Louis Callebat, *Pierre de Coubertin* (Paris: Fayard 1988).

2. Jean M. Leiper's essay, "Politics and Nationalism in the Olympic Games," is a valuable resource, and I used it many times in the 1970s.

Though out-of-date for the scholar, I strongly recommend it for the general reader. It can be found in *The Olympic Games in Transition,* Jeffrey O. Segrave and Donald Chu, editors, (Champaign, IL: Human Kinetics, 1988), 329-344.

3. See *Atlanta Constitution,* 23 September 1990, pp. C1, C3, C5, C6, C7, and 25 September, 1990, 1, A15, B1, C1, D1, E2.

4. Jacques Rogge, "Une grande Europe Olympique," *Revue d'information du comité Olympique Belge,* July 1990, 1-3.

5. Richard Pound, IOC vice president, at the Rhode Island University symposium on "Sport and the Media," 6 August 1990.

6. Dr. Ching-kuo Wu, speech at the USOA, Atlanta, Georgia, 14 June 1990.

7. David Sibandze, interview with author, Olympia, Greece, 23 June 1990.

8. Jim Murray, "The Memories," *Los Angeles Times,* 24 July 1983, Home section, 28.

9. Ahmed Touney, letter to author, 16 August 1989.

10. Pierre de Coubertin, "Does Cosmopolitan Life Lead to International Friendliness?" *American Review of Reviews, 17,* April 1898, 434.

11. J.A. Samaranch, in *Olympic Panorama, 1,* 1989, 13.

12. Samaranch, speech at the IOC Executive Board and International Sport Federations meeting, Belgrade, 24-26 June 1990; see *Olympic Review, 271-272,* May-June 1990, 243.

13. "The IOC's First Century," *Time, 136,* 17 September 1990, 2.

14. Isaac Ofek, letter to author, 22 September 1989.

15. Berthold Beitz, letter to author, 15 June 1990.

16. David Miller and John Goodbody, *London Times,* 10 July 1991, 40.

17. For several helpful essays on these "restless" NOCs, see *Sport and Leisure* [London], *30* November-December 1989, 62. *New York Times,* 7 January 1990, n.p.; 26 January 1990, B12; 15 February 1990, D29; 5 September 1990, B8. Also *Sports Illustrated, 72,* 26 February 1990, 92; *International Herald,* 8 June 1990, 19.

18. Principle 3, which deals with discrimination, does not include the word *gender* and it has angered certain special interest groups worldwide. The Olympic Tripartite and Olympic Games organizers do not believe that they actively discriminate against women, but that global religious and cultural mores conspire against women participating in the Olympic Games. See chapter 13 of the Olympic Charter for an elaboration. Principles 9 and 51 are on pages 8 and 29.

19. Ivan Dibos, interview with author, Tokyo, 15 September 1990. At this same meeting, José D. Vallarino Veracierto, IOC member since 1976,

agreed that "politicians have all the power," but noted, with passion in his voice, "politicians everywhere are aware of the Olympic message, the Olympic idea, and this is especially true during the presidency of Mr. Samaranch."

20. Antonio Rodriguez, letter to author, 5 September 1989.

21. Steffen Haffner, "Der Tausch Daume gegen Bach scheitert am internationalen Widerstand," *Frankfurter Allgemeine*, 21 September 1990, 31.

22. "Action in Athens?" *New York Times*, 7 October 1990, S10.

23. J.A. Samaranch, quoted in *Olympic Panorama* 1-36, Winter-Spring 1986, 29.

The Olympic Games Program: Testing Ground for Compromise and Survival

The IOC and its Program Commission must 'bite the bullet' and halt the near out-of-control growth of Olympic events. The IOC must no longer bow to the hue and cry of having programs that will sell tickets.

C. Robert Paul, *Archivist, USOC*

The program of events represents the heart of both the Winter and Summer Olympic Games, and unless the weight and substance, the quality and configuration of the entire 14 to 16 days of competitions are near perfect—for the spectators, the unseen television audience, and, most especially, for the competing athletes—then no other factor or combination of factors will make the two quadrennial sagas successful. The total winter-summer package

49

must appeal to a very broad spectrum of attending audiences and, just as importantly, to several billion television viewers. To achieve this, the program must be constantly monitored and changed from one quadrennium to the next. An unalterable program of events—frozen, inflexible—would mark the beginning of the end of the Olympic Games. Change is all-important and reminds me of what the Cambridge University music author and critic, Edward Joseph Dent, said: "Music is of all the arts the most subject to change."[1] If this is so, then Olympic sports must approach music in their frequency of change.

The Modern-Day Agenda

The Olympic Games at Chamonix and Paris, France, 1924, resemble in only a small way the 1992 Albertville and Barcelona Games. Rule 43 of the Olympic Charter lists three categories: sport, discipline, and event.[2] In Albertville, France, from 8 through 23 February, 1992, competition in the *sport* of speed-skating will take place, and the men's and women's *disciplines* will be given almost equal emphasis, that is, there will be five men's *events* (500; 1,000; 1,500; 5,000; and 10,000 meters) and four women's *events* (500; 1,000; 1,500; and 5,000 meters). The total of 43 events and 129 gold, silver, and bronze medals to be awarded in 1992 contrasts vividly with the 41 medals awarded at the first Winter Olympic Games.[3] Between 25 July and 9 August 1992 in Barcelona, the Games of the XXVth Olympiad will include 28 sports,[4] 257 events, and the awarding of 771 gold, silver, and bronze medals. In track and field alone, several thousand athletes will compete for 129 medals in 43 events. Some old-timers among the IOC, like the great mountain climber Maurice Herzog, found cause for alarm at such an increase, especially if it were to continue through the 1990s. "The Olympic Games would become a colossus with feet of clay," he wrote as long ago as 1982.[5]

The Winter and Summer Olympic Games' sports are strongly slanted toward European and North American traditions, especially those of British and Scandinavian orientation. There is no central African wrestling at the Summer Games, nor are ancient Eskimo sports a part of the winter festival. Indigenous combative sports of southeast Asia and reindeer racing of the Arctic Circle Laplanders are not part of the Olympic Games and will not be, because of the Olympic Charter.

Rule 43 states that only when most of the world plays a certain sport will the IOC consider that activity for possible inclusion in the Games. Most *of the world* is a paraphrase; the Charter uses the word *nations*. Neither is satisfactory. For example, the Olympic sport of yachting is an international sport on all six continents, but if all serious yachters were to stand up and be counted, they would represent only a tiny fraction of the billions of people in the world. The same could be said of other winter and summer sports.

The Charter uses the wholly ambiguous phrase "only events practised" worldwide will be considered for the Olympic Games. Does this mean practiced by the masses or by only a few highly skilled specialists, but watched by many? The Charter is purposely vague here. Surely, rhythmic gymnastics and synchronized swimming are not popular participatory sports everywhere. Only a very small cadre of talented, dedicated women in several dozen countries practice and contest these two highly specialized activities. Only a few thousand men in the world hurl the 16-pound hammer, and yet it has been an Olympic sport since the Irish-American "whale" J. J. Flanagan won the gold medal in Paris in 1900, with a toss of 167 feet 4 inches.

The unenviable task of the IOC Program Committee is to come up with a balanced sport sequence of traditional "beloved" sports, with sporting activities popular with millions of "ordinary people," and sports that are visually attractive and exciting to millions of attending Olympic Games watchers and compelling to several billion television viewers. Some combination of team and individual sports, plus an ideal mix of subjective and objective refereed sports have to be included in the Games.

John Landy was the world-record holder for the mile (3:58.00) during the early 1950s and a bronze medal winner in the 1500-meter run in Melbourne in 1956, an Olympic participant and an Olympic Games "watcher" for 40 years. The single biggest threat to the future of the Olympic Games, he said, was that

> some events on the Olympic Games summer program are no longer tests of specialized skills. There are dozens of medals awarded to only a tiny handful of sprint specialists. In my sport of track and field, there is absolutely no need for singular speed events, the 100, 200, 400, [or the] 4 × 100 and 4 × 400 relays. They all require the same God-endowed skill of speed. Not all of them belong on the program. The same men and women win them all. How ludicrous it is to award *team* gold, silver, and bronze to such supremely individual events as gymnastics and fencing![6]

If there is a danger in all of this, it is in the inexorable increase in events rather than the proliferation of Olympic Games sports. The Olympic organizers for the 1992 Barcelona Games (COOB) underscored this point and on 5 June 1990, announced that "no excessive numbers of persons will be allowed in the Olympic Village." In support, the IOC declared that many NOCs must reduce the size of their teams.[7] President of the Association of National Olympic Committees (ANOC) at their 1990 meeting in Barcelona, Mario Vazquez Raña of Mexico, was also adamant on this point and told a gathering of journalists that the future of the Olympic Movement lay, partly, in successfully controlling the size of the Olympic Games. "Absolutely no more than 10,000 athletes will be allowed in Barcelona 1992," he announced. "Our idealized goal," he concluded, "is the perfect balance of [168] nations participating without the accompanying threat of runaway gigantism."[8]

The steady stream of international sports not included in the Olympic program that wish to become part of the Olympic Games continues into the 1990s. An IOC resolution passed on 19 September 1990 insisted that to be included in the Olympic Games of 2000 and beyond, men's sports must be practiced in 75 countries and on four continents, whereas women's sports must be widely practiced in 40 countries and on three continents. Previously, the requirements were 50 countries on three continents for men's sports and 35 countries on three continents for women's sports.[9] Olympic historian Paula Welch wrote that "admission to the [Olympic] Programme is a privilege earned, not given."[10] Much earlier, in 1981, the then IOC sports director, Arpad Csanadi, said the same thing, but as if not to dampen anyone's enthusiasm, reminded us that the IOC must allow the Olympic Games to grow—gradually, carefully.[11]

The Summer Games of 1996 will not include demonstration or exhibition sports, a time-honored IOC tradition that allowed the host nation to display a popular domestic sport. "We cannot keep sports that aren't interesting to our youth and not accept sports that are being practiced by hundreds of thousands of people around the world," said President Samaranch.[12] The Soviet Union's Vitaly Smirnov, IOC executive board member and program commission chairman, refused to be pinned down as to the upper limits of the program but implored all to work for slow, forward progress. Completing his tenure at that job, he had this "Parting Word":

> The program determines how athletes prepare for their major events, how money is allocated, what arenas are built, and how the sports departments of the big television networks organize their workload. And it is largely on how well the program is drawn up that the success of the Games hinges.[13]

Retaining and Selecting Olympic Events

Raña, in his double responsibility as leader of ANOC and president of Comité Olimpico Mexicano, believes a formula must be found for the selection of new Olympic sports and the retention of those already on the program. He didn't have an answer, but he said that when one is found, it would do no injury to the NOCs or to any single sport federation. The editor of the Soviet journal, *Olympic Panorama*, said the same thing. "Explicit criteria for the inclusion and removal of [Olympic] sports" must be found, he wrote in 1989.[14] That special interest groups might overexpand the program and in so doing ruin the Olympic Games was C. Robert Paul's message. His 40 years of close involvement with American intercollegiate athletics, the American Amateur Athletic Union (AAU), and the United States Olympic Committee (USOC) gave him cause for concern. "The IOC and its Program Commission must 'bite the bullet' and halt the near out-of-control growth of Olympic events. The IOC must no longer bow to the hue and cry of having programs that will sell tickets.''[15] The IOC has not yet resolved the problem of gigantism, or the out-of-control expansion of its Olympic program, though not for lack of trying.

"Absolutely not," cried Italy's Primo Nebiolo, president of track and field's International Amateur Athletic Federation (IAAF), when it was suggested that the soccer finals might replace the men's marathon as the last event on the program of the 1992 Barcelona Olympic Games. He said that the Fédération International Football Association (FIFA) was out of line. "How would we ever know what kind of a match we were going to get? It would be unbearable to finish an Olympic Games with a match like the one in Rome, the roughest World Cup with the largest number of player penalties in championship history.''[16] Yet if the program commission tends to its task in a conscientious manner, intense study of every event on the program must take place. No Olympic sport is unimportant; there are no minor Olympic sports. And *no* sport on the program is either more important or less valued than any other.

Look at the canoeing, kayaking, and rowing events scheduled for the 1992 Olympic Games. (See Table 5.1.) Meaning no disrespect toward these fine, demanding, aesthetically pleasing sports, but there can be only a few hundred people in the world who know something about their bewildering 26 events. Is there some kind of mandate that they must *all* be included in the summer festival? Risking the anger of the federations, would it be unwise to suggest that the Olympic Movement and the Olympic Games might be better served if a *representative* program of canoeing, kayaking, and rowing events be part of future Games, rather than the whole "kit and caboodle" of more than two dozen spectaculars? Several other Olympic sports, such as swimming and track and field, could be said to fall into this same category of "too much of a good thing."

The Effects of Growth on Quality

On receiving an invitation to serve on the IOC, an offer that surprised many, political activist and two-time Olympic rower, Anita DeFrantz, said that this was her kind of organization, because "the IOC is no longer the cautious, conservative body it used to be.''[17] Another woman, even better known within the Olympic Movement, Monique Berlioux, frequently voiced the conservative view of change in the Olympic program, always in the direction of halting growth. Though never a member of the IOC, she was its director from 1972 until her departure in 1985. Bigger is decidedly not better, she once argued. "Maybe there ought to be 5 or 10 basic sports appearing in every Games and then 30 or 40 on a 'revolving' basis." Such an idea would not be retrogressive. It might help save the Games. "I'm fully aware," she said, that "in any facet of life, you can never go backward, and that's true of the Olympic Games." The Olympic Games and the Olympic Movement

Table 5.1   Summer Olympic Canoeing, Kayaking, and Rowing Events

Men's canoe-1, 500 M	Women's double sculls
Men's canoe-2, 500 M	Women's pair without coxswain
Men's canoe-1, 1,000 M	Women's quadruple sculls
Men's canoe-2, 1,000 M	Women's four oars with coxswain
Women's kayak-1, 500 M	Women's eight oars with coxswain
Women's kayak-2, 500 M	Men's single sculls
Women's kayak-4, 500 M	Men's double sculls
Men's kayak-1, 500 M	Men's pair without coxswain
Men's kayak-2, 500 M	Men's pair with coxswain
Men's kayak-1, 1,000 M	Men's quadruple sculls
Men's kayak-2, 1,000 M	Men's four oars without coxswain
Men's kayak-4, 1,000 M	Men's four oars with coxswain
Women's single sculls	Men's eight oars with coxswain

are swollen with wealth, power, and prestige and, at the same time, "in need of reform, in need of some kind of sport 'Martin Luther,'" she wrote. And a sensible Olympic program of sports, disciplines, and events would be a good beginning.[18]

The Barcelona Olympic Games will host 20 more events than the 1988 Seoul extravaganza and will include baseball and badminton as official rather than demonstration sports. The quality and size of the Olympic sports program as well as the relevance of each event are still unresolved problems of continuing concern to the Olympic Tripartite. "Profound revisions are required," President Samaranch said at a two-day meeting in Rome of the IOC executive board and international sport federation members. "We are aware that today some sports on the program no longer deserve full participation in the Games, while other sports have grown and qualify for greater presence," he said.

There was agreement that thousands fewer athletes and officials will be allowed into the Barcelona Olympic Village, smaller in size than the huge Village and Family Town in Seoul '88. The Spanish city in the summer of 1992 absolutely cannot accommodate more than 15,000 athletes and officials.[19] Twenty-eight sports for Barcelona "is enough," said an IOC spokesperson. Three demonstration sports (Basque pelota, tae kwon do, and roller hockey) will be allowed, but this special category will no longer exist after 1992. Almost with a sense of pique, the IOC executive board announced that for Barcelona, "one team event in archery will be allowed, but none in rhythmic gymnastics." Nor will there be exhibition golf or women's softball: "We must lighten the load."[20]

Vitaly Smirnov and Nadia Lekarska of the IOC's program commission agreed that women's events need fairer treatment and that an increase in the number of women's teams in volleyball, basketball, and handball is likely.

The cautious Lekarska, with 40 years' experience in both Olympic and feminist causes, approved Smirnov's announcement, but added, "To blindly increase women's events in order to equal men's events would be wrong, very wrong."[21]

The June 1990 meeting of IOC and ANOC delegates was and is a classic example of wise men and women seeking solutions to complex problems that would injure no person, insult no special interest group, satisfy the organizing committee, and result in a still exciting, if less than perfect, program. The sports, disciplines, and events they chose might not satisfy everyone but must please the athletes. As long as the Games continue, the athletes must be the cynosure of the festival. To protect athletes' interests, the Olympic program must undergo constant change. Change isn't always progress, but stagnation never is. Modification of the program demonstrates commitment to the athletes. Procrastination by anyone connected with the Olympic movement is tantamount to dereliction of duty. Donato Martucci of the Italian Rowing Federation, demanding action and responsible change in the Olympic program, quoted ancient Latin jurists who held that *quod differtur non aufertur*—what is postponed is not abolished.[22]

With the admission to the General Association of International Sport Federations (GAISF) of sled-dog sports and curling, the number of sports connected to the Olympic Movement increased to 75, and many more are knocking at the gate.[23] The program's growth must not be allowed to go unchecked; only extremely well-conceived additions, modifications, and eliminations of sports will preserve the Olympics' athletic integrity and sustain public interest in the Games. After four decades in the world of sports, the Czechoslovakian leader, Vladimir Cernusak, said sharply, "My IOC colleagues must think seriously about 'retiring' some Olympic sports."[24] Such radical surgery, wherever necessary, must be the result of consensus by the IOC-NOC-sport federations Tripartite. It will not be easy, especially for some who, "as an ox that goeth to the slaughter," fear that their sport might be among those eliminated from the Olympic program.

The perfect Olympic Games program is an impossibility, because human institutions are inherently imperfect. But thoughtful recommendations from everyone interested, offered at the proper time and always with civility, will result in a "cleaner" and, hopefully, smaller Olympic program for future Winter and Summer Games.

Reforming the Games

There are a dozen scenarios for the reform of the Olympic Games program. Avery Brundage, half in jest but still raising the hackles of journalists, suggested reducing the number of women's events, doing away entirely with the winter Olympic Games, and deleting the quarrelsome (in his mind) team sports. More seriously, a small group in pursuit of Olympian egalitarianism advocates dropping those sports that are financially beyond the reach of poorer national Olympic committees and impoverished athletes. At first glance, such sentiments have merit. Unfortunately, there are no inexpensive Olympic sports. Wrestling, boxing, and track and field are costly federation and NOC sports, albeit light-years away from the astronomical expense of yachting, equestrian sports, bobsledding, and figure skating.

A few mawkish reformers would do away with many European-American sports and substitute local and national activities more familiar to the indigenous peoples. They argue that Australian and Canadian native pastimes and African and South American games should be included if Olympic leaders wish to make any effort at being sensitive to special needs of special peoples. The idea is provocative but wholly unmanageable and therefore impossible.

An idea with some appeal is that all Olympic sports that require human, subjective judging and scoring be purged from the program. Modern machines and technology can and should referee Olympic sport. Those events not lending themselves to such impartiality must be struck from the program, say these computer-age reformers.

Not only the sports of the Olympics but the site, too, has been a topic of reform-minded discussion. For example, the Winter Olympic Games could be divided among four Scandinavian countries, and every quadrennium, the Summer Olympic Games could be held in six cities on six different continents, thus solving the problem of single-site gigantism. This suggestion has received no support in Olympic circles.

Nor has the IOC seriously considered the so-called Lucas plan. First outlined 25 years ago, this plan suggests that both the Summer and Winter Games be held in one central European location on a permanent basis.[25] The Greek plan, the Bradley plan, and several other ideas for a permanent Olympic Games location have one thing in common: They allow the program of sports to be better controlled and far better administered at a permanent site by a professional staff who conduct every aspect of the winter and summer programs.

Officials must be in control of their sport at the Olympic Games, not in an Orwellian fashion, but so that every single athlete competes on as "level a playing field" as possible. Every athlete in every event should have the opportunity to compete, to seek personal excellence, to strive for a medal, and to enjoy the effort. A stable program supervised by the best officials in the world should be the goal of all Olympic organizers.

Each sport's competitive nature must be assessed critically. Grossly expensive sports, excessively dangerous sports, and sports wholly unamenable to objective judging should not be accepted for Olympic Games competition. Experiential input from the whole Olympic family, including the athletes, would help assure a better program. The Olympic program commission needs to continue collecting reliable data and then find a quiet place in which to work creatively, boldly, and fairly. If "solitude is a writer's oxygen,"[26] as Nobel Prize winner Camelio José Cela said, then a similar ambiance is needed in which all those who treasure the Olympic sports program can work to make it better as the centennial of the Games approaches.

Notes

1. Edward Joseph Dent, quoted in "The World's Wise Men," *Boston Globe*, 30 July 1936, 16.

2. *Olympic Charter*, 1990, 24-25.

3. Spectators at Albertville and television audiences may select from 43 events: three kinds of freestyle skiing (moguls, ballet, and aerials); the new event of speed-skiing; 5-, 10-, 15-, 20-, 30-, and 50-kilometer cross-country skiing, plus 4 × 5-km and 4 × 10-km relay racing for men and women; biathlon; ice hockey; 2- and 4-man bobsled; single and double luge, for both men and women; ski jumping, 70- and 90-meter; Nordic combined; curling; short-track speed-skating; 10 men's and women's events in speed-skating; men's and women's Alpine skiing (downhill, super G, giant slalom, and slalom); figure skating individual, for men and women; figure skating pairs; disabled skiing, and ice dancing pairs.

   The Calgary Winter games had exactly 50 separate events, see *XV Olympic Winter Games Official Report* (Calgary, Calgary Olympic Development Association, 1988), 531.

4. Rink hockey; tae kwon do; Basque pelota; tennis; archery; track and field athletics; badminton; baseball; basketball; boxing; canoeing; cycling; equestrian sports; fencing; soccer; gymnastics; team handball; field hockey; judo; modern military pentathlon; rowing; shooting; swimming and diving; yachting; wrestling; volleyball; table tennis, and weight lifting.

5. Maurice Herzog, letter to author, 21 January 1982. See also his prescient speech "L'Olympisme: Vie ou Mort?" *Proceedings of the International Olympic Academy*, 1977, 96-103.

6. John Landy, interview with author, Barcelona, 5 June 1990.

7. *Barcelona El Mundo Deportivo*, 5 June 1990, 32, reporting on the ANOC meeting in that city.

8. M.V. Raña, press conference, ANOC meeting in Barcelona, 7 June 1990.

9. *Mainichi* [Tokyo] *Daily News*, 20 September 1991, 10; *Japan Times*, 20 September 1991, 21.

10. Paula Welch, *Olympic Review, 273*, July 1990, 332.

11. Arpad Csanadi, "Gigantism," *Bulletin 6 Congrès Olympique Baden-Baden 1981*, 38-41, 68.

12. J.A. Samaranch, quoted in *Boston Globe*, 23 September 1990, 50.

13. V. Smirnov, "The Olympic Program: 'Where is the limit?' *Olympian, 17*, September-October 1990, 62. He also said that an increase in the number of women's teams in volleyball, basketball, and handball is imminent; *Olympic Review, 273*, July 1990, 309. There will be small but interesting changes in the programs of Albertville and Barcelona in 1992 and at the 1994 Winter Olympic Games in Lillehammer; *Olympic Review, 263-264*, September-October 1989, 439, 444-445.

14. Mario Vazquez Raña, letter to author, 20 June 1990; Alexandre Ratner, "Searching for an Optimum Model," *Olympic Message, 23*, March 1989, 58.

15. C. Robert Paul, letters to author, 19 August 1989 and 23 May 1990.

16. P. Nebiolo, quoted in David Miller's column, *London Times*, 26 September 1990, 40. The 1990 World Cup was a nightmare of unsportsmanlike behavior and misconduct.

17. Anita DeFrantz, quoted in Randy Harvey's article, *Los Angeles Times*, 18 October 1986, 27.

18. Kenneth Reich, "The Madame," *Los Angeles Times*, 24 July 1983, Home section, 20-21, 26; Michael Dubbs, "Olympic Referee," *Washington Post*, 10 July 1984, C1, C10; Simon Barnes, "Martin Luther King of the Olympics. Berlioux Says 'I Have a Dream,'" *London Times*, 13 May 1986, 28.

19. *Washington Post*, 1 March 1990, p. C2. Also "Accés limitat als Jocs del '92," in *Madrid El País*, 5 June 1990, 10.

20. *Olympic Review, 267*, January 1990, 7.

21. *Olympic Review, 273*, July 1990, 309; *Olympic Review, 275-276*, September-October 1990, 458.

22. Donato Martucci, "The Reinsertion of the Athlete," *Olympic Message, 23*, March 1989, 66.

23. *Olympic Review, 266*, December 1989, 553.

24. Vladimir Cernusak, interview with author, Tokyo, 16 September 1990.

25. During the so-called boycott years, 1980-Moscow and 1984-Los Angeles, scores of essays appeared championing the "Greek Plan," the "Bradley Plan," and the "Lucas Plan." See John Lucas, "Olympic Reform," *The Modern Olympic Games* (New York: Barnes, 1980); Lucas, "Let Olympics Play at a Permanent Site," *USA Today*, 16 September 1988, 8A; Lucas, "Pick a Neutral Site," *U.S. News and World Report, 96*, 28 May 1984, 31. Also "Greece's Olympic Gift Horse," *World Press Review, 27*, July 1980, 62; "A Greek Permanent Home for the Olympics," *New Statesman, 99*, 15 February 1980, 231;

and a quite extraordinary essay by Frederic C. Rich, ''The Legal Regime for a Permanent Olympic Site,'' *New York University Journal of International Law and Politics, 15*, Fall 1982, 1-53.

26. Camelio José Cela, quoted by Marca Antonio Velasco, *Iberia Airline Magazine Ronda*, June 1990, 64.

C·H·A·P·T·E·R·6

The Olympic Games Are for the Athletes

I swam well in the 1932 Olympics, but failed to win a medal. For nearly 60 years I've been uplifted and strengthened by that peak experience

Maria Lenk, *Olympic swimmer*

In an essay titled "The Future of the Olympic Athlete," IOC member Raymond Gafner declared that all the competitors in the Games are due respect, recognition, fair treatment, and some form of financial aid. After all, he said, it is the athlete who brings both wealth and prestige to the Olympic movement.[1] After 22 Olympic Games since World War II (and as we approach the end of the 20th century), it has become more confoundedly difficult to keep this dictum to the fore. Every year, scores of essays in English, German, and French alone discuss the Olympic Movement and the Olympic Games and never mention Olympic athletes, those men and women who are the essence of the enterprise. Pretentiously scientific articles on the

61

Olympic Games run on for thousands of words and never mention the athletes in the arena. These writings sometimes succeed only in being facile, despite their specialized sociological and anthropological jargon. Esoteric exercises in the private languages of hi-tech communications and medicine, and the niagara of puffy profit-loss reports on Olympic enterprises in what seem innumerable business journals and newsletters only distract from the real issue. The athletes are what matters. This chapter is a reminder to all who read it that IOC member Flor Isava Fonseca was right when she wrote that what counts is the athlete.[2] The multitalented American artist LeRoy Nieman, who gained international recognition through his sport art portraying the athlete in heroic and existential terms, agreed. Accomplished in several media—oil and watercolor, sculpture, book design and illustration, etching, lithographs, monotypes, and computer graphics—he observed that "there is something a painter and an athlete have in common. Both are achievers trying to reach the limits of human potential."[3]

High-level sport is like a thousand other human enterprises in that it offers young men and women a precious opportunity to transcend their individually perceived physical and spiritual limits. Yet life for Olympic Games aspirants will continue to be precarious through the remaining years of the 1990s. Never in modern history have athletes had to withstand "this bank and shoal" of imminent danger to their whole persons. Despite possible Olympian rewards, the athletes in the next generation need wisdom and perspective as never before. Luc LeVaillant was too optimistic in his soaring reassurance: "Gone are the days of the 'straw-brained Popeyes' who can think of nothing else except sport."[4] North American and European NOCs are offering their athletes new job-training possibilities in their sometimes unsettled postathletic careers. Of course, all of them—gold-medalist or last-place runner in the marathon—will need much more than job training to survive and flourish in the world after their sport careers. Hopefully, most will make the transition uninjured, whole. Olympic champion rower Andrew Holmes was able to say about his own experience, "Rowing has given me self-respect and faith in myself."[5] But thousands of Olympic Games participants, having spent 10,000 hours training and another 10,000 hours traveling over a 10-year period, end up intellectual cripples, with no visible career skills to see them through the remaining decades of their lives. Ninety-five percent of athletes will make no money from post-Olympic sport. Some other, radically different training will be needed.

The USOC, the IOC, and many international sport federations and NOCs have recently included academic rehabilitative programs, permanent career-seeking orientation sessions, and psychological-remedial opportunities for many of their athletes who know nothing but sports. Oh, to be Sebastian Coe of England, with his intelligence, university education, excellent health, and four gold and silver Olympic medals! After 12 years in the "pit" of world-class athletics, he retired from sport, immediately won (with his multiple skills) a place in British politics, and then waved "a last, last good-by."[6]

The marvelously talented Olympic Games filmmaker, Bud Greenspan, grew up in New York City and had as his hero, Jesse Owens, "the greatest Olympian of them all." Greenspan's several books and his television films have focused on the very best qualities of individual Olympic competitors, both men and women, gold-medalists and nonwinners (Bud never used the terms *loser* or *failure*). Greenspan, considered by most experts in the field to be the best producer of sports documentaries in the world, always focuses on the uniqueness of the athlete, the vulnerability, the soaring grace and skill. Greenspan's films have integrity. "There is no embellishment. The documentaries are pure and simple. They allow the stories to tell themselves with unhindered drama," wrote one London film critic.[7] He is simply "one of the greatest storytellers who has ever lived," wrote the USOC's monthly magazine, *The Olympian*.[8] And always, without being maudlin, the childless Greenspan perceived many Olympic athletes, the very best of their kind, to be his own children. "Most athletes at the Olympic level have special needs, are sensible and emotional people, and, frequently, are quite vulnerable," he has said.

Greenspan's "hauntingly evocative" film specials have won praise around the world for 20 years, and yet he remains true to the individual athlete and to what a *Newsweek* critic called Greenspan's special gold medal for "rekindling the Olympics' flickering image."[9] Greenspan's personal philosophy is that of the best Olympic athletes, a saying from Greek antiquity: "Ask not for victory, ask for courage. For if you can endure the struggle, you bring honor to us all. Even more, you bring honor to yourself." Concentrate on the human being and not on the event, is Greenspan's deceptively simple filmmaking modus. Film critic A. P. Montesano wrote that Greenspan realizes the dramatic content of the individual Olympic athlete's story and that he "does not feel the need, like some, to add to what already is the most dramatic story of all, the will of the human spirit to compete."[10] There is a certain soft yet searing sensitivity in Greenspan's films, and he credits these characteristics, in part, to his late wife, Cappy Petrash, and more recently, to his associate, Nancy Beffa. Someone wrote, "Isn't it nice that Bud Greenspan still sees sports through the eyes of a young boy." Greenspan, his eyeglasses perched precariously on his bald head, answered "When I stop doing that, it'll be over."[11] When interviewer Sandra Peris asked him to define the Olympic Movement, Greenspan—never at a loss for words and always wholly sincere—answered,

> I think it's the way of compensating all the men and women connected with the Olympic Games for all the effort involved in training for 3 years, 11 months and 3 weeks for a few seconds or minutes of real competition. I think it's fascinating. For me the Olympic philosophy is that you can win by losing, because you make the attempt.[12]

Participants Redefine *Winning*

Filmmaker Bud Greenspan's opinion that no athlete is ever a loser at the Olympic Games, provided the effort is honest, is borne out by two remarkable marathon runners at the 1984 Games in Los Angeles. I learned so much about myself, remembered Gabrielle Andersen-Scheiss of Switzerland, and they were lessons for a lifetime. Remember the grotesque sight of her tortured figure in the final lap of the women's marathon as she took a quarter-hour to stagger a few yards through the oppressive heat at field level in the Los Angeles Coliseum? Lofty goals and laudable goals must everlastingly be pursued, she told several hundred young people at the 1986 International Olympic Academy (IOA). That goal is frequently not realized, "as was my case in the Los Angeles marathon." Then she concluded, "Seek excellence everlastingly, for if we surrender in life, it spells personal death, both spiritual and physical."[13]

The winner of that memorable first women's Olympic marathon, Joan Benoit, endured her own nightmare. Just 17 days before the American marathon trials, she underwent knee surgery, and the experts said "no way" to her chances of running well in the 42-kilometer classic. She either did not listen or just ignored them and took charge of the race in the first 3 miles, forced the pace, then turned her baseball hat backwards and ran the second half as strongly as she had the first 72 minutes, finally struggling through the last yard to set the marathon's first-run Olympic record at 2 hrs 24 min 52 sec. In a book about her experience, *Running Tide*, Benoit gave her own personal philosophy about handling all future exigencies. "Love yourself," she wrote, "not hedonistically, but essentially. Love what you are, protect your dreams, and develop your talents to their fullest extent."[14] Brazilian swimmer Maria Lenk was 78 when she wrote, "I swam well in the 1932 Olympics, but failed to win a medal. For nearly 60 years I've been uplifted and strengthened by that peak experience."[15]

Standing nearly 2 meters tall and with a massive and powerful body, IOC member Anton Geesink dismissed his memorable gold-medal judo victory in Tokyo in 1964, the first ever by a non-Asian. "My concern is with today's athletes and their future," he stated with a quiet intensity that belied his size. "There are so many more temptations for present-day Olympians. From cradle to the international victory stand, athletes of the future desperately need to be exposed to a moral and Olympian education. There is no other way." He continued that Olympic Games participation was and is a meaningful experience for most, a symbolic as well as physical experience. Yet the athletes of the future must help themselves and be helped by others.[16]

It was a message, a warning, and a call for help not dissimilar to that of Olympic historian John J. MacAloon, who said in an 8,000-word essay that the Olympic athlete, regardless of nation of origin, is capable of enormous influence—such is the symbolic power of the Olympic Games—and simultaneously is surprisingly vulnerable. Living three lives at the same time—that of a private person, a national figure, and a member of an international elite—renders the Olympian's actions especially significant. For inside the Olympic stadium, they are the rulers, MacAloon said, and as such they have the capacity to make certain precious messages meaningful for all of us.[17]

Paying the Price

Most of the world's elite, nonprofessional athletes receive financial aid from universities, governments, business corporations, clubs, and from the Tripartite—NOC, international sport federations, and IOC (called "the Family" by Olympic people). Most need this helping hand because the nearly incalculable hours of training, travel, and competition often result in traumatized bodies, minds, and psyches. Training to win an Olympic gold medal is an unequivocally unhealthy way to spend part of one's life. Clinics, hospitals, sports medicine centers, trauma units, laboratories, first aid infirmaries—all come to the aid of the athletic trainer in the constant, around-the-clock care of the international sports person. More help is to be had from a sophisticated army of sport physicians, sport psychologists, biomechanical engineers, physiologists, motor-learning experts, orthopedic surgeons, even orthodontists and optometrists who specialize in the athlete's unique problems. This is not to mention the role of electromyographers, strength-training specialists, hypnotists, podiatrists, organic chemists, and a swarm of super-specialized coaches—all focusing on the uniquely talented, but not especially healthy, Olympic athletes. And it will continue in this vein for some years. Only the athletes themselves can control the intensity of effort and involvement of this formidable support staff or, if they wish, put a stop to it all.

Some progressive and relatively wealthy national Olympic committees have vocational training centers, post-Olympic career programs, counseling sessions, and "back-to-civilian-life" courses.[18] The charismatic mayor of Paris, Jacques Chirac and his advisor, Monique Berlioux, created a program "pour les athlètes d'elite," which gives some of France's best athletes an opportunity to plan for life beyond the Olympic stadium.[19] The Canadian and United States Olympic committees have job opportunities programs for athletes in training and special education-career preparation courses for athletes after their sporting days. The well-organized Belgian Olympic Committee has a "Comité des Athlètes et Sport de Haut Niveau" to help Belgian young people to constantly seek "high standards in every dimension of their lives."[20] The closing years of the 1990s and the centennial celebration of the Olympic Movement will undoubtedly see an increase in NOC and sport federation support systems for athletes during the "agony and ecstasy" of their frenetic international competitions, but also during the longer and equally important time after their retirement from sport.

Looking Beyond the Days of Competition

The wisdom of Olympic athletes about their own future comes from men and women, young and old, and from every continent. At the New York City Marathon in November 1990, two African Olympians finished first and fourth. When interviewed by veteran television broadcaster Jim McKay, the defending champion, Juma Ikangaa of Tanzania, explained that "the will to win means nothing if you do not have the will to prepare, and both of them are meaningless if not used in life after the marathon.'' Ikangaa finished fourth that day, after running much of the race beside the winner from Kenya, 37-year-old Douglas Wakiihuri, who revealed that "preparing for marathons and running in them is important to me, terribly important. But they are part of the first part of my life and will help me be strong during that second phase.''[21]

Australian Shane Innes (née Gould), said that her adult life was shaped by those intense youthful years of swimming. Innes's family praised her every little success, out of as well as in the pool. All this support was "equally terrific" and has stayed with her, she added.[22] Her two Olympic gold medals in the discus meant a great deal to Germany's Evelin Schlaak Herberg, but so did all the preparation, which "gave me the necessary balance in my life after sport.''[23]

There's so much more of this athlete's wisdom, but too often in retrospect. Ten-time world's champion and Lake Placid silver medalist in figure skating, Jan Hoffmann (now a physician) was convinced that his dozen years of unrelenting discipline had been excellent preparation for his modest efforts "to resolve the existential issue facing humanity, the struggle for peace.''[24]

These are a few of the thousands of Olympic "survivors." But equal numbers have been irreparably damaged by years and years on the training and competitive fields and inside the Olympic arena. So very many athletes in recent times have spent most of their youth consumed by sport that they find themselves, as Canada's Ken Read so aptly put it, "dancing on the razor's edge.''[25] Far and away, the athletes themselves are responsible for their conduct and their achievements, as well as their inactions and moral derelictions. And though assistance programs must be increased, help is close at hand if they, the athletes, will only reach out.

The honest mind of Baron de Coubertin perceived the revived 20th-century Olympic Games as a hymn of praise for the athletes. To him, these young people involved in high-minded competition came first. He knew nothing of commercial endorsements, media complexities, and today's utterly fantastic methods of nurturing a special cadre of physical super-people. Few of us want to turn back the clock, even if we could, but there is today a groundswell against what Robert Creamer of *Sports Illustrated* called the trend to treat Olympians as "little more than actors in a gaudy show.''[26] To state that many of the changes in the Olympic Games have aided both athletes and spectators is only to acknowledge reality, but that in no way suggests that the whole Olympic idea be turned upside down. Olympic athletes must be something more than only actors on one of the world's largest stages. Their concerned voices, IOC President Samaranch promised, will be "increasingly heard and recognized.''[27] Of course, it is only fair, for it was and is these same professional and nonprofessional athletes who have brought to the Olympic Movement in 20 years an awesome level of recognition, prestige, and some $3 billion in income.

Fifty-year-old IOC member Ivan Slavkov, a water polo Olympian and television commentator in Bulgaria, was "100 percent for the athlete." Somehow we must all work to restore a level of joy and spontaneity to the lives of our athletes, he said, "the way that it was for me 30 years ago as we cavorted in our water polo pool." The Olympic family can do it, provided there is "balance in everything" and, most importantly, Slavkov ended, that "we make money *for* sport rather than making money *out of* sport."[28] Another water polo star of the 1960s, and also an experienced IOC member and former president of the United States Olympic Committee (USOC), Robert H. Helmick, said something similar. He admitted that there exists in the Olympic world a narrow-mindedness and malaise that too often prevent its members from seeing "the larger vision of what we are about, a direction for us to go, a place for all of us, especially the athletes, to reside." And that place, ended Helmick, is where all qualified athletes might compete fairly and fully, unencumbered by suffocating layers of bureaucratic restraint.[29] Philippe Chartrier, longtime president of the Fédération Internationale de Tennis and IOC board member, wrote "that by inviting the best athletes—professional and amateur—to compete every 4 years, we are on the right track."[30]

The IOC's 13-person Commission des Athlètes, made up of IOC members and very recent Olympic athletes, is convinced that it can help all Olympians who call for help, today and tomorrow. Anita DeFrantz, a member of that commission, represents the near-perfect melding of Olympic medal-winner (in rowing) and IOC member. Her challenge is to empathize in both directions and to work toward the fulfillment of congruent goals. In an *Olympic Message* issue entirely devoted to "people athletes need," DeFrantz was passionate in her definition of an athlete's family. Everyone can come to the aid of the aspiring athlete: friend, parents, teachers, coaches, sport federations, NOCs, and the IOC. And then let that person work extraordinarily hard and with honest technical assistance and ethically sound medical support, all in this "celebration of human excellence."[31] In the same issue, Japan's great judo star, Nobuyuki Sato, outlined his plan of hard work and public service, a plan for "champions of sport to become champions of life."[32] So often one hears this complaint among Olympic athletes: What do I do with my life after standing center-stage inside the Olympic stadium?

When Lord Philip Noel-Baker, in his 92nd year of a remarkable life, moved to the speaker's platform of the Olympic Congress in Baden-Baden, Germany, on 26 September 1981, a thousand delegates from every nation rose to their feet and applauded the Nobel Peace Prize winner and former Olympic Games athlete (1912 through 1924). They applauded again when the elderly man, leaning heavily on his cane, promised that "if the IOC can make a substantial contribution to both the sport-for-all movement and to the health of elite athletes, then I shall recommend to Norway that the Nobel Peace Prize be awarded to the International Olympic Committee."[33] He died exactly 1 year later, unable to keep his promise.[34] Noel-Baker was the idealized Olympic athlete, the quintessential Olympian. He was a fine athlete—a silver medalist at the 1920 Antwerp Games in the 1500-meter run—and a sensitive and intelligent university scholar, and he had a brilliant career in the diplomatic corps and in the international peace movement. He should stand as a model for athletes, an inspiration for those who make the commitment to lift up the level of their own physical prowess, to begin the process of intellectual perspicacity and personal unselfishness—and to do all three simultaneously. It's a tall order, one that was difficult in Noel-Baker's era but that, in theory at least, should be a little more attainable in the 1990s. Support systems (see chapter 8) for all athletes abound in our time, and the IOC, NOCs, and sport federations need to set aside hundreds of millions of dollars to "save" the post-Olympic athlete. Most of the young men and women will have the motivation, discipline, and staying power to take advantage of such help, but only if the caring is there.

The most thoughtful of our athletes have always, amidst the "battle" of high-level competitions, kept one eye on the future. Al Oerter won four consecutive Olympic gold medals from 1956 through 1968. He threw the discus a million times and always claimed that it was preparation for "life-after-sport" as a computer engineer. Winning in sport and satisfaction with one's life career are related, he suggested. The point is not to win, but rather to be well focused, so that the effort of 4 years of training would culminate on just one day. "You're focusing the sun's rays through a magnifying glass, and you're right in the little spot of heat." He retained this laser-like "spot of heat" and at 50 years of age, was still ranked among the best discus throwers in the world—along with being a very successful engineer.[35] Thus, for the elite athlete, the Olympic athlete, the future is rooted in the past and it becomes a duty for those who touch the lives of these athletes to come to their aid—now. There's so much more that they can do for themselves, and yet honest empathy from others can be effective.

A certain educational futurist talking about students said that "the future will arrive ahead of schedule."[36] The Olympic Games of the 1990s will be high-voltage experiences and, for the aspiring Olympian, a tortuous trip, one embarked on willingly, but one implicitly difficult. Every national Olympic committee and all sport federations, during the remaining years of this century, must make extraordinary efforts to encourage their athletes about the quality of their lives in the next century, and to serve these young men and women in ways that are clear, lofty, utilitarian—and not necessarily in that order.

Notes

1. Raymond Gafner, "The Future of the Olympic Athlete," *Olympic Message, 2*, September 1982, 29-37.

2. Fonseca, "What Counts Is the Athlete," *Olympic Review, 267*, January 1990, 25.

3. Nieman, quoted in *Olympic Review, 260*, June 1989, 273.

4. Luc LeVaillant, "Retraining: Top Level Athletes Seek Careers as High-Flyers," *Olympic Review, 258*, April 1989, 151.

5. *Olympic Review, 266*, December 1989, 559.

6. Sebastian Coe, *Olympic Review, 269*, March 1990, 154-155.

7. Sam Barnes, "The Olympiad: The Very Best," *London Free Press*, 28 February 1976, n.p.

8. "The Olympic Storyteller," *The Olympian, 17*, July-August 1990, 7.

9. Harry F. Waters, *Newsweek, 87*, 24 May 1976, 98.

10. Anthony P. Montesano, "Medal Contenders," *American Film, 13*, September 1988, 57-63.

11. Bud Greenspan, quoted in Lawrence Van Gelder's column "At the Movies," in the *New York Times*, 11 November 1988, C6. Greenspan (1927-   ) has, to date, written three books: *Play It Again, Bud!*; *We Was Robbed*; and *Glory of Their Times*. Some of his acclaimed Olympic Games films are: *Jesse Owens Returns to Berlin; An Olympic Symphony; Wilma; Numero Uno; The 1932 Summer Olympic Games; Glory of Their Times; The Olympiad; Sixteen Days of Glory 1984; An Olympic Dream; Time Capsule: The 1936 Berlin Olympic Games; Calgary '88: 16 Days of Glory; Seoul '88: 16 Days of Glory; The Golden Age of Sport*; and, in preparation for the 1992 Olympic Games, *For the Honor of Their Country*. His "Great Moments in Sport" was a gold-record album. In 1985, IOC President Samaranch awarded Greenspan the coveted Olympic Order.

12. Greenspan, "My Dream Is to Film the Barcelona '92 Olympics," *Olympic Review, 274*, August 1990, 371. The Olympic Movement and the Olympic Games are not synonymous. The former includes international sport on every continent and during every week of the year; the Olympic Games are periodical competitions.

13. The everlasting desire to do one's best in every endeavor, she said, can lead one "to increased standards and personal growth," Gabrielle Andersen-Scheiss, "Olympic Experience," *Proceedings IOA 1986*, 254.

14. See Ross Atkin, "Joan Benoit Samuelson Eyes Olympic Marathon Repeat," *Christian Science Monitor*, 7 March 1988, 18.

15. Maria Lenk, letter to author, 30 June 1990.

16. Anton J. Geesink, interview with author, Tokyo, 14 September 1990. Marie-Hélène Roukhadzé wrote an illuminating biography of Geesink in *Olympic Review, 269*, March 1990, 139-142.

17. MacAloon's message was delivered to an audience at Olympia's IOA and published in the *Olympic Message, 3*, December 1982, 22-36, and in the *Proceedings IOA 1982*, 132-148.

18. There are hundreds of such athlete help programs around the world. Several are discussed in Patrice Ragni, "Athletes Psychoanalysed," *Olympic Review, 265*, November 1989, 501-505, and Donato Martucci, "Return the Athlete to Society," *Olympic Review, 269*, March 1990, 143-145.

19. Guy Drut and Monique Berlioux, *Jacques Chirac—La Victoire du Sport* (Paris: DPS, 1988), 132-135.

20. See Paul Urbain's essay in *News Olympic of the Comité Olympique Belge*, September 1990, 14.

21. Both Africans interviewed as part of the American Broadcasting Company (ABC) telecast of the 21st New York City Marathon, 4 November 1990. Between them, Ikangaa and Wakiihuri have run more marathon races (42 kilometers) under 130 minutes than any other pair in the history of the sport. See the *New York Times*, 5 November 1990, 1, C1-C7.

22. Shane Gould, in David Hemery, *The Pursuit of Sporting Excellence* (Champaign, IL: Human Kinetics, 1986), 240.

23. E.S. Herberg, "Olympic Experiences," *Proceedings IOA 1986*, 255.

24. See Hoffman, "Impressions," *Proceedings IOA 1988*, 235-236.

25. Ken Read, ibid, 218.

26. Robert Creamer, in *Sports Illustrated, 44*, 26 January 1976, 9.

27. Samaranch, at the IOC's 95th Session in Puerto Rico, 29 August 1989. See *Olympic Review, 263-264*, September-October 1989, 431.

28. Ivan Slavkov, interview with author, Tokyo, 19 September 1990.

29. Robert Helmich, interview with author, Philadelphia, 9 October 1990.

30. Philippe Chartrier, letter to author, 17 August 1989.

31. Anita L. DeFrantz, "Families in Sport," *Olympic Message, 18*, August 1987, 15.

32. Nobuyuki Sato, "Pride Goeth Before the Fall," *Olympic Message, 18*, August 1987, 22. Other essays in this issue include Hall-of-Fame figure skater Courtney J.L. Jones on "Fairness First"; Olympic champion and Romanian NOC president, Lia Manoliu, "From the Stadium to the Office"; and France's gold-medal fencer, Philippe Riboud, with Olympic "greats" Pal Schmitt, Ken Read, and Michelle Ford, "The Athlete and His Future." Their message was that athletes need information, more information, and the lightest hand of help in order to make it into the altogether-more-important world beyond the Olympic Games.

33. Philip Noel-Baker, *Olympischen Kongres Baden-Baden 1981* (Berichte und Dokumente zum 11, 1982), 185.

34. The *New York Times* of 9 October 1982, 30 carried Noel-Baker's obituary. After 70 years of Olympic Games watching, he commented in the *Olympic Review* of May 1981:

> The victory ceremonies in the Olympic Games are a supreme example of this marriage of national and international patriotism and pride . . . and are a witness, more precious perhaps, than any other in any realm of Man's activity, to the unity of the human race, to common interests, the shared ideals and friendship, of all nations everywhere.

35. "Al Oerter Breaks the Age Barrier With Every Toss," *Christian Science Monitor*, 2 April 1990, 1-2.

36. Steve Benjamin, "An Ideascope for Education: What Futurists Recommend," *Educational Leadership, 47*, September 1989, 12.

C·H·A·P·T·E·R·7

Olympic Entrepreneurship:
The Search for the *Golden Mean*

There is a new professionalism in the air and sponsorship is seen as a part of the promotional package.

Investor's Chronicle

The most discouraging comment on Olympic leadership and the direction of the Olympic Movement came from gold-medalist and professor of philosophy at Karlsruhe University, Hans Lenk. Lenk's love affair with the Olympic idea goes back more than 30 years, to the pope's Italian summer home, Castel Gandolfo. At nearby Lake Albano, the German rowing-eight, using the very latest scientific knowledge of shells and rowing techniques, swept to victory in the 1960 Games. Lenk sat in the middle that day, but over the next 2 decades, he moved to the front in mathematics and philosophy. His published works in these two areas and in the subdiscipline of sport philosophy were prodigious, but when asked about the future of the Olympic Games, he wrote,

I am not really working in scientific problems of the Olympics any longer, since I am rather suspicious about its future. On the one hand it will remain to be a great spectacular televisionary success, a tele-economic super spectacle so to speak, but on the other hand most of the value-orientations have been pushed aside or ignored.[1]

In a 1987 lecture to several hundred delegates at the 11th United States Olympic Academy (USOA), I commented that my search of journal literature had uncovered not a single essay on Olympic philosophy, 1 essay each on Olympic Games history and Games philosophy, 33 technical papers on Olympic buildings and stadia, and 131 articles on Olympics-related business, marketing, advertising, and profits and losses. Then I asked, "Is my research deficient, incomplete?"[2] The answer was—and still is—an emphatic *no*. For every article dealing with scholarly and educational matters of the Olympic Games, there are several dozen pieces on Olympic cash flow in magazines such as *Advertising Age, Business World, Business Week, Forbes, Fortune,* the *Wall Street Journal, Financial Times, The Economist, Broadcasting, Marketing News,* and the *Journal of Advertising Research.* Two dozen others address television, marketing and sales, corporate sponsorship, packaging, and, worst of all, "selling the Olympic rings."[3] The question is not whether the Olympic Movement should be generating a huge cash flow. Of course it should, and it is doing so successfully, honestly, and with dignity. Of deeper concern is the growing public opinion that the Olympic Games and the Olympic Movement are no more than gigantic money-making machines.

The 1981 conference in Baden-Baden, Germany, was a watershed for the international Olympic Movement. President Samaranch gave the green light for the IOC and the Olympic family to go into areas hitherto forbidden. The dissolution of the unenforceable "pure amateur code" was the first substantial and partially successful effort to blend the IOC, the NOCs, and all the international sport federations into a like-minded semidemocracy. Just as important, the 11th Congress struck boldly in the direction of increased television revenues and initiated straight-line negotiations for huge sums of money. No previous congress could boast such a near "three-out-of-three" success.

The venerable Giorgio De Stefani, the Italian tennis star of the 1930s and, for more than 40 years, an influential IOC member wrote about this all-important congress that so very much was done—and all of it for the athletes. "We put to rest some old myths, addressed straightforwardly the threats of terrorism, boycotts, and political intervention. We also explored untapped and nearly unlimited sources of revenue for the Olympic movement, almost all of which would be spent for the athletes."[4] Modern Olympic entrepreneurship began at Baden-Baden in 1981. A disquieting note to this historic meeting was a conversation with Otto Szymiczek, dean of the International Olympic Academy from 1961 until his death in 1990. Szymiczek shook his head at an acrimonious meeting in which NOCs from several underdeveloped nations demanded a larger share of television monies. The fifth IOC president, Brundage, ''was not a reactionary; he was a futurist,'' volunteered Szymiczek:

> As early as 1960, Brundage saw that television monies would eventually create massive Olympic disharmony. Did you notice the wholesale preoccupation with money at this morning's meeting? Mr. Brundage would not have been surprised.[5]

Both President Brundage and Dean Szymiczek[6] were correct, of course. But what they failed to understand is that the Olympic Movement of the 1990s, like any family, can survive disharmony if the real benefits are substantial, sustaining, and, in the case of scores of NOCs, bridge the difference between mere survival and partial support of a country's athletic population.

The Olympic Games are the largest regularly recurring event in the modern world.[7] Television has brought the Games to all six continents and to an audience of half the world's population. More than a billion dollars is involved. Several hundred of the world's largest corporations are willing, even eager, to spend another billion dollars for exclusive rights to display on their goods the most recognized of all logos, the Olympic rings. The combined incomes to the IOC, from television companies and international business firms, complement one another, allowing the IOC to avoid putting all its financial trust in one or the other. Olympic committees of the 1990s are sitting in the ''catbird seat'' as the money rolls in. But caution is necessary; as Mario Vazquez Raña, president of the Association of NOCs (ANOC) said, ''We must take great care and avoid immoderate commercialisation.''[8]

The IOC and Television Entrepreneurship, 1988 to 1994

Amid the blizzard of IOC enterprises, but not necessarily at its center, is the serious business of making money through contracts with television networks around the world. IOC agreements with corporations in Europe, Africa, South America, Canada, the Soviet Union, Australia, and Japan are worth millions of dollars and represent a potential source of revenue for the IOC. Yet their combined monies do not approach the sums received from the United States and its three major networks, the American Broadcasting Company (ABC), Columbia Broadcasting System (CBS), and the National Broadcasting Company (NBC).[9] ABC's agreement with the IOC for the Calgary '88 Winter Olympic Games was $326 million (Canadian), and NBC finally agreed to pay the IOC a guaranteed $300 million with an additional

$200 million on a risk-sharing basis, a total of $500 million for the Summer Games in Seoul.[10]

The "financial engine" known as the IOC, despite deriving credibility and permission from its own Charter,[11] is certainly not free from internal cautionary notes, usually from the more conservative members of the Olympic family. In an expertly written essay by William O. Johnson and Anita Verschoth, titled "Olympic Circus Maximus," the IOC's Count de Beaumont replied to a question about the state of the movement: "It is only a question of money . . . pouff."[12] The president of the French NOC, Nelson Paillou, warned that the two great dangers facing the Olympic Tripartite are excessive political chauvinism and excessive mercantilism. But it need not fall prey to such if its members are men and women of honor and common sense. He concluded, "I agree with my fellow countryman, Montaigne [16th century essayist and philosopher], who said it is better to have 'a head made for thinking rather than full of thoughts.' "[13]

CBS outbid NBC "by a lot" to win the broadcasting rights to the 1992 Winter Olympic Games in Albertville, France. Because of its failing popularity ratings compared to those of ABC and NBC, CBS paid the IOC $243 million and was back in Olympic TV business for the first time since Rome 1960. NBC moguls blasted CBS for paying such an "absurdly high sum." Annoyed NBC sports president Arthur Watson said, "You always want to be a winner. But you don't want to commit suicide at the same time."[14] When the dust settled, and the IOC found itself richer by nearly half a billion dollars for the two Olympic Games in 1992 (thanks to CBS and NBC), it was the IOC that expressed "high spirits"—not the television executives. Michael Janofsky of the *New York Times* was there and described IOC senior officials as "almost giddy with satisfaction and relief." I never expected to get so much money, said President Samaranch. "So the contract we got is a very good one, no?" he asked rhetorically.[15]

ABC got out of the business of televising Olympic Games in March 1989, having broadcast 10 Olympic Games since 1964. "We do not intend to bid for the 1994 Winter Games in Lillehammer," was how they put it. (There had been "stunned silence" at the IOC meeting on 15 September 1988 in Seoul when it was announced that the little Norwegian resort town of Lillehammer had won the coveted prize—until the usually taciturn Scandinavians "erupted with joy and flag-waving, pinched themselves and began to celebrate.")[16] The two remaining American television giants began serious bidding, and on 24 October 1989, CBS again won the contract, this time for $300 million. Mark Harrington of CBS began plans to send 1,500 technicians to Lillehammer "in groups of 500 at a time."[17] On 23 April 1990, the Norwegian Parliament gave its full political, moral, and financial support to the Lillehammer Olympic Organization Committee (LOOC), their collective voice "Norway is proud" supported by the allocation of 7 billion Norwegian kroner ($1 billion). "This will be the largest sporting event Norway has ever organized, but we have the resources," said Prime Minister

Gro Harlem Brundtland. The president of the LOOC, Gerhard Heiberg, said the money would be well spent, repeating the litany of previous organizing leaders, "Our winter Olympic Games will be the best ever."[18] It was comforting to the IOC that the collective brain power of the whole, mammoth Olympic family seemed to have everything well in hand: the imminent Olympic Games in 1992; a national mandate for a successful 1994 Winter Games; powerful social, cultural, political, and multibillion dollar support for the 1996 Summer Olympic Games in Atlanta; and another dozen cities clamoring for the privilege of hosting either the 1998 festival or the Olympic Games in the millennial year 2000. For the IOC it seemed that, to parrot Dickens "it was the best of times." Only a natural catastrophe or, more likely, some human global cataclysm can put an immediate end to these best-laid plans.

Corporate Sponsorship Provides More Balance

There was a time not so long ago when the IOC depended on television for 95% of its income. No longer. The international Coca-Cola Company spent $22 million at the Seoul Olympic Games to guarantee that no competitive soft drink be allowed to display the Olympic rings or to sell their products at any Olympic stadia. The Olympic Programme (TOP) is the worldwide sponsoring agent of the IOC, and they are joined by the expert marketing consortium, International Sports and Leisure (ISL). TOP was first discussed at the New Delhi meeting of the IOC in 1982, and the Swiss-based company ISL was created the same year, following the soccer World Cup in Madrid. Slowly, discreetly, small numbers of billion-dollar corporations have been invited into the TOP-ISL-IOC inner circle, and by 1991, the sums of money earned by the IOC began to approach 50-50, or equal amounts of IOC income earned from television and other corporations.[19] Diversity had nearly been achieved, because the IOC hierarchy anticipated a possible decrease of television monies in the second half of the 1990s.

There seemed to be no crisis at the 1990 meeting of the IOC in Tokyo, where some of the world's richest corporations lined up and signed up with the TOP-ISL-IOC, all for the privilege of Olympic five-rings exclusivity (see chapter 3). There were new wrinkles, but it was a very old game. Older than Coca-Cola at the 1928 Olympic Games and Kodak film at the first modern Games in Athens 1896, was the first automobile sporting event in 1887, supported by the French magazine *Velocipède*. The British journal *Investor's Chronicle* recently chirped, "There is a new professionalism in the air and sponsorship is seen as a part of the promotional package."[20]

Some of France's biggest and best corporations (the SNCF French National Railways; Renault; AGF Assurances Générales de France; IBM; and others) formed a consortium, called Club Coubertin, and nearly 2 billion French francs (FF) are anticipated, with the Albertville organizing committee, the corporations, and the IOC to share the wealth.[21] Not far away, Barcelona's organizing committee (COOB '92) was working hard on a projected final $140 million profit from services rendered, ticket sales, accommodations, lotteries, stamp, medal, and coin sales, and of course, the great "double-dip"—television and corporate sponsorship.[22] Professionalism in the packaging and selling of the Olympic Games is a new phenomenon and the Olympic Movement has entered this entrepreneurial arena with all—possibly more—of the enthusiasm and skill of older and more experienced competitors. The IOC and its affiliated NOCs and sport federations have made the decision to go this direction, because, as their leaders say, they are inexorably drawn there, and the entire future of the international Olympic Movement lies in the direction of *shared* funding from most of the world's governments and from some of the biggest and best business corporations.

The IOC Climbs Into the Marketplace

During the Winter and Summer Olympic Games at St. Moritz and Amsterdam (1928), at Lake Placid and Los Angeles (1932), and the double German Games of 1936 in Garmisch and Berlin, 95 to 98% of the thousands of competitors made no money from their participation, not a franc, dollar, or mark. In other words, only a small, smart-looking cadre of superstars profited at all from their dearly-won gold medals. We know them well: Paavo Nurmi, Charley Paddock, Sonja Heine, Maribel Vinson, Eleanor Holm, Buster Crabbe, Glenn Morris, Ray Barbuti, Willy Ritola, and several other marketable Olympic champions. Two generations later, nothing has changed, except the sums of money involved. In the 1980s and 1990s, 90% of Olympic athletes came away with memories, good and bad, but absolutely nothing more. To be sure, there were those in North America, Asia, and Europe who became "as rich as Croesus." That hasn't changed in 60 years—and yet almost everything else is different in the Olympic story.

The single, biggest development has been the democratization of the Olympic Movement today and with it, the attendant bedfellow, capitalism. In the old days of elitist Olympic administration, that athletes should profit monetarily was anathema. Even today, the mounting profits being made by the Olympic Tripartite and by some highly visible Olympic champions have roused a far louder criticism than in the past—and in the 1920s and 1930s, there were legions of Olympic Games critics. The nature and intensity of today's faultfinding is different from yesteryear's (see chapter 11).

Nowhere in the world is it well known that most of the money earned by the Olympic network reverts back to the athletes. What is better understood by the media and the public is that there is very big money out there in the Olympic world, that a great many Olympic-related people are living well, and that a relatively small number of superathletes are being treated in an idolatrous manner, that is, they are allowed to make a great deal of money.

There is some public disenchantment with this in Europe and North America, and as the 1990s continue, more criticism of national Olympic committees, domestic and international sport federations, and the IOC itself will occur. This last company of 7 women and 85 men (as of early 1991) has made an effort to counter this poor publicity by underscoring the importance of the Pierre de Coubertin-created movement, *Sport-for-All*. Every third or fourth speech of IOC President Samaranch has emphasized the moral urgency of the Olympic family moving in this direction of mass sport, school physical education, and healthy, safe recreational activities for the millions. There seems to be a blind spot in many societies, however, when it comes to providing modest financial assistance to aspiring Olympic athletes not yet ranked in the "Top Ten" in their event. Almost no NOC or sport federation is giving much real help to these very talented young men and women.

The drumbeat of concern, questioning, constructive criticism, and plain written and verbal censure, directed at the IOC especially, continues in regard to a perceived unapologetic preoccupation of the Olympics with high finance. It is not enough that these critics are told (perhaps too infrequently) that they do not fully understand that this money is returned in an honest and efficient manner to those people and institutions that need it most. The Olympic family talks to itself, through blizzards of letters, notes, telegrams, and the newly ubiquitous fax sheets when it needs to talk to the *world* and explain the disposition of these monies. It needs a better system by which to better inform all branches of the media, perhaps requesting that they in turn write interesting, even provocative features about Solidarity monies, grants to NOCs and ISFs, and the hundred imaginative ways in which deserving athletes around the world are given tiny but still helpful financial grants. (Developing such a system should preoccupy Olympic bureaucratic specialists for the rest of the 1990s.) For example, there seemed to be no visible support or condemnation from the IOC when American tycoon Ted Turner bought 50 hours of television time for $50 million, in order to sell cable "pay-per-view" of the Barcelona Games. In fact, NBC sold 600 hours of Olympic Games events for $500 million to three simultaneous-broadcast pay channels.[23] These were exciting, extraordinary, and honest business deals. And yet, because it is a nonprofit sporting organization, the IOC must be ever responsive to the all-too-frequent criticism that, since the days of its previous presidents, Brundage and Killanin, it has moved like a shot in the direction of a monopolistic, international business syndicate.

TOP-I was the successful ISL-IOC marketing plan for the 1988 Olympic Games. An even more ambitious TOP-II plan for the double games of 1992, involving Coca-Cola, Eastman Kodak, 3M, Ricoh, Matsushita, *Sports Illustrated*, Visa, and the U.S. Postal Service's international express mail service, brought in "more than $120 million" to the IOC coffers[24]. British television historian, Steven Barnett, warned the IOC to resist what he saw to be an ever-growing American demand for their Olympic pound of flesh. If we are not careful, the Olympic Games could be hijacked by an obsessively competitive American television industry, whose money will eventually corrupt completely the original [Olympic] spirit.[25]

Similarly, Steven Aris's acid article in the *London Financial Times* supplement said that Baron de Coubertin would have found fault as "the lordly IOC climbed down into the market place."[26] Money and the IOC are synonymous in this "growing commercialism of the Games" was the overstated comment in the *New York Times*.[27]

There have been a hundred warnings and many harsh words leveled against the Olympic committee,[28] but John Rodda, the veteran Olympic Games journalist from the *London-Manchester Guardian*, possibly summed it up best when he said that although the enormous new wealth enjoyed by the IOC has the capacity to erode Olympic democracy, impartiality, and independence, this has not yet happened. And because the benefits to athletes everywhere are enormous, Rodda concluded, the perilous experiment with big business should be allowed to continue.[29]

During the titanic years of money-making in American history (1880-1910), men like John D. Rockefeller, J.P. Morgan, Charles Schwab, Andrew Mellon, George Pullman, and Andrew Carnegie spent their vigorous years accumulating wealth, rose in power almost equal to that of the federal government, and then, without exception, moved to unprecedented generosity. The Olympic Movement, especially the IOC, is bedazzled by its newfound avenues of financial opportunity and will continue exploring them for some years to come. By the millennial year 2000, the IOC will have accumulated in properties, investments, credits, and cash sufficient billions of dollars so that it can "ease off." It will pull back appreciably from this financial focus and be able at last to devote nearly all of its vast power, influence, and new wealth to educational and altruistic efforts at an even higher level and through a more universal presence than are now possible. Jacques Rogge, editor of *Sport Europe*, voiced the concern of many: "The Olympic Movement should control this financial [preoccupation] and keep its soul."[30] Balance, control, and historic perspective are everything in this blending of the Olympic past, present, and future.

Notes

1. Hans Lenk, letter to author, 9 August 1989.
2. John Lucas, "Contrasting Faces of the Olympic Ideal," *Proceedings USOA 1987*, 168.
3. One of my graduate students, more skillful with a computer than I, located 2,000 references to the Olympic Games and television alone.
4. Giorgio De Stefani, letter to author, 22 January 1982.

5. Otto Szymiczek, interview with author, 11th Olympic Congress in Baden-Baden, Germany, 21 September 1981.

6. Dean Szymiczek died in August 1990, a hero to both the Hungarian and the Hellenic Olympic Committees, having served the latter with honor for 58 years.

7. Eric W. Rothenbuhler used the word *probably* in a similar statement in the *Journal of Communication, 38*, Autumn 1988, 64.

8. Raña, quoted in *Sport Europe. AENOC Official Magazine, 1*, 1990, 25. The ANOC Constitution (p. 6) states that one of its objectives is to "formulate recommendations to the IOC regarding the utilization of the television funds provided for the NOCs."

9. There are at least a dozen texts on sport television. Four representative books are Jim Spence, *The Inside Story of Network Television Sports* (New York: Atheneum, 1988); David A. Klatell and Norman Marcus, *Sports For Sale—Television, Money, and the Fans* (New York: Oxford University Press, 1988); Steven Barnett, *Games and Sets. The Changing Face of Sport on Television* (London: BFI, 1990); and Terry O'Neil, *The Games Behind the Games* (New York: Harper & Row, 1989).

10. The ABC and NBC agreements for both Olympic Games in 1988 may be substantiated by consulting the *Official Report XV Olympic Winter Games* (Calgary: ODA, 1988), 79-81; *Maclean's Magazine, 101*, February 1988, 98-102; *Sports inc.*, 15 February 1988, 1; *New York Times*, 20 November 1988, sec. 8, 11; *Television and Radio Age, 35*, 7 March 1988, 37-39, 121; Vincent Jean Riquart, *The Games Within the Games. The Story Behind the Seoul Olympics* (Seoul: Hantong Books, 1988); Kim Un-Yong, *The Greatest Olympics: From Baden-Baden to Seoul* (Seoul: Si-sa-yong-o-sa, 1990); and *Olympic Review, 254*, December 1988, 688-691.

11. Olympic Charter '90, By-laws 6 and 51, 36-37, cover all forms of exclusivity regarding the Olympic rings and mascots, and the commercial use of these immediately recognizable symbols.

12. *Sports Illustrated, 65*, 27 October 1986, 43.

13. The *Magazine of the Organizing Committee for the XVIth Olympic Winter Games 1992*, October 1990, n.p.

14. Watson's quote is in the *Wall Street Journal*, 26 May 1988, 32. Much more literature exists. See *Sports Illustrated, 68*, 6 June 1988, 30-32; *Dallas Morning News*, 25 May 1988, Sport section; *Sports inc., 1*, 20 June 1988, 49; *Advertising Age, 59*, 30 May 1988, 3, 70; *Broadcasting, 114*, 30 May 1988, 24; and the *New York Times*, 30 May 1988, 32.

15. *New York Times*, 6 December 1988, B22.

16. See "ABC Will Stop Being Olympic Torchbearer," *USA Today*, 24 March 1989. Norwegians celebrate: see *New York Times*, 16 September

1988, D19, D21; *International Herald Tribune*, 16 September 1988, 17; the *Christian Science Monitor*, 16 September 1988, 18; Randy Harvey in "Longshot Lillehammer" quotes IOC Vice President Richard Pound: "One thing I've learned in 10 years on the IOC is that nothing is a surprise." See *Los Angeles Times*, 16 September 1988, part 3, 3; and the *Korea Herald*, 17 September 1988, 3.

17. *Newsflash 1*, April 1990, newsletter for the XVIIth Olympic Winter Games; also the *London Times*, 25 October 1989, 52.

18. *Frankfurter Allgemeine*, 27 November 1989, 32; *Lillehammer 1994 Budget Facts and Figures* (LOOC: August 1990), 5; *Newsflash 2*, June 1990, 2-3; Status Report address by LOOC President Heiberg to the 96th Session of the IOC, Tokyo, September 1990.

19. Several helpful articles (from a cache of several hundred references) are "IOC-ISL: The TOP," *Review, 213*, July 1985, 384; *Advertising Age, 59*, 30 May 1988, 48-49; *Olympic Message, 24*, July 1989, special issue on marketing and Olympism; *Marketing Communications*, January 1989, 18-26; Richard W. Pound, "The International Olympic Marketing Programme," *Olympic Review, 220*, February 1986, 84-86; Randy Harvey, "IOC Chief Hurdles Financial Bag," *International Herald Tribune*, 13 September 1989, 18; " 'Ambush' Marketing," *Journal of Advertising Research, 29*, August-September 1989, 9-14; *Olympic Review, 263-264*, September-October 1989, 445; *TOP Worldwide Sponsorship of the Olympic Movement* (23-page brochure, International Olympic Committee, Lausanne, Switzerland, 1990).

20. *Investor's Chronicle*, 14 July 1989, 14.

21. "Club Coubertin '92," *Olympic Review, 257*, March 1989, 75-77, and "Club Coubertin: L'Important c'est de Parrainer," *Le Magazine du Comité d'Organisation Des XVIes Jeux Olympiques D'Hiver D'Albertville*, June 1989, 10-11. In October 1990, Alcatel, France Télécom, and Thomson joined the "club"; *Flash Cojo, 37*, 30 October 1990.

22. Mary Beth Double, "Barcelona Olympics Will Open Doors for U.S. Business," *Business America, 110*, 28 August 1989, 2-5; *Press Dossier 1990* (COOB '92, S.A.).

23. *Advertising Age, 60*, 28 August 1989, 6; *Advertising Age, 61*, 22 October 1990, 55; *Wall Street Journal*, 12 February 1990, B1, B4; *Los Angeles Times*, 14 February 1990, F1, F9. "By the year 2000, most major sports will be available only on cable TV," wrote David A. Klatell in *Sports for Sale* (New York: Oxford University Press, 1988) in a chapter titled "The Future."

24. *Advertising Age, 61*, 30 April 1990, 23. General Motors and McDonald's joined in late 1990, paying very big money. Also *Advertising Age, 61*,

29 October 1990, 3, 62; *USA Today*, 16 November 1989, 16c (for postal service full-page ad).

25. Steven Barnett, *Games and Sets. The Changing Face of Sport on Television* (London: BFI, 1990), 134.

26. "The Great Olympic Soap Sell," *London Financial Times Supplement*, 11 June 1988, 1.

27. *New York Times*, 12 September 1988, sec. D, 6.

28. For a sample of these "red-flag" warnings, see "The Price of Gold," *London Guardian*, 24 September 1988, p. 21; "Kamikaze Competition," *Fortune, 122*, 19 November 1990, 95; "For the Glory of ABC and Skippy," *Maclean's, 101*, 22 February 1988, 60; and "The Olympics: A Better Way," *Washington Journalism Review, 10*, October 1988, 57. Hugh McIlvanney talks about "The Sleaze," in the *London Observer*, 11 September 1988, 16.

29. Rodda, in the *Olympic Message, 23*, March 1988, 6-15.

30. Jacques Rogge "Editorial," *Sport Europe. AENOC Official Magazine, 3*, 1990, 3.

Olympic Solidarity:
Largesse Mixed With
Unseen Problems

[Solidarity's aim] is to coordinate and work together for the
further advancement of the human being to find what are our
common denominators in the Olympic World and not what are
our differences.

Lord Killanin, *former IOC president*

If the previous chapter succeeded in underscoring the perception that the
International Olympic Committee is engrossed in the business of making
money, then this one will outline one way in which the IOC returns to
"family" a small portion of these funds. Most IOC money is set aside for
the organizing committees of the Winter and Summer Olympic Games, for
the legally recognized international sport federations, and for essential
administrative functions of the 168 national Olympic committees (to help

pay for athletes, trainers, coaches, and judges to come to the Olympic Games). Another important IOC donation is to the Olympic Solidarity Fund, which helps the NOCs in scores of ways, utilitarian and educational, with special emphasis on assistance to underdeveloped countries. Although the sums are insufficient to meet all national needs, the grant amounts have risen and by 1991 amounted to $25 million.[1] All well and good; there is gratitude for the monies, but already some NOCs see in these funds a perpetual supplement to budgets that are never big enough.

John J. MacAloon, a University of Chicago anthropologist-historian, correctly pointed out that "the Olympics are the closest approximation to a truly global ritual system that humankind has yet generated."[2] But in the working person's "trenches" of the sport federations and NOCs, especially in poor countries, this important observation frequently goes unnoticed during the frantic quest for financial aid. All during the 1980s and at increasing levels in the 1990s, Solidarity grants have frequently made a difference in some countries' abilities to serve their athletes, administrators, and young scholars of the Olympic Movement. The late Sheikh Fahad al-Sabah, IOC member from Kuwait and president of the Olympic Council of Asia at the time of his assassination in August 1990, wrote that Solidarity monies were useful even in the wealthy nations he represented, but increasingly indispensable "in poorer developing countries where even increased financial and technical support from the IOC are not enough."[3] The Saudi Arabian NOC leader said the same thing: In a five-page letter, Faisal Fahd Abdul Aziz detailed "IOC generosity in the creation of coaching courses, in sending athletes and officials to the Olympic Games, and for NOC administrative improvements."[4]

The Swiss Olympic administrator, Myriam Gross, in her role as head of the Solidarity Secretariat, outlined the scope of activities as "extensive." Athletes' and coaches' clinics dominate, but there are also sports medicine courses, acceleration of women's competitions, Olympic Day races, Sport-for-All recreational experiences, and the payment of all expenses for several hundred young men and women from around the world to attend the annual International Olympic Academy.[5] Millions of dollars are involved, monies only recently acquired by the IOC. From its inception in 1894, the modern Olympic Movement has projected a double image: First, it filled a void for elite international athletic competitions; and second, and less visibly (except in the mind of Baron de Coubertin), it offered the possibility of mutual understanding, a kind of specialized solidarity that might contribute to universal harmony.

But Coubertin's dream was more metaphysical than earthly, and for 80 years the IOC was without any source of income and in no position to help NOCs in the same boat. Only after the ultraconservative Calvinist warrior-leader of the IOC, Avery Brundage, completed his tumultuous 20 years of leadership (1952-1972) was the movement allowed to even think about profit-making. Change took place in the Killanin years, 1972 to 1980.

American television corporations began sending monies to the Château de Vidy, and small residual monies were then directed toward the already established but slumbering Solidarity committee, established, ironically, in the middle of the Brundage administration. Samaranch arrived on the scene in 1980, and nothing less than jet speed could describe the increase in Solidarity monies and the worldwide dissemination of financial grants engendered by his leadership during the 1980s and well into the 1990s.

Helping the Struggling Nations

Throughout this chapter the phrases "Third World," "underdeveloped nations," and "developing countries" are used. There are no fully developed nations in the world; some are only more developed than others. High gross national product (GNP) and high technology are visible and measurable criteria for a so-called advanced society, and yet that country may have many deficiencies.[6] In any case, the IOC defines a *developing country* to be one poorer in most visible and materially sustaining goods compared to those nations in which average annual incomes and GNP are among the highest in the world.

The IOC's Solidarity program is a modest but real effort to raise the level of elite sport, recreational Sport-for-All, and athletic education in every country, but with special emphasis on those societies that are "not rich." From the beginning of the Solidarity movement in 1961 (and *before* the IOC had any money), the founder, France's Count Jean de Beaumont, and the IOC made a commitment to help those nations struggling to emancipate themselves from colonialism. The story is one of the most praiseworthy chapters in Olympic history—always anticipating that Solidarity's best days are still ahead.

At the 58th Session of the IOC in Athens (1961), Count Jean de Beaumont (in his 11th year of membership) took the initiative and set up the Commission for International Olympic Aid (CIOA) intending to help the African and Asian countries that had just achieved their independence. Assisting him were Constantine Andrianov, S. Gabriel Gemayee, G.D. Sondhi, Reginald Alexander, and Ahmed Touney. Little could be done for a decade when, in 1971 at the Luxembourg IOC meeting, the name was changed to the Commission for Olympic Solidarity, with new leadership from Raymond Gafner, Colonel Raoul Mollet, and the vigorous stewardship of Guilio Onesti, and the financial backing of his Rome-based Italian Olympic Committee (CONI).

Solidarity secretary Edward Wieczorek pointed out in 1974 that scores of recently emerging Third World NOCs were in desperate need of any kind of help. The number of NOCs had grown to 132 by 1974, and some Solidarity aid had to be used for "the promotion of sport from the school room to old age." Coaches' clinics, scientific sport textbooks, and technical equipment were needed and supplied, and 115 sport-related scholarships were awarded.[7] In those early days, the most frequent request from underdeveloped countries was that their athletes and coaches be helped to attend sophisticated training centers in North America and the Soviet Union for scientific training courses, the prize for the precious 8-week Solidarity courses being an invitation to the famed facility in Leipzig, Germany.[8] In 1976, the IOC paid for 624 individual scholarships, stimulated by poorer nations' interest in attending regional and Olympic Games. In that same year, 92 NOCs requested Solidarity grants for new equipment, the construction of athletic facilities, local coaching schools, travel abroad, the purchase of scientific sporting literature, and "full scholarships to attend the International Olympic Academy."[9]

Television Revenue Boosts Solidarity

Solidarity's effectiveness was given a boost in 1972 by the television monies earned from the sale of broadcast rights to the XIth Winter Olympic Games in Sapporo, Japan, and the Games of the XXth Olympiad in Munich. At the historic Varna Congress in 1973, President Killanin announced a plan to more closely integrate the Solidarity program with similar programs in the NOCs and international sport federations, and in so doing "avoid overlapping of efforts."[10] Solidarity efforts began to heat up at two IOC meetings in Santo Domingo, Dominican Republic (2-5 March 1974), and Tehran, Iran (29-31 August 1974), culminating in a publication titled *Solidarity* and edited by Secretary Wieczorek, whose altruism and optimism could not be hidden:

> Olympic Solidarity of the IOC will contribute to develop and reinforce the bonds uniting it to the NOCs that they will serve to promote even further Olympism and amateur sport in the world, and that they will be carried out in very close collaboration between the IOC, the NOCs, and the IFs.[11]

At the Tehran meeting, Lord Killanin delivered a 3,900-word oration on the enhanced Solidarity efforts and emphasized the new financial importance of television. Solidarity monies would be spent largely for scientific and technical help to athletes, trainers, and coaches. Financial assistance would go to those nations who need it most, but they must have the infrastructure to use the money honestly and effectively. Killanin's statement is the clarion call of the Solidarity movement to this day. Self-help and realistic desires to improve oneself are prerequisites to any aid. Always, Killanin repeated, the Olympic code of honesty, sportsmanship, and fair play would surround all proceedings. Solidarity's aim, he ended, "is to coordinate and work together for the further advancement of the human being to find what are our common denominators in the Olympic World and not what are our differences."[12]

In 1980, the offices of Solidarity were transferred from Rome to Lausanne, and in 1982, J.A. Samaranch, assisted by ANOC president, Mario Vasquez Raña, took charge. By the mid-1980s, millions of dollars poured into IOC headquarters from television companies and international business corporations, with the Solidarity Commission benefiting. The 1985 *Solidarité Olympique Rapport* pointed out that sport federations and NOCs joined in requesting 239 coaching clinics.[13] The Solidarity engine, for the first time supplied with sufficient fuel, was moving determinedly forward. Shoe companies and the international sporting goods industry donated millions of dollars in equipment and a blizzard of technical and scientific literature. The movement had arrived at a point where to stand still was to fall behind. Solidarity director Anselmo López was pleased and reminded all that absolute honesty of all parties was necessary and that only vouchers—never cash money—should ever be involved. Special Solidarity bank accounts were set up to keep the whole affair both philanthropic and businesslike.[14]

Enrichment programs in portions of the vast African continent were working, but Amadou Lamine Ba, secretary general of both the Association of African NOCs (ANOCA) and the Supreme Council for Sport in Africa (SCSA), was concerned. "Things are not running smoothly," he confessed to a journalist from the Brazzaville, Congo newspaper *Le Stade*:

> Underdeveloped countries have special difficulties . . . and a good atmosphere of cooperation between Solidarity and state authorities is not always easy, despite the fact that President Samaranch recommends to all NOCs that they encourage collaboration with governments. State intervention and aid is essential. The important thing is for the governments to understand and respect the characteristics and ideals of Olympism.[15]

Solidarity spent $5 million in 1987, and $11,388,000 during the Olympic year 1988. The largest single item was for transportation of athletes and coaches to the Seoul Olympic Games ($5 million); the rest went toward clinics, equipment, sport facilities, sports medicine seminars, worldwide play days for children, local sports activities, Sport-for-All festivals, "Olympic Day-June 23rd" celebrations, young adult scholarships to the IOA at Olympia, Greece, and partial financial aid for athletes not yet "stars." The great unknown, of course, is how effective these efforts were in the "propagation of Olympic ideals, of its philosophy of fair play," and in the inculcation of Olympian education for those young people touched by the Solidarity program.[16]

Olympic Solidarity devotes most of its energy and money helping those NOCs that are "least well off," but Director López has been careful to point out that Solidarity also "rewards the largest NOC delegations" for their own domestic growth and contributions to the worldwide Olympic movement.[17] It seems no one is ignored by the 23 members of the Commission for Olympic

Solidarity.[18] Each Olympic Games year sees an increase in Solidarity spending, because several thousand athletes receive partial payment for transportation to the site. (Details of such expenditures for the 1988 Games were explained by Antonio Aguilar of Mexico, general coordinator in America of Olympic Solidarity.)[19] The program has "grown like Topsy" and, therefore, has had operational problems, such as lack of cooperation from some NOC leadership in returning their administrative, technical, and financial reports to Solidarity headquarters—together with proof of their expenditures. The always alert Amadou Lamine Ba recognized the danger of such carelessness:

> We are once again forced to deplore the fact that very few end-of-course reports were received. . . . This state of affairs puts us in a very embarrassing position.[20]

Everything connected with Solidarity originates in and emanates from a four-story building in downtown Lausanne, Switzerland, two kilometers from the IOC's Château de Vidy. In 1990, the modern, hi-tech offices were home to Director López, the hard-working head of the Olympic Solidarity Secretariat Myriam Gross, four secretaries (each with specific geographic responsibilities), and one accounts secretary.[21]

Several Solidarity programs are functioning well, notably (a) programs for sport administrators, (b) programs for coaches and trainers, (c) financial aid for elite athletes, (d) financial aid for promising male and female athletes, and (e) young adult scholarships to the International Olympic Academy at Olympia, Greece. By means of these far-flung Solidarity enterprises, (surpassing $30 million in costs each quadrennium), the Commission in its rather high-minded, ambitious way has demonstrated its intention to do more than aid in the production of athlete-gladiators. All Solidarity teaching efforts include the concepts of sportsmanship and fair play (the two terms are not synonymous)[22], as well as efforts to heighten individual and collective physical skills. Yet, even in this second generation of Solidarity largesse, athletes, coaches, and administrators (let alone the larger public) still imperfectly understand that educating the mind is of equal importance to training the body. There are many examples of this Solidarity mind-body effort.

The theme of the 1990 IOA at Olympia was "Women and the Olympic Movement." Not surprisingly, though for the first time, more women than men attended the meeting, and Solidarity scholarships were mainly responsible for the attendance of both. At the Second Caribbean Conference on sports medicine, 36 physicians and 7 physiotherapists focused on the latest, most sophisticated sport science techniques, with lectures by Professor de Rose of Brazil and Robert Voy, MD, and Charles Dillman, PhD, from the United States. The clinic cost Solidarity $25,000, but it must have been worth it, for the evaluation report called the meeting "successful; let us extend it to a week next time."

In Ulan Bator, Outer Mongolia, a boxing clinic taught by Peter Stoytchev of Bulgaria (and costing $15,000) included every aspect of boxing theory, practice, administration, and "medical and pedagogical controls." The 32 participants heaped praise on the program and asked that "refereeing and judging" be included in future meetings. Athletes with "real potential" are invited into the Olympic Scholarship program at a special training center for 4 months, renewable by Solidarity, provided the "progress and the conduct" of the athlete is good. Even higher standards were attempted (though not all were attained) in the "Schools for Sports Leaders-Administrators"—170 of them in a 3 year period.

"A great river of runners"—a million youths—seems testimony enough that the IOC-Solidarity Sport-for-All "Olympic Day-June 23" is working. A coaching clinic in the People's Republic of the Congo drew 48 participants, cost $16,000, and helped 18 coaches earn FIFA certification. Some courses were postponed, a few cancelled, and, disconcertingly, some evaluation reports "have not yet been received."[23]

And lastly, the push for successful, whole world representation at the Albertville and Barcelona Olympic Games engendered massive support from the IOC:

> For Albertville, 3 athletes and an official plus the sum of US $6,000 paid to each NOC for its delegation's equipment, and free accommodation and meals at the Olympic Village for the official whose expenses are taken care of. For Barcelona, air tickets and the Village will be paid for 6 athletes and 2 officials, and each NOC will receive US $8,000 for equipment. The sum of US $800 will be allocated for all other athletes, and stay in Olympic Village will be free in both Albertville and Barcelona.[24]

Thus it has become fact: In a single generation, the Olympic world, the family of international sport federations and national Olympic committees has come to depend on Solidarity stipends, financial allowances that have taken on a life of their own. For many NOCs, any decrease in monies would be a hardship. None of us knows how long the present financial superabundance flowing into IOC coffers will continue, nor can we predict what might happen should tomorrow's precious overflow, now earmarked for Solidarity generosity, fail.

The Hazards of Solidarity Dependence

Olympic sport federation leaders and chiefs of all NOCs, rich and poor, must not allow themselves to depend too much on Solidarity benefits. In the United States such bounty is called "soft money," and it represents recognition of competency and work well done. However, only skill in engendering a regular income ("hard money") and vigilance in resisting the unconscious inclination to expect and depend on these gifts will save federations and NOCs from some possibly rude future shock. Like any national institution, Olympic-related sports bodies must, if they have not already done so, learn to make it alone. Solidarity monies were never intended to fully support international nonprofessional sport bodies, but rather to marginally supplement their efforts. If there is a reversal in the economic flow of monies into IOC banks after the retirement of President Samaranch, there will be a reduction in (and possibly the eventual elimination of) *all* IOC Solidarity monies. All nations should be encouraged to become self-sufficient.

It is the responsibility of the IOC not to encourage, directly or indirectly, the perception that Solidarity monies for NOCs and federations will increase for the remainder of this century. The IOC must fashion a set of limitations, certain financial parameters that will say clearly that these grants are no free lunch and that sport federations and national Olympic committees must be largely self-supporting from domestic sales, corporate donations, and government grants. Only under these circumstances will the concept of Olympic Solidarity be perceived correctly as *contributing* to the quality of recreational and elite sport in every nation in the world.

In 1983, James Nafziger expressed uncertainty that international sport and the Olympic Games had the ''cathartic capacity to diminish aggressive impulses,'' but he had no doubt that these same competitions ''offer a highly visible alternative in the global living room.''[25] He was correct, of course. Uncertainty and optimism must live together in the larger world as they surely do in the Olympic family. What must be grasped by all is that we are not some fatalistic flotsam incapable of modifying the future. We can make a difference, and Olympic Solidarity, well done, can improve the quality of life in a small but measurable way.

Notes

1. David Miller, ''Figures Show Value of Fund,'' *London Times,* 26 April, 1989, 46, and in the *Olympic Review, 259*, May 1989, 204-205.
2. John J. MacAloon, '' 'La Pitada Olympica': Puerto Rico, International Sport, and the Constitution of Politics,'' *Proceedings of the Ethnological Society,* 1984, 315.
3. Sheikh Fahad al-Sabah, letter to author, 17 June 1990.
4. Faisal Fahd Abdul Aziz, letter to author, 16 October 1989.
5. Myriam Gross, ''Olympic Solidarity Administration School Management Training,'' *Proceedings International Olympic Academy 1988*, 158.
6. As far back as 1974, K.A. Doxiades wrote, ''All nations are underdeveloped; every nation is developing.'' See his *Anthropopolis* [City That We Need] (New York: Norton, 1974), 349.
7. Edward Wieczorek, ''Solidarity,'' *Olympic Review, 85-86*, November-December 1974, 602.

8. "IOC Solidarity," *Olympic Review, 99-100*, January-February 1976, 35.
9. "Olympic Solidarity," *Olympic Review, 101-102*, March-April 1976, 151-152.
10. Killanin's "Final Statement," *Proceedings Olympic Congress Varna 1973*, 163.
11. Edward Wieczorek, Ed., *International Olympic Committee—Olympic Solidarity, Problems of Sports Organizations and Management* (Lausanne: IOC, 1975), 38.
12. Lord Killanin's "Address," *Olympic Review, 82-83*, September-October 1974), 399.
13. *Olympic Review, 228* October 1986, 610-611.
14. "Olympic Aid: An Assessment," *Olympic Review, 231-232*, January-February 1987, 22-23; also "Half-Time Score," *Olympic Review, 240*, October 1987, 513-515.
15. Ba's comments can be found in *Olympic Review, 242*, December 1987, 636, 638.
16. *Olympic Review, 246*, April 1988, 181; *Olympic Review, 249*, August 1988, 357; *Olympic Review, 250-251*, September-October 1988, 447-449; *Olympic Review, 253*, November 1988, 620; *Olympic Review, 270*, April 1990, 205; and *The Olympic Movement* (Lausanne: IOC, 1984), 64.
17. Anselmo López, "Who Gets What? Solidarity's System of Aid," *Olympic Review, 257*, March 1989, 98.
18. Though it seems like an unwieldy number, the Commission's 23 members include the president and 1 vice president of the IOC; 6 IOC members; the IOCs director general, deputy administrator, and secretary general; 7 members of ANOC; 2 people from the international sport federations; 1 Olympic athlete; the IOC's director of sports; and the Solidarity director. See *Olympic Solidarity Report 1989*, 1, and *Sport Europe. AENOC Official Magazine, 1*, 1990, 59.
19. Antonio Aguilar, "Olympic Solidarity," *Proceedings IOC 1989*, 77.
20. Ba, quoted on page 50 of the 1989 Solidarity Report.
21. *Olympic Solidarity Objectives and Realization.* A 1990 document distributed by Olympic Solidarity.
22. Sportsmanship can be defined as some athletes' gracious act before or following the game or contest. Fair play has been arbitrarily defined as an act of compassion during the "heat of competition" when the issue of winner is still in doubt. See the 31-page document, *Declaration on Fair Play* (Paris: International Council of Sport and Physical Education, 1978).
23. Several of these Solidarity examples are found in *Olympic Solidarity Report 1989*, 22, 111, 257, 259, 265, 267, & 276. Other anecdotes were located in *Sport in the USSR, 312*, March 1989, 2; *Olympic Review, 266*, December 1989, 566-569; *Olympic Review, 271-272*, June 1990,

257; *Olympic Review, 260,* June 1989, 254. The *Revista Olympica, 271-272,* May-June 1990, 256, trumpeted, "No dormirse en los laureles" ([Olympic Solidarity] must not rest on its laurels).

24. "VIIth ANOC General Assembly," *Olympic Review 273,* July 1990, 307.

25. James A.R. Nafziger, "Nonaggressive Sanctions in the International Sports Arena," *Case Western Reserve Journal of International Law, 15,* 1983, 329.

C·H·A·P·T·E·R·9

Olympic Games Overkill

The importance of life is not so much in triumph or winning as in the struggle itself, the prime essential is not so much to have conquered as to have performed honorably and well.

Baron Pierre de Coubertin, *founder of the modern Olympic Games*

The Olympic motto, *Citius, Altius, Fortius* (Faster, Higher, Stronger), is dichotomous in that in its original 19th-century sense, it represented the greatest physical and moral glory of the athlete, but for some late 20th-century Olympians it means gambling with death, not sport at all. Any physical activity, including sport, when taken to extremes thus risking life, is an abandonment of personal morality and humaneness. As philosopher-Olympic champion Hans Lenk said, sport extremism is "genuinely marginal in the existential sense."[1] Without ethics, morality, and fair play infused into all sport from kindergarten games to the Olympic 100-meter final, there is no sport, only mindless physical activity and gladiatorial athletic superlatives. Because "Faster, higher, stronger" has infinite, no-limit connotations and because the human body in its *natural* state is finite and very much limited, the Olympic code has dangerous implications physiologically, psychologically, morally, and chemically. Much more than policing athletes is needed. The whole Olympic household of NOCs, sport federations, and the IOC must urge and help implement a new-old worldwide educational moralism. Such a serious code of sporting ethics, quoting Lenk again, "has hardly yet reached even a rudimentary stage of development."[2]

Defining the Olympic Motto

My own 15 years of competition in long-distance running (including the 1952 American Olympic trials), combined with another 15 years of coaching, have resulted in my personal Olympic motto: "*Citius, Altius, Fortius . . . within rational and ethical boundaries.*" I'm sure Père Didon, who first used the three Latin words, and Pierre de Coubertin, who made them the Olympic motto, *implied* the restraints of rationality and morality. Henri Didon (1840-1900), a French Dominican friar, was preacher-writer-school sport leader and preceded Coubertin in emphasizing the potential physical and spiritual values of sport well conducted. Father Didon also visited British public schools and exclaimed, "The English help to emancipate their pupils, we confine them." Addressing his own French students at Arcueil College in Normandy, his white gown flapping in the outdoor air, Didon pronounced, "*Citius, Altius, Fortius!* Ever Faster, Higher, Stronger!" The new Olympic leader, Coubertin, seized on the good priest as one of his own and invited him to present at the 1897 Olympic Congress in Le Havre his oral dissertation titled "Moral Effects of Athletic Sports":

> Physical exercise in the open air is definitely beneficial and has a powerful educational, moral, psychic, as well as physical benefit. Sport helps young people in an activity satisfying to their nature, their need for movement, and helps to make them complete, and paves the way for a proper school spirit . . . the strengthening of the body, and temper[ing] the soul.[3]

In a 16 November 1894 speech at the Athens Parnasse Society, Coubertin said, amidst a great many points, "I envy the words of Père Didon,"[4] and not just the neat Latin phrase, but the whole package of competitive sport wed to high-minded education. One of Coubertin's earliest biographers said of the baron's views, "Rather than being a formal religion or formal philosophy, his ideas are a new secular way to meld science, metaphysics, and sport."[5] And so Coubertin added essential moral baggage to his Olympic Games, adopted the Didon motto as the Olympic motto, and did so with full confidence that generations of Olympic athletes would understand the larger message with its implied moral imperative. Most did; many did not.

Some years later, on 24 July 1908, in a speech delivered at the official banquet given by the British government in honor of the officials of the

Games of the Fourth Olympiad, Baron de Coubertin delivered another of his stirring speeches, pointing out that the previous Sunday, the bishop of Pennsylvania had addressed the Olympic athletes about the danger of abandoning their belief in the lofty concept of 'Fair Play' and that he, the bishop, had noted that "the importance of these Olympic Games lies not so much in winning as in taking part."[6] Let us all return to this grand idea, continued Coubertin, who added his own athletic homily:

> The importance of life is not so much in triumph or winning as in the struggle itself, the prime essential is not so much to have conquered as to have performed honorably and well.[7]

For nearly 75 years no one knew the name of this American bishop. Norwegian historian Ture Widlund discovered his name to be Ethelbert Talbot (1848-1928).[8] Exactly what Bishop Talbot said in his Sunday sermon on 19 July 1908 had not been known until I discovered in the archives of the Episcopal Church in July 1988, exactly 80 years after Talbot's presentation, his 2,000-word sermon titled "The Inner Life." He was thrilled that athletes had come from all over the world to the London Olympic Games. Ever superior to the glory of a strong and robust athletic body, he said, are the unseen things, the invisible and spiritual virtues that mark the realm of God. The Olympic stadium, he continued, is correctly the beginning of a new "era of internationalism"; but in that same arena lurks "an element of danger," and we must all, therefore, return to the idealism of the ancient Greeks and their games where "the games themselves are better than the race or the prize." And finally, Talbot promised,

> our prize is not corruptible, but incorruptible, and though only one may wear the laurel wreath, all may share the equal joy of the contest. All encouragement, therefore, be given to the exhilarating—I might also say the soul-saving—interest that comes in active and fair and clean athletic sports.[9]

It seems that Coubertin did not quote Talbot exactly, but borrowed the essence of his remarks, added them to his own strong athletic idealism, and created what would become, in 1932, the unofficial Olympic code.[10]

The gist of all this is that the unofficial Olympic code of Coubertin, with some inspirational help from the bishop of Central Pennsylvania, appears to be at odds with the older Father Didon–Pierre de Coubertin official Olympic motto, *Citius, Altius, Fortius*. All this is no mere hair-splitting, for the code deals with an overarching, philosophical ideal about Olympic Games competition, whereas the motto seems to imply that the role of the athlete is everlasting effort to improve physical skills, the unremitting concentration on finding ways to run faster, jump higher, and become physically stronger. The first is extremely difficult to achieve psychologically without risking athletic mediocrity; the second carries within its message potentially grave dangers to one's health and psychic sense of proportion.

The beleaguered Prince Alexandre de Merode, IOC chairman of the Commission Médical, has been thus far frustrated in his efforts to eliminate drugs from the Olympic Games. To do so, he said, must be an evolutionary process. "The ancient motto *Citius, Altius, Fortius* is still valid, provided it is understood in its context," he told the editor of *Olympic Review*, ending with the observation that "if society is not possible without a moral base, then sport is not possible without rules."[11] Tying together, as Merode tried to do, the Olympic motto, the scourge of harmful drugs, and some higher moral law is extremely difficult, because each is fraught with complexities. The laudable Olympic motto when carried to its ultimate physical and motivational conclusion will too often result in disintegration of the body and a willingness, even eagerness, to resort to the use of exotic and sometimes dangerous chemicals. In our modern miracle society, there are thousands and thousands of drugs, and to call some OK and others "dangerous and, therefore, illegal" is a pharmacological, medical, and surveillance impossibility. The discovery of some Olympian "higher moral law" acceptable to almost all the athletes is a tall order and if ill-conceived may fall on deaf ears. (I shall try to elaborate on these points in the next chapter, because the motto, *Citius, Altius, Fortius*, and the Olympic Games' problem with doping are related.)

Historian Widlund found ever so much more soothing and less threatening than the *Citius, Altius, Fortius* dictum, the unofficial Olympic "device" (as he called it): "The important thing in the Olympic Games is not winning but taking part, for the essential thing in life is not conquering but fighting well." This lofty sentiment should replace the arrogant, and potentially dangerous, official IOC motto. Let us rid the Olympic Charter of the *Citius, Altius, Fortius* mind-set, concluded Widlund.[12]

In the United States, a nation known for its competitiveness, the Pacific Northwest Amateur Sports Foundation, an organization with USOC support, adopted for 1991 an agenda with the motto Faster, Higher, Stronger.[13] This agenda is "for children in kindergarten through grade 3," and I tremble at the thought of how poorly such a program might be managed. Without enlightened coaching, children engaged in competitive athletics can and have been misled, educationally and technically, to believe that the only reason for such activities is record-breaking performance, that the end of sport, games, and athletic competition is *Citius, Altius, Fortius*. It is not. It is but one dimension of organized sport in which *some* children should be encouraged to participate. Yet for athletic youth to reach full physical potential without damage to body, mind, or spirit, the education of these children *must* begin in kindergarten. The risk is great, the possible reward is significant.

Athletes everywhere must avoid at all cost embracing a Machiavellian athletic philosophy that says in essence, "I will run faster, jump higher, become physically stronger—no matter what it takes, no matter what I must do.'' In the present era of moral relativism, the Olympic motto, *Citius, Altius, Fortius,* can mean anything that one wishes it to mean. Eternal vigilance is necessary in the Olympic garden, where the Olympic flag and the Olympic motto fly from the mast.

Adding the Moral Dimension

Pierre de Coubertin helped accelerate a Western European culture already running hell-bent in the early development of high-level sport competition. Symbolism, ritual, an underlying fervor, and tooth-rattling competition mark the modern Olympic Games, and therefore, as one scholar said in 1990, "Coubertin can no longer be regarded as a dreamer."[14] But the mindless, lemming-like obedience of those who insist on Higher, Faster, Stronger from their athletes by whatever means is coming to an end. John Hoberman, who has spent years studying German and Soviet "super-elite" sports peoples observes that it should only be a matter of time before responsible people in large numbers begin to express "doubts about the rigors of high-performance sport."[15] To win an Olympic gold medal, one need not, one should not, resort to any device, but this does not mean that the task is anything less than 30 hours a week of painfully hard work. Two Americans, Brad Lewis and Paul Enquist, won gold medals in double sculls rowing at the '84 Olympic Games, and in *Assault on Lake Casitas,* Lewis exposed "with dental-drill precision, the raw-nerve pain and sacrifice at the heart of the greatest quest in amateur sport"—Olympic gold.[16]

The Olympic motto is a Coubertin-inspired code, an idealized Athenian rendering melded to an ethereal 19th-century Victorian sentiment that may never have been, but only existed in the mind's eye. It may be only that—a vision. What this *Citius, Altius, Fortius* code is *not* is the vulgar statement of the world's fastest sprinter in the year 1990, Leroy Burrell, who told a *Wall Street Journal* writer, "We're not in this sport because we like it or we want to earn our way through school. We're in it to make money."[17] Contrast this attitude with Olympic historian Arnd Krüger's belief that "the Olympic Games . . . become a symbolic midsummer festival in the life cycle of the athlete."[18] The Olympic Games should be the triumph of the individual as athlete and trustworthy member of the human race. An important, relevant, and hugely exciting challenge, the Olympic motto can contribute to that end. For when practiced successfully as part of one's larger life and thus viewed in its full effulgence, it can be a living liberation.

In obedience to the Olympic code, the athlete can give all within the boundaries of fair play and medically sound health practices, and in possession of a mind-set that values the athletic experience higher than the money. The amateur spirit, which always races slightly ahead of the gold coin, is the working embodiment of this code. (The "spirit" of Leroy Burrell must value the prize more than the struggle, if we believe his bald admission.)

It is the spirit that matters most in Olympic competition. The famous foreign correspondent, Dorothy Thompson said, "Though stripped of every armor, be a warrior—a warrior of the spirit,"[19] an image that Coubertin would recognize instantly.

In the end, true understanding and pursuit of the Olympic *Citius, Altius, Fortius* ideal lies with the innermost person. Obedience to the wider, deeper meaning of the Olympic code is unenforceable by outside agencies. It cannot be taught, but it can be learned. Morality and purity of human action must somehow fit into this whole picture, too, and, ever and always, they must be self-imposed. The Olympic code can be either a license for vacuous amorality or a reminder of untapped powers; either a clarion call for the awakening of positive, hitherto undiscovered personal qualities, physical and spiritual, or permission for the disregard of ethics and, as one journalist wrote, "the absence of all restraint."[20]

The Olympic Charter covers only a fraction of what an athlete may and may not do, a kind of legislative bull's-eye in the target of the dilemma. The outer rings and the area outside the target represent Free Choice, the freedom to do anything we wish. It is the middle rings of the target that are germane to the Olympic motto, a directive which states that we must strive everlastingly for excellence, but implies *within bounds*, never to excess, never to the detriment of intellectual and spiritual realms which we all possess. The Right Honorable Lord Moulton, British judge and parliamentarian during World War I, called these nebulous but important middle rings of life's target, "the domain of Duty, Public Spirit, Good Form, the domain of Obedience to the Unenforceable."[21]

This principle of obedience to the unenforceable is no mere theory, for the Olympic athlete lives primarily *not* in the world of rules and regulation nor in the nether world of lawlessness, but in the middle ground of personal decision making. In today's complex society of international sport, more and more athletes explain away their misconduct and disobedience to the rules by using the limp argument that they only did what their coaches, physicians, trainers, or agents told them to do. Such limpness of thought is the epitome of personal irresponsibility. Each athlete *must* seek within himself or herself some pristine moral goodness that will, in most cases, prevent compromises between what is right and what is wrong in athletic competitions. No one can accurately define *right* and *wrong,* but most should know the difference between them when confronted with the dilemma.

The Olympic Games is a tiny copy of the larger world, but because it is "tiny" there is contained within it the greater possibility for controlled aggression, the exploration of new and complex strengths, and the flowering of skill and virtue. Olympic television commentator Jim McKay was sincere when he said that "the Olympic Games are the most important sporting event in the world."[22] He did not say why, but I have my own reasons for agreeing with him. The possibility of individual disharmony and dysfunction exists at every turn in the Olympic Games arena. So, too, does the capablity of seizing by force an extraordinary "joie de vivre." But as Soviet poet Yevtushenko said, "Sport is one of the basic joys of life . . . and must be seized by force." But "to seize things by force, a sound mind and sound muscles are needed."[23] I'm sure that had he been asked, Yevtushenko would have agreed to the suggestion of adding a moral dimension to his mind-and-muscle description of idealized sport. I wish no proscription of the present official Olympic code, *Citius, Altius, Fortius*, but I cannot escape thinking that a superior sporting philosophy, one that in no way diminishes the glory of individual athletic achievement, would be the Coubertin-Talbot maxim: The important thing in the Olympic Games is not winning but taking part. The essential thing in life is not conquering but fighting well.[24]

The ancient Greeks and Romans conducted Olympic Games from 776 BC to 393 AD—nearly 1,200 years, and though uneven in their capacity for good, these games did contribute to the glory that was the Greek spirit: "To rejoice in life, to find the world beautiful and delightful to live in."[25] At their best, the ancient Greeks have much to share with us at the end of the 20th century and in celebration of the modern Olympic Games' first century of uneasy existence. But Faster, Higher, Stronger is an inferior philosophy and conveys a confusing double message. Better, much more appropriate as an Olympic "shingle" to display in the stadium, would be "Aretê and the flowering of human worth and potential." (There is no need for a footnote, for the quote is mine.) Sir Maurice Bowra in *The Greek Experience*, wrote three full pages defining the all-important "aretê" concept, which glorifies the special worth of all humanity and urges us all to work hard toward the fullest realization of our individual physical, intellectual, and spiritual potential, that is "to develop his [her] aretê, or inborn capacities, so far as he [she] possibly can."[26]

There are those who believe that Pierre de Coubertin made a more than acceptable effort at transporting over the centuries a life philosophy, an athletic code relevant to the modern age, and did so with "aristocratic elegance."[27] I count myself as one of these believers. His "inspiration," Father Didon, was a good and holy man, by all accounts, and, I think, a wise priest. If they were with us today, they might be willing to withdraw the provocative *Citius, Altius, Fortius* and substitute something even better. A modern Olympic philosophy (code, dictum, or maxim), widespread and well understood by the entire Olympic world, has more chance of being grasped and practiced by all athletes. Doing so would be to heap praise on themselves and, in the highest sense, to "seize" what Sophocles said about the very best of men and women: "There are many strange wonders, but nothing more wonderful than man."[28]

Notes

1. In my view, Dr. Lenk was never better than in his "Humanity," *Bulletin du Congrès Olympique Baden-Baden 1981*, 54.

2. Ibid.

3. Didon, quoted in Monique Berlioux, "The Reverend Father Didon," *Olympic Review, 28*, January 1970, 9-11. See also *Bulletin du Comité International Olympique, 52*, 15 November 1955, 56; *Coubertin Leben, Denken und Schaffen eines Humanisten* by Klaus Ullrich (Sportverlag Berlin, 1982), 170; *Pierre de Coubertin* by Louis Callebat (Paris: Librairie Arthéme Fayard, 1988), 109; and *Le Mouvement Olympique* (Lausanne: IOC, 1984), 71.

4. Coubertin, "L'athlétisme dans le monde modern et les jeux Olympiques," *Bulletin du Comité International des Jeux Olympiques, 2*(3), January 1895, 4.

5. Ernest Seillière, *Un Artisan d'Energie Français—Pierre de Coubertin* (Paris: Henri Didier, 1917), 45.

6. Coubertin, "Speech at the Government Banquet," *The Fourth Olympiad London 1908 Official Report* (London: BOC, 1908), 793.

7. Ibid. Coubertin's speech was published in French; the translation is mine.

8. See Widlund's 71-page essay, "Det Olympiska valspråket—bakgrund och tillkomst," in *Idrott Historia Och Samhälle* (Schmidts Boktryckeri AB, Helsingborg 1982). There is a brief summary in English, 68-71. Also, see Widlund's abbreviated version in *Olympic Review, 187*, May 1983, 294-295.

9. Talbot's long-lost essay, "The Inner Life," is in the archives of the Episcopal Church in Austin, Texas, and was published in a Church of England newspaper, *The Guardian*, 22 July 1908.

10. Widlund said on page 70 of his essay that on the giant Olympic Games scoreboard in Los Angeles 1932, and in a recorded radio speech by Coubertin at the Opening Ceremonies of the Berlin Games of 1936 were the words, "The important thing in the Olympic Games is not winning but taking part. The essential thing is not conquering but fighting well."

11. de Merode, "The Fight Against Doping: Ongoing Evolution," *Olympic Review, 262*, August 1989, 384.

12. Ture Widlund, "The Background and Origin of the Olympic Device," *Olympic Review, 187*, May 1983, 295.

13. "Academy Announces Programs," *Academy Quarterly* (Pacific Northwest Amateur Sports Foundation), Fall 1990, 2.

14. Ove Korsgaard, "Sport as a Practice of Religion: The Record as Ritual," in John M. Carter and Arnd Krüger, *Ritual and Record: Sports Records and Quantification in Pre-Modern Societies* (New York: Greenwood Press, 1990), 121.

15. John M. Hoberman, "The Transformation of East Germany Sport," *Journal of Sport History, 17* (Spring 1990), 68.

16. Book review of Brad Lewis, *Assault on Lake Casitas* (1990), the *Washington Post*, 30 October 1990, E2.

17. Leroy Burrell, quoted in Peter Waldman, "Track Stars Get Set to Dash for the Cash," *Wall Street Journal, 216*, 3 August 1990, B1.

18. Krüger represented Germany in the 1500-meter run at Mexico City 1968. See his statement in his book *Ritual and Record*, 142; Note 15.

19. Dorothy Thompson, quoted in frontispiece, Peter Kurth, *American Cassandra: The Life of Dorothy Thompson* (Boston: Little, Brown, 1990).

20. Rushworth M. Kidder, "The Three Great Domains of Human Action," *Christian Science Monitor*, 29 January 1990, 13.

21. John Fletcher Moulton, "Law and Manners," *Atlantic Monthly, 134*, July 1924, 1.

22. McKay, quoted in Anthony P. Montesano, "Medal Contenders," *American Film, 13*, September 1988, 57.

23. Yevgeny Yevtushenko, "A Poet Against the Destroyers," *Sports Illustrated, 25*, 19 December 1966, 128.

24. The United States Olympic Committee's official *Report of the Games of the XIVth Olympiad 1948*, edited by Asa S. Bushnell, featured this maxim in its frontispiece.

25. See back cover jacket in Edith Hamilton, *The Greek Way to Western Civilization* (New York: Mentor Books, 1959; originally published in 1930).

26. C.M. Bowra, *The Greek Experience* (New York: Mentor Books, 1959), 211.

27. Antonio Gnoli, *The Glory of Olympia* (Milan: Arnoldo Mondadori Editore, 1985), 134.

28. Sophocles on "Man" from *Antigone*, in *The Portable Greek Reader*, edited by W.H. Auden (New York: Viking Press, 1958), 471.

Bulgarian Olympic Committee Bulletin

C·H·A·P·T·E·R· 10

The Olympic Drug Crisis:
Seeking a Level Playing Field

I don't call it cheating. My definition of cheating is doing
something nobody else is doing.

Charley Francis, *track & field coach*

The International Olympic Committee is consumed with outrage and fear
that wholesale promiscuity of illegal drug use by Olympic Games athletes
will reduce the credibility of the 100-year-old competition and lead to its
premature demise. However, the president of Chile's national Olympic
committee, Sergio Fantini, wrote, "Doping can destroy athletes and therefore
the movement. Massive education first, and along with it strict enforcement
[are] the only way out of this nightmare."[1]

Of course, the whole fuss and furor might be unnecessary. Charley Francis,
who coached Canadian sprinter Ben Johnson (barred from competition for
two years after testing positive for steroids during the 1988 Olympics), said
that he didn't consider the regular and long-term administering of anabolic

steroids to athletes to be cheating. "My definition of cheating," he said, "is doing something nobody else is doing."[2] All well and good for the prevailing North American relativistic philosophy of the 1990s. But just how does Francis's atavistic comment square with the Olympic Charter, which states that the Olympic Games "unite competitors of all countries in fair and equal competition"?[3]

The whole unseemly dilemma of drug use in the Olympics, which saw no solution before the Albertville and Barcelona Games, has ramifications relating to the physiological, psychological, legal, ethical, and philosophical (and undoubtedly other) aspects of all human endeavors. It brings to mind Sir William Osler's comment that "the desire to take medicine is perhaps the greatest feature which distinguishes man from animals."[4] No one, absolutely no one, is an expert on the subject of drugs and athletic performance. There is still no answer to the question, What foods, medicines, chemicals, supplementary aids, substances, drinks, and drugs can be administered to athletes that are both enhancing and safe?

The official Olympic list of dangerous substances is alarmingly long, and it is growing. Scores of drugs are listed, among them stimulants, narcotics, anabolic steroids, beta-blockers, diuretics, peptide hormones and analogues, drugs used for pharmacological, chemical, and physical manipulation, plus "classes of drugs subject to certain restrictions (alcohol, marijuana, local anesthetics, and corticosteroids)."[5] The list is there, but IOC Vice President Richard Pound admitted, "We still have no clearly stated definition of what doping is."[6] We are not yet at the absolute limits of human physical achievement, but some in the elite athletic world are moving rapidly in that direction with the help of drugs, however ill defined.

The Olympic Drug History

In the United States, unconfirmed rumors of drug use among competitive professional athletes have circulated since the antebellum era of professional footracing in the 1840s and 1850s. Scores of inferential and anecdotal stories have come down to us about drug use during the nightmarishly difficult 6-day "go-as-you-please" 144-hour, 600-mile indoor "shuffles" of the American post–Civil War era, 1870 to 1890. Later, at the first four Olympic Games, rumors abounded that stimulants and alcohol were consumed during the marathon races. Almost no corroborative evidence exists about drugs inside the Olympic stadium during the nine Olympic Games between the World Wars.

Drug abuse began in earnest during the 1950s and 1960s and was discussed by Prince Alexandre de Merode, founder of the IOC's Commission Médicale, in the Belgian newspaper *Le Soir*. Merode ended his essay on an admittedly optimistic note: "Let us look forward to a time soon when Olympic gold medal winners will not feel the need to make a detour to their local drug

store.''[7] Everyone recognizes that drugs are not the "magic bullet" to victory, but they can be, sometimes, a small but significant "boost" in that direction. This is enough for a growing minority of athletes, coaches, and medical doctors who believe that within certain parameters and inside the Olympic stadium, the end does justify the means. These same people might find irrelevant philosopher-theologian Michael Novak's comment that the Olympic Games experience should be "a testing ground for virtue . . . an exhibition more about the beauty that the human spirit might create than about some new distortion of the body."[8] To participate in the Games with unalloyed honor, concluded Novak, is to have in perfect placement every human element and in so doing "to hit the mark exactly."[9] Seeking the aid of coach, physician, and scientist in stretching the outer limits of human physical achievement is legitimate provided all those involved do not "worship success" or fall prey to the "lust for international glory."[10]

Draconian emergency drug-testing procedures were enacted following the Ben Johnson incident in late September 1988. Another world conference on antidoping in sport took place in November 1988, despite similar conferences in September 1986, October 1987, and June and September 1988. Robert O. Voy, MD, one of the conservative, alarmist voices raised against the use of drugs in sport had already stated categorically that "only drug education and drug testing" in close concert can control, though not eliminate, drug use among Olympic athletes.[11] The Pierre de Coubertin International agreed with Dr. Voy, stating that education and "repressive punishment" should be administered simultaneously to offenders, though "education is of greater importance than repression."[12] At an emergency meeting in Vienna on 6 December 1988, the IOC, still groping for solutions to the proliferation of banned drugs among Olympic athletes, pleaded that the entire Olympic family find a solution. "If the Olympic movement fails in this area, everyone can go home," said Australian Kevan Gosper.[13] Prince Merode, with surprising candor, admitted that besides the reasons of ultranationalism and personal gain that some athletes give for making drugs a part of their lives, there was also the worldwide, cynical perception of "top-class athletes as mere workers performing a job, exercising a profession."[14] In the United States alone, there were an estimated half million adolescents using anabolic steroids in 1988, and, according to one researcher, the fault lies not with the athlete alone, but with the whole of society and its "addiction to sports." Charles E. Yesalis concluded that something other than money must dominate the sport world before meaningful change can take place, and "only when individuals and teams are willing to act unilaterally by renewing their commitment to fair play and no longer tolerate, actively or passively, the abuse of anabolic steroids" will real reform take place.[15]

Athletic performance-enhancing substances, especially steroids, failed to lose any appeal in 1990 and 1991. The IOC's elaborate and very expensive plans for a "flying airplane drug laboratory" seemed to fall on deaf ears; Anita DeFrantz's hard-line Olympic "death penalty" (proposed to begin after the Games in '92) lingered in uncertainty; track and field champions Randy Barnes, Larry Myricks, and Butch Reynolds claimed innocence when faced with 2-year banishments, and Germany's *Stern* magazine blackened the names of a host of athletes who allegedly took steroids over a period of several years. The list seemed endless.[16]

The biggest "bomb" was the publication of the *Dubin Report*, a 638-page indictment of drug offender Ben Johnson, but also a cutting criticism of many Canadian athletes, coaches, trainers, sport physicians, government officials, Canada's track and field federation, and its national Olympic committee. From 11 January through 3 October 1989, 119 witnesses appeared before the Honorable Charles L. Dubin, the recorded testimonies stretching to 14,817 pages. "The use of banned performance-enhancing drugs is cheating, which is the antithesis of sport," wrote Judge Dubin, sounding like someone from another era. So many people kept quiet as the Canadian drug problem grew within and without the athletic community. With the publication of this report, said the judge, "the conspiracy of silence has now been broken and the truth revealed." The Olympic Charter and its high-minded principles had been wounded, he wrote, and this "unprincipled pursuit of wealth and fame at any cost now threatens our very social fabric."

Dubin went on, page after page, extolling the pursuit of excellence, but "never at any cost and the loss of ethics and fair play." He talked about the absolute essential nature of "the level playing field":

> One of the excuses of Canadian athletes who used banned substances was that they had to do so to compete with athletes from other countries who were also using drugs. This may have levelled the playing field for the cheaters, but it put those athletes who competed honestly at a great disadvantage.[17]

Scores of recommendations poured from the shocked and outraged lawmaker, many of them technical, medical, administrative, and governmental, as well as legal in nature. Judge Dubin's run-on criticisms of collective greed, his statement that there exists a giant void of ethical practice were, some critics said, needless blanket indictments of the whole Canadian nonprofessional athletic system. But the essence of the mammoth report is that of a morally indignant, old-fashioned, concerned citizen and patriot. The document will be read for years to come either as a rallying cry for sanity and honesty or as the ramblings of an Edwardian gentleman wholly out of step with the sharp pragmatism of this very modern age.

Doctor Robert Voy, for 5 years the United States Olympic Committee's chief medical officer, was also of a conservative bent and his views coincided with Judge Dubin's. He insisted that there were too many loopholes in the American drug-detection system and a massive assault against all those guilty had to be initiated immediately. His sweeping prescription for drug reform included heavy punishment, improved research, increased educational efforts, and a societal change of attitude regarding all drugs. Effective, practical testing procedures were needed that involved the right people, the athletes. He had other suggestions: Hire an independent agency; start the plan now; build a better Olympic system, including clubs and a highly select group of corporate sponsors; reward progressive thinking; restrict volunteerism in the USOC system; keep clean records; and "dump the gold medal mentality."[18] Our Olympic committee, stated the incautious Voy, "is managed without vision, altruism, or determination."[19] They had to return to a consecration to Olympic ideals—"a treasure worth fighting for," he ventured.[20] It was too much, too fast for the USOC, and in March 1989, Dr. Voy was forced to resign.[21]

Solving the Problem

Like everyone else, I have no easy answer to the problem of drugs and the Olympic Games. As the intensity of drug use in the larger society subsides, it will abate within the athletic arena. But that is no answer at all. What must be done? First, the IOC must more clearly define *doping*. The Olympic Charter by-law to Rule 28 "is a disaster," stated a senior professor at Quebec City's Laval University, Fernand Landry, who knows so much of the Olympic world, philosophically and scientifically. "One cannot have a bare-faced statement, 'Doping is forbidden,' and then fail to clearly, scientifically, unambiguously define that word," stated physiologist Landry. It seemed "a blatant sin against logic" that doping be forbidden, and yet the Charter does not define the word.

Furthermore, Landry went on, it is against "legalistic logic" for all sport-governing bodies to attempt to enforce that which has thus far remained undefined. The concept of the level playing field and equality of opportunity in international competitive athletics does not stand up to critical logic. The very purpose of modern-day scientific training is to gain an advantage over one's opponents. There can never be a level playing field in big-time athletics, and, he concluded, to insist on such equality is

> a philosophical paradox . . . if not a dire contradiction. Coubertin himself struggled for a long time with his own paradoxical sporting philosophy, his search for what I call "minimal intellectual dissonance" between the Olympic motto *Citius, Altius, Fortius*, and "la recherche de la *mesure* dans la *demesure* [the search for the limits of excess or immoderation]." Doping is nothing as compared to what recent developments in biotechnologies, molecular biology and human genetics may bring to bear on the complex matters of talent, selection and/or development of high athletic performance before the third millennium turns upon us! I recall the first two lines of Henry David Thoreau's beautiful yet sobering poem *Sic Vita*: "I am a parcel of vain strivings . . . tied by a chance bond together."[22]

A "laundry list" of substances *not* allowed by the IOC (and the list is very long) is an unacceptable way of defining drugs, or, as it is called in the Olympic vernacular, doping. In much of the world, especially among the so-called Western tradition societies, the motivation to win Olympic medals is so powerful as to turn the motto *Citius, Altius, Fortius* on its head—to seek gold wherever it can be found and, too often, at whatever price. The Olympic leadership and most of us must live with this and with the omnipresence of "special substances" given to athletes or taken by them. That last phrase is important: Drugs can be administered to an athlete who is oblivious to their effects, or that same Olympian can demand to know the exact nature of every medication recommended to him or her. The solution to the Olympic drug problem is complex, but it can begin with the main actors on the stage, the athletes, demanding to know exactly what their trainers and physicians are putting into their bodies.

Ten years ago, multiple Olympic champion, Sebastian Coe, speaking on behalf of the athletes and unaware of the awful complexities of the doping question, called for "a life ban on offending athletes and coaches and on the so-called doctors who administer this evil."[23] It may be that, all these years later, British politician Coe might amend and expand his dictum with an exact definition of what constitutes "this evil" before exacting lifetime punishments. With all the vagueness and inexactitude regarding drugs, the Olympic Games, and fairness for all (i.e., a level playing field for all the competitors), I present several alternative scenarios for the 1990s.

OLYMPIC DRUG ALTERNATIVES FOR THE 1990S

1. Reverse current IOC policy, withdraw all forms of testing and surveillance, and eliminate punishment for the use of chemical substances by athletes. (Such a "solution" would save hundreds of millions of dollars in a single quadrennium.)

2. Adopt a new policy clearly defining the words *drugs* and *doping*.

3. Convene a meeting of medical doctors, physiologists, chemists, pharmacologists, legal scholars, ethicists, and moral philosophers to discuss and (improbable as it might seem) agree on the definitions of *dope* and *drugs*, and then publish, in the Olympic Charter by 1996, the exact natures of chemical substances that *may* be taken voluntarily and with full knowledge by the Olympic athlete and of those that *may not*.

4. Spend a billion dollars during the remainder of the century to enact a massive, "hard-line" drug-testing program on every continent, at most major international sporting events, and at the Winter

and Summer Olympic Games. Using "flying drug laboratories," announced and unannounced testing would become commonplace, with immediate lifetime banishment of all offenders so detected.

5. Develop a massive educational program, coordinated by the entire Olympic family of IOC, NOCs, and sport federations, for all pre-Olympic and Olympic Games athletes. The body of drug information should be wholly value free, devoid of any moral imperatives, and be, in every way, the latest scientific, disinterested, factual material. Thus informed, each athlete could decide what to do with his or her life.

6. The Olympic family in each country of the world educates its own athletes, from elementary school through university, in sport clubs and on national teams, in simple concepts of drug use and abuse. Such a massive effort would expose these vulnerable young minds to messages from educators, teachers of ethics, advocates of sportsmanship and fair play, moral philosophers, and theologians about making wise personal decisions that are neither self-injurious nor unjust to others.

7. A combination of alternatives 4 and 5 would find widespread support within the Olympic community without engendering any sense of conflict or contradiction.

Other approaches are possible, other combinations might work. What I find unacceptable is the position on doping mandated by the 1990 Olympic Charter, though I recognize the enormity of the risk that the IOC took in supporting President Samaranch's position. "Doping equals death"—death of the body, the intellect, of the moral and spiritual person, he said at the opening session of the IOC meeting on 12 September 1988. The IOC will take a firm stand against "this plague," he went on, for

alas, the thieves of sports performance, like their criminal counterparts in society, are forever striving to find new methods, often assisted by specialists who attach little importance to their oath or the code of ethics they are supposed to respect.[24]

Only a few weeks later, *Der Spiegel* published a lengthy and revealing essay titled "Doping—The Logical Result of the Pathetic, Commercial Circus in Seoul. Athletes Commit Chemical Castration."[25] Samaranch would have agreed with the second half of the headline, but he would have wholly rejected the first.

A Look Into the Future

The future is grim, not only for the Albertville and Barcelona Games, but for all Olympic festivals through the remainder of the century. In September 1991, IOC bulletins went out to all NOCs to reduce their Olympic Games delegations for Barcelona, because no more than 10,000 athletes and 5,000 support personnel will be allowed in the Olympic Village. As a result, some medical doctors and medical investigators must be left at home. The general feeling among some elite athletes is that most Olympians, both in the United States and abroad, are using performance enhancement drugs and that there are only a few great athletes in the world who are not using them (opinions reported by researchers Steven Ungerleider and Jacqueline M. Golding in an October 1990 report called the *Elite Athlete Project*).[26]

Not all is without hope. Energetic attempts to stop the increase in drug use among athletes have been initiated by the IOC, some sport federations, and some NOCs. It seems to be the best that they can do, but if consistent scientific information is melded with a renewed sensibility about fair play, then elite athletes of this century's remaining years may act from an improved motivational base. Some of these athletes, already suffused with this sense, find it strange that 2 years after his censure for having *knowingly* cheated at the Olympic Games, the great sprinter Ben Johnson could drive a $325,000 car and make frequent celebrity guest appearances at $3,000 to $5,000 each.[27] Thoughtful people in the Olympic arena know full well that something is amiss, that some of society's values and their own are askew, and that, at this very moment, there is need for personal reassessment of those values.

Medical and scientific models alone will not succeed in resolving the Olympic drug dilemma. There also must be communicated to athletes young and old "the plain message that there is something fundamentally wrong in misusing any substance." Clinical psychologist and teacher of psychiatry at University of Pittsburgh School of Medicine, Robert M. Schwartz, was of the opinion that much of youth everywhere are "moral orphans," lacking consensus that abuse of drugs is not only physically damaging but wrong. The concept of virtue must be made respectable again, and

> if there is a war to fight, let it be to reintroduce into our national vernacular the language of moral virtues—of self-control, discipline, balance, and moderation.[28]

The athlete aspiring to become a member of his or her national Olympic team may need to hear this message as much as, if not more than, any other person in society.

Science has served us very well throughout the century and will continue to do so, but some of us have hit bottom spiritually, and another road must be traveled, one called by futurists John Naisbitt and Patricia Aburdene "the direction of the nonrational."[29] When our Olympic athletes combine unambiguous scientific facts about anabolic steroid pharmacology and toxicology with what the United States secretary of health and human services, Louis W. Sullivan, called a "culture of character,"[30] then there will be better Olympic Games in 1994, 1996, 1998, and 2000. Facts and philosophy are the only intellectual team that will save the Olympic Games from being a dumping ground for a hundred drugs, ranging from the mundane to the latest athletes' "fix," the synthetic hormone rEPO. (Called "the cutting edge of cheating technology,"[31] this genetically engineered substance, as of this writing, cannot be detected in the body.)

Ultimately, the solution to the serious problem of athletes eating, drinking, chewing, ingesting, and injecting anything that might give them an edge will appear when these same men and women engage in the kind of serious introspection that Alvin Toffler calls a move away from muscle-and-money to mind as the main instrument of social control.[32] The real salvation of our Olympic athletes (and of the Olympic Games) will be a collective reassertion that ethics, morality, and fair play really do matter. For as Ray Monk said in his Ludwig Wittgenstein biography, "after science is done, the deep problems remain."[33] Olympic athletes must pay heed to these deep problems—now!

Notes

1. Sergio Santander Fantini, letter to author, 28 February 1990.

2. Charles Francis, quoted in Merrell Noden, "A Dirty System," *Sports Illustrated, 73,* 17 December 1990, 27.

3. Olympic Charter '90, 6.

4. Sir William Osler, quoted in Anthony Smith, *The Body* (New York: Viking Penguin, 1986; originally published 1968), 527.

5. *International Olympic Charter Against Doping in Sport 1990, Annex 2,* 2.1-2.12. The USOC's *Drug Education Handbook 1989-92* is an impressive 59-page document. It has everything in it, except, unfortunately, instructions on how athletes should take direct and personal responsibility for their behavior, their expenditures, and their actions.

6. Richard Pound, letter to author, 7 July 1989.

7. Alexandre de Merode, "LeCIO veut gagner la guerre de la pureté," *Bruxells Le Soir,* 12 September 1988, 9.

8. Michael Novak, "Sports and the Moral Life," *Creative Living, 13,* Spring 1984, 4. "The Olympic Games," he said, "are a celebration of the deepest strivings and most sharply etched acts of beauty that constitute civilization" (2).

9. Ibid.

10. Marie-José Mimiague, "The Doping Problem in Comparative Penal Law, Part II," *Olympic Review, 82-83,* September-October 1974, 460.

11. Robert O. Voy, "Education as a Means Against Doping," *Bulletin Fédération Internationale d'Éducation Physique, 57*(3), 1987, 8.

12. *A Declaration of the Pierre de Coubertin Committee Concerning Doping in Sport* (Paris: Coubertin Committee in France, 1987), 4.

13. *New York Times*, 8 December 1988, p. D27. Also Anita DeFrantz, IOC member and president of the Los Angeles–based Amateur Athletic Foundation, "Sports Devastated—Steroids Are Destroying Our Athletes," Los Angeles: AAF, 1988.

14. A. de Merode, "The Fight Against Doping: Ongoing Evolution," *Olympic Review, 262*, August 1989, 383-384. In the same issue, IOC Vice President Richard W. Pound hoped that the Ben Johnson affair marked the beginning of meaningful reform, "the point at which the turn-around began" (391).

15. Charles E. Yesalis, "Steroid Use Is Not Just an Adult Problem," *New York Times*, 4 December 1988, 125; "Anabolic-Androgenic Steroids . . .," *Clinical Sports Medicine, 1*, 1989, 126; "Winning and Performance-Enhancing Drugs, Our Dual Addiction," *Physician and Sportsmedicine, 18*, March 1990, 167; "The Strengths and Frailties of Drug Tests," *New York Times*, 4 February 1990, 105.

16. *Olympic Review, 275-276*, September-October 1990, 446-449; *Washington Post*, 30 August 1989, n.p.; *USA Today*, 6 November 1990, 11c; *New York Times*, 7 November 1990, D27-D28 and 30 November 1990, B15; *Sports Illustrated, 73*, 17 December 1990, 27; and *London Times*, 29 November 1990, 43.

17. Charles L. Dubin, *Commission of Inquiry Into the Use of Drugs and Banned Practices Intended to Increase Athletic Performance* (Ottawa: Canadian Government Publishing Centre, 1990), 547-548. Also xxi-xxii, 516-519. The report is summarized in *Maclean's, 103*, 9 July 1990, 18-19. Also John J. MacAloon, "Steroids and the State: Dubin Melodrama and the Accomplishments of Innocence," *Public Culture, 2*, Spring 1990, 41-62.

18. Robert Voy, with Kirk D. Deeter, *Drugs, Sport, and Politics* (Champaign, IL: Leisure Press, 1991), 198-199.

19. Ibid., 137.

20. Ibid., xviii.

21. Michael Janofsky, "Voy Is Still a Voice, Without Portfolio," *New York Times*, 13 March 1989, C6.

22. Fernand Landry, interview with author, Quebec City, 21 October 1990.

23. Sebastian Coe, quoted in "Olympic Congress Bucks Drug Fight," *International Herald Tribune*, 29 September 1981, 13.

24. J.A. Samaranch, quoted in *The Seoul Olympian*, 13 September 1988, 6.

25. "Doping—die logische konsequenz im erbarmungslosen, kommerzialisienten artisenzirkus von Seoul. Wirkt wie eine chemische kastration," *Der Spiegel, 40*, 3 October 1988, 290. The day before, 2 October 1988, the *London Sunday Times* published a different kind of article on Olympic Games drug taking. See "Cheats Can't Kill the Flame," B2. In October 1988, I collected more than 100 essays published dealing with Canadian sprinter Ben Johnson, his medical, business, and coaching entourage, and their collective greed and irresponsibility regarding the use of anabolic steroids. Also, Michael Janofsky published a massive five-part series, "Steroids in Sports," in the *New York Times*, 17-21 November 1988. The bibliography seems endless on this subject—a testimony to the collective shock and outrage, the general ignorance of the subject, and the importance of the Olympic Games to the media and among many peoples of the world.

26. Ungerleider and Golding, "Elite Athlete Project," presented at The Athletic Congress [TAC] annual meeting in Seattle, December 1990. The data are presented in a more elaborate format in a book entitled *Beyond Strength: Profiles of an Olympian* (Dubuque, IA: Brown, 1991).

27. D'Arcy Janish, "A New Race for Gold?", *Maclean's, 103*, 9 July 1990, 18. If Johnson races Carl Lewis in 1991, it will be for a $2-million "gate" according to Peter Corrigan in "Addicted to Revenge in the Dirtiest Running Battle," *London Sunday Observer*, 28 October 1990, 23.

28. R.M. Schwartz, MD, "For Drugs, a Moral Model," *Christian Science Monitor*, 2 November 1990, 19.

29. Naisbitt and Aburdene, *Megatrends 2000: Ten New Directions for the 1990s* (New York: Morrow, 1990), 295.

30. Louis Sullivan, MD, reviewed the government text, *Healthy People 2000*, and listed 22 areas of medical concern. But above all else, he said, we must cultivate "a culture of character," to be sensitive to

> the need to take control of our lives, to become free and independent, to overcome . . . constraints that limit our potential achievement . . . to be ever cognizant of our responsibility to others (*Health Promotion, 5-6*, September-October 1990, 5.).

31. Merrell Noden, "A Bad Boost," *Sports Illustrated, 73*, 26 November 1990, 29.

32. Toffler, quoted in Guy Halverson, "Toffler's *Powershift* Based on Knowledge," *Christian Science Monitor*, 22 November 1990, 7.

33. Ray Monk, *Ludwig Wittgenstein: The Duty of Genius* (New York: Free Press, 1990); reviewed by Thomas D'Evelyn, "A Philosopher's 'Why?' ", *Christian Science Monitor*, 12 December 1990, 13.

C·H·A·P·T·E·R· 11

The High Tide
of Olympic Criticism

The Olympics are of emotional value without intrinsic value.
Their disappearance would be of no great loss to society.

Derek Johnson, *silver medalist*

This book is an effort to illuminate virtually all aspects of the Olympic Games and the larger entity, the Olympic Movement. Much of it is complimentary, occasionally even laudatory, of certain athletes, administrators, and scholars within this whole structure. But perspective, historical accuracy, and attention to one's craft of trained observer compel me to point out what has been obvious to Olympic scholars for three generations: the Olympic Movement and Games have been forcefully criticized from day one in 1896, and criticism continues unabated to this day. Olympic critics come from every direction: athletes and Olympic bureaucrats; genuine scholars and pseudo-intellectuals; concerned, informed journalists and their less worthy brethren, whose primary interests are sales and higher television ratings. It is impossible to always disentangle the one from the other. So the critical as well as the eulogistic Olympic face must be revealed, for as historian Barbara Tuchman said, "Leaving things out because they do not fit is writing fiction, not history."[1] This chapter attempts to list the criticisms leveled against the Olympic Movement, especially the IOC, during the Games of 1988. The second half of the chapter has a dual purpose; it points out those criticisms that are factually incorrect, out-of-date, or otherwise misleading or exaggerated while examining weaknesses in the contemporary Movement and suggesting reforms that might be made before the next Olympic Games.

Criticism Against the Olympic Movement

Julius L. Patching, president of the Victorian Olympic Council, a division of the Australian Olympic Federation, found it helpful to divide criticism into derogatory (expressive of a low opinion) and destructive (designed to ruin or destroy) categories.[2] There is merit in his dual gradation of Olympic criticisms, but I have not taken advantage of such in this chapter. The flood of criticism against the Olympic Games and the Olympic family, especially the IOC, is beyond the capability of a single researcher to collect, though none of it should be ignored. Most Olympic fault-finding, unflattering essays fall into these five categories:

- Expressions of discontent by political self-interest groups
- Complaints of commercialism gone berserk
- Persistent vexation against the IOC
- The "muddiness" of Olympic philosophical principles
- Olympic Games as 'war without weapons'

The upbraiding of the Olympic Games and the Olympic Movement by the whole spectrum of critics (from scholarly, thoughtful critics to sensation-seeking nincompoops) needs study and reflection by historians, reformers, members of the Olympic Tripartite, and all those with a sustained interest in this most important sporting event. This chapter presents a representative sample rather than a definitive discussion of Olympic fault-finding. For those "in the Olympic family," this discussion might be useful in a cathartic, self-healing sort of way. For media professionals, scholars, and concerned lay persons, this chapter might engender further constructive criticism, and when such examination is insightful it can only enhance the credibility of the whole Olympic research enterprise.

In a sense, the Olympic world is the larger world. Journalist Hugh McIlvanney of the *London Sunday Observer*, after discussing rampant commercialism, crude nationalism, "eager subservience to the arrogant power of television," the abandonment of ethics, and pervasive drug abuse, noted wryly, "What more could we ask to make us feel at home?"[3]

Discontent of Political Self-Interest Groups

Olympic historians in the next century may write that no quadrennial festival received as much worldwide criticism as did the '84 Summer Games in Los Angeles. They were unique and unsettling in so many ways. Two Canadian critics called them a grandiose, vulgar, and unsuccessful expiation of America's sins in a wrongful Vietnam war.[4] The Games of the XXIVth Olympiad in Seoul, South Korea in 1988 were only slightly less criticized, whereas the Winter Games in Calgary 7 months earlier had invited mostly domestic deprecation.

Half a world away and 2 years earlier, the gigantic Seoul City had hosted with great success the Asian Games of 1986. From that day to the Opening Ceremonies of the 1988 Olympic Games, the English-language newspapers in Pyongyang, North Korea—the *People's Korea* and the *Pyongyang Times*—issued an endless vilification of the Games in Seoul. The South Korean government-controlled organs, *Korea Herald, South-North Dialogue in Korea, Vantage Points . . . in North Korea*, and the more scholarly *Korea and World Affairs* and *Far Eastern Economic Review*, more than held their own in condemning the People's Republic of Korea in the north while boasting of the amazing economic vigor in the south. It was old-fashioned Stalinist communism versus the newest brand of Asian capitalism. But the voices of discontent directed at the very existence of this international experiment, this Olympic anomaly, continued loud, persistent, and directionless.

All is illusion, myth, and misrepresentation regarding Olympic peace, solidarity, and human enrichment, was the neo-Marxist message of Michel Caillat and Jean-Marie Brohm in their *Les Dessous de l'Olympisme*—the "hidden underside" of the Olympic Movement. "There's nothing new about the Olympic philosophy. It continues to be a cruel deception, just another of the world's illusions," concluded the two French critics.[5] One of Brohm's pupils, Philippe Simonnot, wrote a rambling tirade in *Le Figaro* called "Physique et Métaphysique du Sport." He talked about the death of God, about "Coubertin's substitution of sport as the new religion," and of the godless, pharmacological, drug-infested arena that was the Seoul Olympic Stadium.[6] Olympic historian Yves Pierre Boulongne also found the Simonnot essay "arresting," and reminded that

> Philippe Simonnot is a disciple of Brohm, with a Marxist-Freudian orientation. Although Simonnot and his ilk are not held in high esteem here among Parisian intellectuals, his articles are frequently picked up by *Le Figaro* and *Le Monde*.[7]

A last barb by Simonnot called the Olympic Games a devious kind of warfare, the death of sportsmanship, and the birth of neopaganism. Richard Gruneau seems to be cut from the same neo-Marxist cloth in his insistence that the whole Olympic leadership is constitutionally incapable of separating itself from its historic ultraconservatism and from the "class and gender biases of Victorian athleticism" that render it incapable of honestly representing universal human values.[8] Similarly disposed ideologically was the Alexandrakis and Krotee essay, "Dialectics of the IOC," which accused the committee of being capitalistic, feudalistic, imperialistic, monopolistic, and viciously unfair in not having its membership made up of one person from each nation of the world—a true democracy of cooptation.[9]

The entire structure of the Olympic Games reflects a Western civilization bias and represents, historian Allen Guttmann said, the norms shared by Europeans and North Americans. Almost reluctantly, Professor Guttmann observed that within the Olympic framework there exists a conflict between "the universalistic ideals of the movement" and the obvious "cultural imperialism" ingrained in the system. Pierre de Coubertin's first Olympic Games in 1896 were exclusively European and that domination continues nearly 100 years later.[10] Coming from a different direction was Kenneth Reich of the *Los Angeles Times*, who so ably covered the '84 Games and reported them for 3 years in his newspaper's Home Forum and Metro sections, as well as in the sport pages. He wrote me that despite his overall support of the Movement's high ideals, the institution is full of contradictions and paradoxes—a veritable Tower of Babel. The IOC has a long way to go, he said, "to really be an august group." He wasn't sure, but

> it may be that the Olympics actually breed tension by screwing up emotions [and] patriotic fervor to ridiculous extremes. It may be that in the bloody 20th century it is just too much to expect that such an event could really do much to bring peace and good feeling.[11]

Fault-finder Alan Tomlinson, author of *Five Ring Circus*, looked to Pierre de Coubertin for many of today's Olympic ills, calling him a "displaced or dislocated aristocrat . . . his pacifism derived from military humiliation; his declared egalitarianism concerning the politics of the body bounded by principles of privilege and patronage and misogyny." Tomlinson concluded that to this day the Olympic Movement has been unable to shed this Coubertinian heritage.[12] Ideologues of all persuasions have criticized the Olympic Games and Movement, the founder of the modern festival, the present leadership, and, with special fury, the alleged discernible drift toward excessive preoccupation with commerce.

Commercialism Gone Berserk

It is not true that criticism of the growing cache of IOC monies (well in excess of $1 billion) comes only from socialist and former communist societies. American, French, German, and especially British writers have relentlessly "cut up" the IOC and its family for functioning more like multinational corporate executives than as guardians of traditional Olympic ideals.

The Calgary Olympic Organizing Committee did everything it could to aid and abet organizational honesty and efficiency, but it could not escape corruption in the guise of illegal advance sale of tickets. The director of ticket sales, under suspicion of stealing money, was fired. Soviet and Canadian writers took note of the Calgarian "money-making machine" and the "distressing news of Big Business" at work.[13] Britisher David Dawson, writing in the *Listener* and *The New Leader* found much wanting in Calgary, pointing out that western Canadians had raised the meaning of the phrase "going for the gold" to new heights—or depths. It's gold money they're after, pure and simple, he wrote. The "new commercial spirit of the Olympic Games" is no more manifest, wrote Dawson, than the vulgar display at the 15th Winter Olympic Games.[14]

Half a world away in the quintessential nation of commerce, a spokesman for the *Japan Quarterly* called the Seoul festival "a money-making circus . . . that had defiled the spirit of the games."[15] The USA supplies most of the money and gets little gold [medals] in return, complained one *Fortune* magazine contributor, while, improbable as it may seem, ABC-TV boss Roone Arledge said that from a financial viewpoint, "the IOC has treated us very badly." Still another American commented on "the selling of the Olympics," offering the opinion that the Games were now a "run for the money."[16] But again, British "Olympic bashers" seemed to have the most dramatic command of the English language.

When Jürgen Lenz, the executive vice president of ISL (see chapter 7) pontificated that "it is marketing's role to support the Olympic movement financially and materially and not vice versa,"[17] several London journalists jumped all over him. Lenz's "hard sell" was disgusting, wrote Harold Jackson in *The Guardian*, as he described the IOC's pitch-man and his cheerful "search for corporate fat cats to pick up the ever-expanding Olympic bill." Steven Aris was no less rough on Lenz in his *Financial Times Supplement* article titled "The Great Olympic Soap Sell":

> Exactly what Baron de Coubertin . . . would have made of Jürgen Lenz . . . is difficult to say. It is possible they would have hit it off, for Lenz is as devoted in his way to the prosperity of the Olympic movement as the baron ever was. In every other respect, though, the two men could not be more different.

Both Jackson and Aris epitomized the journalistic cynicism regarding the image of the once lordly IOC climbing down into the marketplace.[18] Theirs were not the only complaints. Mary Grimm, watching the Seoul Olympic Games on her advertisement-free television sets in Rome and Athens would have agreed with David Miller, sports editor of the *London Times*, that "the Olympic Games, for better or worse, are a colossal commercial force." Grimm lamented to her readers in the *New Yorker*,

> Why should Americans have to sit for hours of brain-dead commercials, thereby subsidizing the games for Greeks, who get off scot-free? Without advertising, the games become a whole religious drama, with

athletes waiting, pacing, tensing, getting psyched up, then the moment
of repose before they burst off the mark. Why clutter this sacred ritual
with Budweiser horses?[19]

Persistent Vexations Against the IOC

"What has God wrought!" exclaimed Samuel Morse in the first electric
telegraph message on 24 May 1844. The same might be said of Juan Antonio
Samaranch, the main architect of the Olympic Tripartite's billion-dollar
treasure chest. His has been no evolutionary effort, but rather a long decade
(1980-1991) of revolutionary Olympic legislation and Games stewardship.
But there was a price to pay, and in an interview in his handsome Château
de Vidy office, he voiced his concern: "I worry more about the legitimate
criticism of our Movement than I do about baseless, false accusations. Both
are disturbing to me, to us; and all those who love the core of Olympic
philosophy must work to [supplant] the latter with the former," he said in
his slow, precise English.[20]

President Samaranch and most of his colleagues had wrestled with the
dilemma of reconciling their disgust for South Africa's policies of racial
separation with the powerful dream of having every nation on earth
participate in the same Summer Olympic Games this century. The IOC
reluctantly expelled South Africa from membership in 1970, and despite a
hundred Samaranch speeches condemning apartheid, at least one critic, John
Hoberman, was outraged at even very cautious IOC overtures toward
reinstatement. Samaranch had repeated, "never, until apartheid is dead,"[21]
but Dr. Hoberman insisted that the IOC's "racist heritage" accounted for
its sudden interest in restoring South Africa's competitive rights even though
apartheid still existed.[22] The world, especially the black African world,
monitored very closely every IOC overture toward South African reentry,
and politically astute Samaranch seemed to say all the right things. "The
final solution will have to come from our African friends themselves," and
only then would South African athletes be welcomed back into the Olympic
Games, Samaranch repeated at the Tokyo IOC meeting in September 1990.[23]

"I have 15 reasons why I shall not go to Seoul," wrote former editor of
the London Times, Sir William Rees-Mogg. His list seemed a recitation of
all the perceived ills and weaknesses in the whole Olympic structure,
beginning with the loss of idealism. The Games have become "a grotesque
jamboree of international hypocrisy" representing those things "most rotten
and corrupt in the modern world," he wrote in the new London paper, the
Independent. Ultranationalism, racism, vulgar bureaucracy, the exploitation
of talent, "the glorification and self-assertion of totalitarian state regimes,"
IOC moral bankruptcy, mindless warrior athletes who retain "a dishonest
patina of amateurism," a sickening preoccupation with drugs and the
exploitation of child athletes, the encouragement of terrorism, and runaway
commercialism, concluded Rees-Mogg, all point to "the decline of the

Olympics into physical and moral squalor."[24] For many like Rees-Mogg (although less strident), the recent rule changes welcoming almost all professional athletes into the Olympic Games is proof that the Tripartite IOC-NOCs-sport federations have utterly abandoned the lofty principle of the "amateur spirit of joy and altruism," forsaken sentiment for profit, and exchanged the laurel wreath for the cash box.

The "Muddiness" of Olympic Philosophical Principles

With possibly one exception (the Olympic plunge into big-time commercialism), nothing alternately saddens and enrages some Olympic watchers more than the IOC's alleged abandonment of its historic "lofty amateur spirit." No issue "stirs the blood" more than the recent allegations that well-paid warrior-gladiators now dominate the Olympic Games. For the first decades of the Olympic Games, 99 percent of the competitors were amateur, non-paid participants. Even 30 years ago, 90 percent of the Olympic athletes expected no money payments, and got none. But since the 1970s, with the new Olympic monies, world-wide television, and involvement of scores of major corporations, more Olympic athletes are making money, possibly as high as 20 percent of all competitors. There is no longer any argument that the narrow definition of athletic amateurism was not antique Greek in origin, but rather a 150-year-old English tradition, "an ideological means to justify an elitist athletic system that sought to bar the working class from competition," wrote David C. Young.[25] Baron de Coubertin adopted this elitist English code, called it the "Olympic principle," and to his dying day was unsure that he had done the right thing, exclaiming to a French journalist in 1936, "How very stupid has been this Olympic history of amateurism!"[26] No defender of pure amateurism himself, Thomas Keller, former president of the rowing federation (FISA) and former boss of all the Olympic federations (GAISF), sought a reasonable balance but had found none in late 1986, when he confessed that "materialism has replaced idealism."[27] The true amateur spirit, argued Coubertin in the 1930s and the London Times's David Miller in the 1980s, is "an attitude of mind" and not "a preoccupation with an absence of financial reward, but a celebration of the spirit of competition."[28] The loss of innocence regarding the unalloyed athletic amateur spirit, we are told by some of those disillusioned by the recent drift, has led to the Olympic family's unparalleled preoccupation with money, which in turn has seduced many athletes into using drugs in their pursuit of gold. "Should the Chariots of Fire be for hire?" asked one commentator. The same writer snarled at by-law 26 of the Olympic Charter which says, in part, that a non-professional athlete can make all the money he or she wishes provided it is placed in a trust fund until after retirement from Olympic Games competition. However, there is a caveat to this restriction. Any athlete having an "emergency" at home may withdraw monies from the trust in order to take care of the emergency. As a result, some successful athletes are having 10 or 20 emergencies per year. There must be a need, Frank McCoy quipped, "as in 'I need a Mercedes to get to practice.'"[29] Willi Daume, the IOC's consummate idealist-pragmatist, acknowledged the IOC's legitimate, growing need for big money but said that some of the things that are taking place "would set Brundage whirling in his grave" ("Brundage würde sich im Grabe umdrehen").[30]

Absolutely nothing has accentuated the public's confusion about the Olympic Charter's fundamental principle number one, which talks about moral qualities, peace, international understanding, and goodwill among athletes, than the case of Ben Johnson in Seoul 1988. There may have been hundreds of athletes taking steroids at those games, but "poor Ben" made world sport headlines on every continent. Some said that he and his entourage were no more than an aberrant band of very greedy specialists. Others saw a direct line of fuzzy, ever-changing, and even impossible to follow Olympic rules and regulations with profit rather than principle as their main operational thesis, which in turn carried Ben and many others into the swirl of chemical manipulation. It all made for some extraordinary headlines.

The high-principled activist and new IOC member, the first black woman on the committee, Anita DeFrantz, cried in anguish, "Ben Johnson is a coward." Three sport veterans in the *London Sunday Times* of 2 October 1988, roared that "an athletic Armageddon" was upon us, that the "age of innocence is truly over," and, worst still, that "the Olympics wallow in a vat of urine." Hyperbole or honesty—who could say? A grossly muscular gladiator, "Big Ben, has led us to the bottom of the pit," wrote Pierre Hurel in *Paris Match*. "Tarnished gold," wrote *Asiaweek*; Geoff Dyer in the *New Statesman and Society* found the "monomaniac" Ben Johnson's actions a kind of "life in the Faust lane."

Worst of all was Johnson's worldwide popularity *after* his shame, which earned him several hundred thousand dollars in Japanese appearance fees and $25,000 from French television—for his expert advice on anabolic steroids.[31] Ben Johnson was tarnished, but so was the whole Olympic Movement. Greed rather than glory, sleaze rather than principle, at least for the moment, had overwhelmed all.

Olympic Games as 'War Without Weapons'

Chapter 4 discusses this topic of patriotism-gone-awry, but it can never receive too much attention, even in the last decade of this century when, it seems to me, other Olympic-related crises take precedence. Former world-champion runner, Christopher Chataway, and his colleague Philip Goodhart wrote an interesting book in 1968—*War Without Weapons*. They agreed with George Orwell that international sport, the Olympic Games, were "war minus the shooting." To be sure, admitted Chataway and Goodhart, they are a kind of warfare, "but war *without* the weapons."[32] They were not the first to see the similarity. Criticism of the Olympic Games as mock war began at the first

Athenian Games in April 1896, and there has not been a single summer festival free of such accusations, and that, of course, includes Seoul 1988.

Scores of nations promised big money to any of their athletes who returned from Seoul with a medal—any medal. Philippine president Corazon Aquino showed her nation's gratitude for a light flyweight's bronze medal finish with an $18,000 gift. Korean pride was Everest-high, and all of its gold medalists were awarded pensions of $16,600 a year for life. No nation has greater pride than the French, and they awarded "200,000 F pour l'or; 100,000 F pour l'argent, et 75,000 F pour le bronze."[33] Seoul City during the Games was so thick with patriotic fervor, said Blackie Sherrod in the *Dallas Morning News*, "it was like going to bed with a cobra's head in your grasp."[34] Silver medalist in the 800-meters, Derek Johnson, wrote the British prime minister in early 1980 protesting that nation's boycott of the Moscow Olympic Games; but he changed his mind, and later, in the *Daily Mail*, he stated,

> frankly, it does not matter what happens to the Olympic Games. They have become such a political thing that it is actually desirable that they should be cut down to size. The Olympics are of emotional value without intrinsic value. Their disappearance would be of no great loss to society.[35]

When the official film of the Korean Olympic Games Organizing Committee (SLOOC) was released, professional Olympic critic, Simon Barnes, wrote a well-balanced essay, but he was angry that the whole 2-1/2-hour piece was one great, saccharine-sweet, ultranationalistic, Korean love-feast, filled with "half-baked cliches, soft-soap, flannel, [and] lies" produced "for the gratification of the Seoul City Fathers."[36] Interestingly, Barnes had much praise for some things that took place at the 16-day festival. No such compliments came from the pen of Ian Buruma in a lengthy essay in the *New York Review of Books*. Korean chauvinism, hysteria, power politics, ritualized patriotism, and an excess of "shamanistic incantations" negated whatever good there was at the '88 Games, wrote Buruma.[37] On the eve of Seoul's Opening Ceremonies, one author wrote that there was every indication that the world would have inflicted upon it supernationalism, zealousness-to-extreme, sexism, racism, runaway commercialism—a sociological garden of what the games were *not* supposed to be all about.[38] And finally, the saddest note of all was a reminder from the Royal Canadian Mounted Police that millions of dollars must be spent on Olympic Games security, that "constant, creative planning, as well as vigilance, meticulous coordination, analysis, and communication" must be utilized to keep out maniacal terrorists.[39]

Exploring Olympic "Sinkholes"

Chronicles of one's own era have always said that we dwell in tumultuous times, that most of us are living "on the edge." I confess to being one of their number, and with regard to the Olympic Games, I believe strongly that during the remaining years of this century the Olympic Games will move more strongly either in the direction of "circus" or the other way toward controlled majestic drama and the glory of human dignity and athletic performance. The Games cannot stand still. They are dynamic, living entities and will take one course or the other.

Olympic Games' organizers, without exception, whether Greek, Italian, Norwegian, Mexican, Australian, American, Canadian, or Korean, have always tried to portray their stadium world as a reflection of the larger universe—only grander, greater, more heroic. Always, from Athens to Seoul, they have both succeeded and failed. I have no patience with those who describe with excruciating accuracy every human foible inside the Olympic stadium from Paris 1900 through Moscow 1980. Such mindless reiteration of error is no more good history than is reducing world history in the 20th century to the Battle of the Somme, the St. Valentine's Day Massacre, Pearl Harbor, the Tet Offensive, the Charles Manson murders, and the 1990 rape of Kuwait. Any writer taking the opposite, hopelessly Pollyannaish view of Olympic history is equally irresponsible.

President Samaranch revels quietly in his job as IOC president. He may be better at it than any of his six predecessors, especially in the sensitive realm of dealing with political heads of state. When Samaranch retires from his post, the new leader, whomever he or she may be, will have difficulty maintaining such pacific diplomatic relations. The old leadership and the newer men and women coming along must guide the IOC, the national Olympic committees, and the several score of wildly dissimilar international sport federations—the Olympic family—in ways that will not disenfranchise political heads of state.

"Playing ball" with diplomats, without at the same time abandoning Olympic principles, will be the single most challenging task of the family throughout the remainder of the century. Balance is everything, and Olympic leadership must continue dealing with the politicians of the world without following the seductive siren call of those who would suggest unacceptable compromises of the political and the athletic.

Future Olympic leadership must convince a very great many people that the Olympic Games and the Olympic Movement are a truly good enterprise, not just an athletic superchallenge or a money-making machine, but an international happening that is the embodiment of myth, vision, and genuine heroics. There must be about these future Olympic Games a perpetual aura of goodness, a sense of "metaphysical sanity" as one Boston University philosophy professor said.[40]

I have a vision of an Olympic financial scenario in which, by the year 2000, the IOC will have earned, invested, and saved so much money that, unlike the nouveau riche who think too much about wealth, the IOC will be able to devote nearly all its energies in other directions.[41] I wish it to be so, because much of the world is entering the "new altruism," or as author

Tom Wolfe put it, "We are leaving the period of money fever that was the Eighties and entering a period of moral fever."[42] Such a scenario would be the best thing that could happen to the Olympic Tripartite.

The IOC is dramatically not the same organization that it was in the past or even as recently as the 1970s. Vexing problems will continue to challenge a modern IOC membership which, in the 1990s, will be younger, better educated, multiracial, made up of rich and poor with every key working subcommittee composed of men *and* women. It must be this way or it cannot survive, and after conversations with most of the membership, the IOC knows this full well. Of course, there remains intellectual "dead wood" on the IOC, which must be pruned away no matter how well intentioned or well placed. Eventually the IOC must rid itself of any vestige of fatalism and believe implicitly that, even though politicians *do* rule the world, the destiny of the Olympic Games is in IOC hands. One of the wisest voices of American journalism, Flora Lewis, said at the end of 1990, "More and more people are coming to realize that they can choose their history. What is is neither immutable nor inevitable."[43]

Balance is everything, and the Olympic leadership around the world is learning how to amend its rules, regulations, and charters in order to effectively meet modern exigencies without jettisoning the very best of what was given to them by Coubertin; Count Henri Baillet-Latour, the third IOC president; Sigfred Edström, the fourth leader; Brundage; Killanin; and Samaranch. Some entity (the IOC) must be at the head of the Movement, but greater parity, *real* parity, must exist in the Olympic framework, the NOCs, the sport federations, and the growing voice of the athletes. Each must respect the independence of the others and, at the same time, fully understand, emotionally and intellectually, that their collective existence depends on cooperation. The Olympic Charter must clearly reflect this greater need for wholeness, the comprehension and acceptance of diverse viewpoints which, taken together, will most benefit the entire Movement.

The Olympic Games have never started a war, contrary to rumor (like that that claimed violence at the Central American and Asian Games resulted in regional wars). Neither can the Olympic Games bring peace to the world or any part of the world. They *have*, for a long time, enhanced the quality of life for a great many people in and out of the arena and brought pleasure to a mighty large if unseen television audience. "War without weapons" is only an interesting cliche, and though democracy versus communism was an Olympic ideological phenomenon from 1952 through 1984, this particular war was not fought in Calgary or Seoul 1988, nor did it have much meaning for the Games before World War II (and this includes the 1936 so-called "Nazi" Olympic Games). Seoul, Korea, 1988 marked the first time that the Olympic Games were truly world encompassing. This placed extra responsibilities on the IOC, according to John Rodda of *The Guardian*, among them maintaining fiscal responsibility, "selling" the idea of internationalism, remaining apolitical in its ideology but not in its daily machinations, and expanding "further the notions of democracy within the Movement."[44] Buried deep within the ideological superstructure of the Olympic Games and the global Olympic Movement is the biological paradox, so well stated by the modern-day French-American bacteriologist, René Dubos, that all humans remain always and everywhere fundamentally the same, "whereas [their] existential expressions and social aspirations constantly fluctuate."[45]

The players in the Olympic Movement have taken a great deal of heat over the years. Games' organizers, the Olympic Tripartite, the blizzard of entrepreneurs, and some of the "family" of judges, officials, trainers, coaches, and athletes have been found wanting. Honest accusations, accurate revelation of shortcomings, and constructive criticism of past Olympic efforts have helped the Movement to improve itself slowly. But life moves more rapidly as the millenium approaches, and in fact, as futurist Alvin Toffler said, "from now on the world will be split between the fast and the slow."[46] My hope is that the whole of the Olympic world gets on the fast track while refusing to relinquish its 100-year-old transcendental heritage.

Notes

1. Barbara Tuchman, "An Age of Disruption," in Rushworth M. Kidder, ed., *An Agenda for the 21st Century* (Cambridge, MA: M.I.T. Press, 1987), 46.

2. Julius L. Patching, letter to author, 22 September 1989.

3. Hugh McIlvanney, "Games That Rise Above the Sleaze," *London Sunday Observer*, 11 September 1988, 16.

4. Richard Gruneau and Hart Cantelon's exact words were, "Future scholars may well see the Los Angeles Olympics as a cultural event that dramatically signified the final assuagement of the feelings of impotence and confusion following the Vietnam experience and the Iranian hostage-taking." See page 362 in Jeffrey O. Segrave and Donald Chu, editors, *The Olympic Games in Transition* (Champaign, IL: Human Kinetics Books, 1988).

5. Michel Caillat and Jean-Marie Brohm, *Les Dessous de L'Olympisme* (Paris: Cahiers libres: Éditions la Découverte, 1984), 163. Brohm is the single-most persistent critic of the Olympic Games, a professional in the field. Among his writings are *Sport—A Prison of Measured Time* (1978); *Le Mythe Olympique* (1981); "Conversation with Jean-Marie Brohm" and "Le Sport Capitaliste," in *Éducation Physique et Sport, 181*, May-June 1983, 37-41, and *214*, November-December 1988, 80.

6. *Le Figaro*, 11 October 1988, 2F.

7. Boulongne, letter to author, 1 January 1989.

8. Richard Gruneau, "Television, the Olympics, and the Question of Ideology," in Roger Jackson, ed., *The Olympic Movement and the*

   Mass Media—Past, Present and Future Issues (Calgary, CAN: Hurford Enterprises, 1988), 7-26.

9. Ambrose Alexandrakis and March L. Krotee, "The Dialectics of the IOC," *International Review of the Sociology of Sport, 23*(4), 1988, 325-344.

10. Allen Guttmann, "'Our Former Colonial Masters': The Diffusion of Sports and the Question of Cultural Imperialism," *Stadion, 14*(1), 1989, 56.

11. Kenneth Reich, letter to author, 7 January 1985.

12. Alan Tomlinson, in Roger Jackson, ed., *The Olympic Movement and the Mass Media—Past, Present, and Future Issues* (Calgary, CAN: Hurford Enterprises, 1988), 73; also *Five Ring Circus* (London: Pluto Press, 1984), 85.

13. *Canadian Business*, November 1987, 56-66; *Sport in the USSR, 288*, March 1987, 7.

14. *Listener*, 11 February 1988, 9-10; *The New Leader, 72*, 9 January 1988, 9-10.

15. Chūjō Kazuo, in *Japan Quarterly, 36*, January-March 1989, 75-78.

16. David J. Morrow, "How to Quit Losing the Olympics," *Fortune, 119*, 24 April 1989, 265-274; Roone Arledge, quoted in Mark McDonald's column in the *Dallas Morning News*, 20 November 1987, p. 12B; Richard Manning, "The Selling of the Olympics," in *Newsweek, 110*, 28 December 1987, 40-41.

17. See Lenz's speech in Roger Jackson, ed., *The Olympic Movement and the Mass Media—Past, Present, and Future Issues* (Calgary, CAN: Hurford Enterprises, 1988), 103.

18. Harold Jackson, "The Price of Gold," *London Guardian*, 24 September 1988, p. 21; Aris's Lenz-Coubertin comparison appeared in *Financial Times Supplement*, 11 June 1988, 1.

19. Mary Grimm, "Notes and Comments," *New Yorker, 64*, 17 October 1988, 31. Miller's assessment is in an essay, "Taking Gold in a Greater Game," *London Times*, 16 September 1988, 14.

20. J.A. Samaranch, interview with author, 26 February 1990.

21. Samaranch, quoted in "South Africa Gaining but Still in Disfavor," *New York Times*, 26 January 1990.

22. J. Hoberman, quoted in Rachel Shuster, "IOC Urged to Keep South Africa Ban," *USA Today*, 10 August 1990, 2C.

23. *Program 96th IOC Session*, Opening Ceremonies, 16 September 1990, 8-9.

24. William Rees-Mogg, "The Decline of the Olympics Into Physical and Moral Squalor," *London Independent*, 19 April 1988, 16. He concluded

that absolutely nothing good would take place at the Seoul Olympic Games: "It will be repulsive. It will be boring . . . And, thank God, I will not be there." Dr. Don Anthony replied to each of these accusations in an essay called "Keep the Flame Burning Bright!" in *Sports Teacher* [England], May-June 1988, 4-6. Regarding exploitation of child athletes, Rees-Mogg was referring to the large number of preteen female gymnasts who train for 40 hours a week.

25. David C. Young, "How the Amateurs Won the Olympics," in Wendy J. Raschke, ed., *The Archaeology of the Olympics* (Madison: University of Wisconsin Press, 1988), 56. Ronald A. Smith said the same thing, after independent research in a different direction. See his *Sport and Freedom: The Rise of Big-Time College Athletics* (New York: Oxford University Press, 1988), 166; also John Lucas, "From Coubertin to Samaranch: The Unsettling Transformation of the Olympic Ideology of Athletic Amateurism," *Stadion, 14*(1), 1988, 65.

26. In the French journal, *l'Auto*, 28 August 1936. Coubertin's statement is paraphrased by Marquis Melchior de Polignac in the *Bulletin du CIO, 6*, September 1947, 12.

27. Fekrou Kidane, "Thomas Keller—Leader of the Opposition," *Continental Sports, 34*, September-November 1986, 30.

28. Coubertin, quoted by Norbert Müller in *Bulletin 1, Congrès Olympique Baden-Baden 1981*, 7; David Miller, "Professionalism and the Olympic Games," *Proceedings IOA 1989*, 87.

29. See Frank McCoy's essay in *Business Week*, 26 September 1988, 70; David Anderson wrote in the *New York Times* that "Rule 26 is an Olympic joke" (7 February 1984, p. B7). Mark McDonald of the *Dallas Morning News* interviewed 14 IOC members on Olympic amateurism and ended up dizzy with confusion. See his full-page survey, *Dallas Morning News*, 21 August 1988, 1B, 18B.

30. Willi Daume, quoted in *Der Spiegel, 1*, 1986, 133.

31. *Los Angeles Times*, 28 September 1988, part 3, 3; *London Sunday Times*, 2 October 1988, A30, B1; *Paris Match, 2054*, 6 October 1988, 49; *Asiaweek, 14*, 7 October 1988, 46; *New Statesman and Society, 1*, 7 October 1988, 14; *Japan Quarterly, 36*, January-March 1989, 77; *USA Today*, 29 November 1989, 2C.

32. Christopher Chataway and Philip Goodhart, *War Without Weapons* (London: Allen, 1968), 158. Chataway also wrote "An Olympian Appraises the Olympics," *New York Times Magazine* 4 October 1959, pp. 50-58; also "War Minus the Shooting," *London Sunday Times*, 24 April 1966, 12.

33. *Asiaweek, 14*, 14 October 1988, 45, 53; *Le Figaro*, 2 October 1988, 13.

34. Sherrod, in the *Dallas Morning News*, May 1989 (exact date and page not available).

35. Johnson, quoted in Neil MacFarlane, with Michael Herd, *Sport and Politics: A World Divided* (London: Willow Books, 1986), 222.

36. Simon Barnes, "Seoul-Searching Stops Short of the Truth," *London Times*, 18 November 1989, 48.

37. Ian Buruma, "Playing for Keeps," *New York Review of Books, 35*, 10 November 1988, 44-50.

38. Pat McNeill, "Sport and Leisure," *New Statesman and Society, 1*, 16 September 1988, 30.

39. *Police Chief, 56*, March 1989, 39-40.

40. Peter Kreeft, quoted in Thomas A. Stewart, "Why Nobody Can Lead America," *Fortune, 123*, 14 January 1991, 45.

41. The 3,000-word essay, "Fools' Gold: How America Pays to Lose in the Olympics," left me with the impression, a quite convincing image, that unless the IOC and the USOC devote much more time to making money, they will not survive. See Robert Z. Lawrence, with Jeffrey D. Pellgrom, *Brookings Review, 7*, Fall 1989, 4-10.

42. Tom Wolfe, quoted in Alan Farnham, "What Comes After Greed?" *Fortune, 123*, 14 January 1991, 43. The phrase "new altruism" belongs to Farnham.

43. Flora Lewis, "People Make History," *New York Times*, 29 December 1990, 23.

44. John Rodda, "The IOC Since 1972," *Olympic Message, 23*, March 1989, 9.

45. René Dubos, "The Biological Basis of Urban Design," in K.A. Doxiades, ed., *Anthropopolis* (New York: Norton, 1974), 262.

46. Alvin Toffler, *Power Shift: Knowledge, Wealth, and Violence at the Edge of the 21st Century* (New York: Bantam Books, 1990), 397.

C·H·A·P·T·E·R·12

Women in the Olympic Movement: The 52 Percent Solution

Le temps travaille pour nous [Modern times are working in our favor].

Monique Berlioux, *former IOC director*

At the close of the Moscow Olympic Games of 1980 and at a women's sport symposium in Dublin, Ireland, the IOC's director, Monique Berlioux, told the cosmopolitan audiences that there were no female members on the Olympic committee, that women in positions of power were nearly nonexistent in the NOCs and international sport federations, and that in Moscow that summer, only 3% of all officials were women. "Is it possible to envisage a greater servitude?" asked Berlioux, an employee of the IOC, but not a member.[1] Much has changed since then, but not nearly enough in many portions of the world. In sport and the world at large, most national heroes are men. Eighty percent of all biographies are written by men or are about men, because, by inference, the ideal woman of the past "has been silent, self-effacing, and therefore without a story to tell."[2] Fifty-two percent of all humankind is female, but Olympic Games competitors have never even remotely approached any kind of "52 percent solution."[3]

Pierre de Coubertin was a great man in many ways, but because he was a consummate Victorian-Edwardian gentleman, he found it impossible during his 29 years of IOC leadership to encourage vigorous "ladies' events" at the Summer Olympic Games. IOC presidents Baillet-Latour, Edström, and Brundage were benignly neglectful of active campaigning for more women in the Olympic arenas and in executive administrative positions, unable to perceive that all of human progress is retarded when there is universal failure to know that the ultimate triumph "lies in the cooperation and complementarity of women and men."[4] Two hundred years ago, Mary Wollstonecraft, in *A Vindication of the Rights of Women*, insisted that the rights of humankind should not be based on sex, that "what they say of man I extend to mankind."[5] And so, here "at the edge of the 21st century," *Time* magazine devoted a special Fall 1990 issue to "Women and the Road Ahead," the managing editor insisting that women's "endeavors deserve no less a word than *revolution*—in expectations, accomplishments, self-realization, and relationships with men."[6]

Olympic Leadership Acknowledges the Imbalance

Clearly the Olympic leadership is moving in the right direction. In Paris 1900, there were 2 sports for women; 80 years later in Seoul, the number had risen to 17. At Calgary '88, women represented 39% of all athletes; at Seoul, 36%. Merely raising the number of female Olympians is not the issue. Rather, Nadia Lekarska hinted, those nations least receptive to women as athletes must increase their participation in order to balance the always eager Soviet, German, Canadian, English, Australian, New Zealand, and American women.[7]

Increasing the number of female administrators in the worldwide movement is an even more challenging task, because each nation moves at its own speed toward equal opportunities for both sexes. Somehow more, talented women must find their way into local, national, and international administrative sporting positions and, exactly like men do, over time, move up the ladder. Young women graduates of university management programs and retired female athletes frequently can reach the top through hard work, proven skills, and many years of dedication. They only need to market their talents with quiet aggressiveness, which is the way that most men break into the inner circle of Olympic administration. Of the 88 employees inside the IOC's headquarters Château de Vidy in 1991, 58 were women. Samaranch's 1990 appointment of a seventh female IOC member—Canadian Carol Anne Letheren—was an encouraging move, one based on her merits.[8] It might be difficult to disagree with futurist Alvin Toffler who said that "at the edge of the 21st century," education and information represent the source of the highest-quality power of all and are "gaining importance with every fleeting nanosecond."[9] Better educated women are not the sum and substance of the search for more women Olympic administrators, but it can go a long way in that direction, said the young IOC Museum archivist, Fani Kakridi-Enz, speaking to the 3rd International Session for directors of national Olympic Academies. [10] A modern education, available equally to qualified men and women, is the kind of future world envisioned by another writer. "Young women do not want to slip unnoticed into a man's world," wrote a *Time* magazine contributor. "They want that world to change and benefit from what women bring to it."[11] At age 65, Monique Berlioux, administrative assistant to the mayor of Paris (and for 15 years the IOC director), said the same thing in a 1990 speech, "La Femme dans le Mouvement Olympique," ending prophetically, "le temps travaille pour nous [modern times are working in our favor]."[12]

International feminist scholar and activist, Margarita Papandreou, noted that without exception there is no society in the world that is not male-dominated.[13] Clearly then, all members of the Olympic Tripartite, no matter how well intentioned, are constrained regarding the recruitment of women into the dual realms of athletic competition and sport administration. They must move circumspectly forward, putting in order their houses, and hope that the best men and women share the athlete's rostrum and the administrator's chair. "More female role models would provide encouragement for girls in sport, and this means the role models in all domains—in the family and school, high-level coaching, Olympic committees, government officials concerned with sport, athletics, and so on," wrote Dr. Patricia Vertinsky, associate dean at the University of British Columbia.[14] Knowing whereof she speaks, the IOC's Anita DeFrantz spoke to all young women: "Stop believing that we have no role in sport past the playing field. Coaching, the media, countless administrative positions, as well as sport belong to all of us. We must fight to make [them] ours."[15] The logical extension is that the International Olympic Committee and all its associates around the globe have been issued a challenge but also a window of opportunity to harness the brain power and physical energies of highly accomplished members of more than half the world's population—women.

When UNESCO ministers and senior officials responsible for physical education and sport met in Moscow in the fall of 1988, one of their conclusions was that "in the cause of humanism," women have the "right to practice sport [as] one aspect of their right to education."[16] There were no visible stirrings in the developed and wealthier nations, for most of them considered the suggestion a fait accompli. Neither were there many in the Third World or in economically underdeveloped countries toward instituting significant changes that would encourage girls and women to participate in sport and fitness and give them opportunities to compete among the world's best at the Olympic Games. Only Olympic Solidarity monies (see chapter 8) gave a very few young women a chance. In Kenya, Olympic silver medalist (1972), Dr. Mike Boit said, "Women generally do not expect more from life than a low status job or marriage."[17] This attitude is not endemic to east Africa, and only constant pressure and better education can effect a change in it by the end of the century.

There was, during the 1980s, a gradual awakening among some Japanese, Korean, and Chinese women of a desire for personal and collective recognition, a belief that all women should be able "to choose what they want to do on the basis of their capabilities and inclinations" and to seek what one Korean called "women's self-actualization and personhood."[18] "Women's consciousness" is slowly spreading throughout India, even in the rural areas, according to one Indian feminist. There is hope for women in Latin America and the Caribbean, wrote one woman, despite their having borne "the brunt of the region's past 10 years of economic decline." Some Saudi Arabian women want reform in the two most important areas: "expanding available fields of university study, then allowing women to work side-by-side with men."[19] In 1983, Monique Berlioux was pessimistic about the prospect of women *inside* the Olympic Movement and told Morley Myers of United Press International, "I don't see any women on the IOC executive board for some time, and we certainly won't have a woman president this century."[20] She was wrong in the first instance, and she might be wrong in the second. By 1991 there were seven women on the IOC, one on the IOC executive board, and at least two women with the potential of reaching the presidency early in the 21st century.[21]

Defining a Solution

The "52 percent solution" will be difficult to accelerate. Talented women, like gifted men, are on our every side, and to use both expeditiously in every area, including sport, requires more than new laws. Canadian Pat Vertinsky said that such fairness will require, not a "revolution or imposition," but rather "a continuous process of redefinition."[22] There is no greater proof of how difficult it is to open up the Olympic world to women than what happened in Monte Carlo from 31 October to 3 November 1990, when the General Assembly of the General Association of International Sports Federations (GAISF) met for its 24th annual congress. Of the more than 500 delegates, only a handful showed up at a featured presentation on "Women and Sport." David Miller, chief sports correspondent for the *London Times* was in the audience and was angry at the shortfall of members present. "The absenteeism ironically proved the need for the debate," he wrote, continuing,

> when a male squash official suggested that women had more time for midweek sports activity than men, the women present politely fell off their chairs laughing. . . . The fundamental issue is not one of conversion

of the prejudiced, but education from the first days of childhood thought: by parents, teachers and all religious, social, cultural and political leaders.[23]

Miller must be correct. The hope is with the young, where there are no life-long biases that need to be reversed and for whom the future may become, as José Cagigal said in the *Olympic Review*, "a truly human society."[24] When Frenchwoman Alice Milliat, in 1921, created international track and field for women out of nothing (i.e., nearly no history), it was a man, George Pallet, who came forward with congratulations, pointing out that "she lit a candle which has spread a flame round the world."[25] The elusive goal of the Olympic leadership is that women from every country—all 168 of them—participate in the Winter and Summer Olympic Games as athletes, trainers, coaches, and administrators and representative officers in the NOCs, the sport federations, and the IOC. It is unacceptable that Britain, America, and the Soviet Union increase their numbers of women representatives without, at the same time, Central and South America, Africa, and all Islamic nations also sending female members. Ancient cultures and customs must be respected; deep-rooted religious beliefs cannot be disregarded. Still, as Nawal El Saadawi said in *The Hidden Face of Eve*, "more and more women are being drawn into the [women's] struggle for social transformation."[26] Her comment, as much hope as reality, should be emblazoned on all national Olympic committee banners.

It no longer seems utopian that the Olympic Movement—the two dozen international sporting festivals around the world that receive IOC backing, and the tens of thousands of athletic manager-administrators on six continents—can become a model of full rights for women. There are more female than male specialists inside Lausanne's Olympic headquarters, and they make an important difference in the efficiency and ambiance of the far-flung Olympic ship-of-state. Françoise Zweifel, Michèle Verdier, Ann Beddow, Madeleine Ricard, Myriam Gross, Annie Inchauspé, and Fani Kakridi-Enz are key people (admittedly, not policy makers) in the orderly operation of this largest of all sports organizations.[27] A tally of the women in key administrative posts on the IOC, inside NOC headquarters in 168 countries, within 40 international sport federations (recognized and affiliated), and associated with hundreds of national sports governing bodies would be immediately outdated as the numbers continue to rise. "Knowledge yields the highest-quality power," said futurist Alvin Toffler,[28] and those women well placed in the Movement do not necessarily present a women's view, but rather a universal and Olympian face to their knowledgeable work.

An unforgettable moment at the 1984 Olympic Games in Los Angeles was when a young 5-foot, 2-1/2-inch Casablancan, Nawal El Moutawakie, won the gold medal in the first-ever women's 400-meter hurdles. Her king, Hassan II of Morocco, was overjoyed and ordered a national celebration. As for Nawal, "she took the customary victory lap, waving her national flag, and said she had never been happier.''[29] At Calgary '88, it was a "golden moment" for Vida Ventsene of the Soviet Union in the women's 10-kilometer ski race. Her victory smile confirmed what journalist Frank Deford said: These Games did not just begin. "They glowed. They smiled. They sparkled. They sweated. They sang.''[30] Some say that it will take women of the 21st century to surpass the marks of the American "dynamic duo," Jackie Joyner Kersee and Florence Griffith-Joyner. For me, something equally memorable would be to see mounting the victory platform at the 1998 (Winter) and 2000 (Summer) Olympic Games young women from Chile, Mongolia, Albania, Nepal, and Niger. Professor Joan S. Hult of the University of Maryland was correct when she concluded her essay, "The Female American Runner: A Modern Quest for Visibility," with the statement that women as well as men should be "freed to discover . . . both the agony and the ecstasy of being human.''[31]

The Worldwide Challenge

Islamic societies, economically underdeveloped areas of the world, and a certain small number of countries in which the Catholic Church has traditionally "compartmentalized" boys and girls to play out very specific roles will find it especially challenging to release athletically-inclined women into arenas, gymnasia, and stadia. Another less well-understood obstruction to the emergence of the female athlete may be what Kathryn Kish Sklar called the strong-state, weak-state paradigm. It seems, she wrote in *American Historical Review*,

> that traditions of limited government in the United States opened wide opportunities for women reformers, but women's options remained much more restricted in countries with traditions of strong, centralized government.[32]

Smart, active, and politically astute national Olympic committees, working with their colleagues on the IOC and in the far-flung sport federations, can work toward finding the very best male and female athletes, coaches, trainers, sport specialists, and administrators and do so with firm civility and without disrespect to their individual cultures, traditions, and religions.

The gentle but persuasive Lia Manoliu of Romania was talking about that very thing when she said, "Never stop pressing. Move forward with your message, gently, persistently." Manoliu, one of the world's greatest discus throwers for 15 long years (and Olympic champion, finally, in 1968), rose to the presidency of her national Olympic committee. "All my adult life I was determined to help athletes, and now I am in a position to do so," she revealed.[33] Her ascendancy wasn't a reversal of tradition, but, as Manoliu would probably agree, a result of the steady march of talented, caring women toward their dreams. All over the world, Geneviève Rail told us at the 1990

International Olympic Academy, "women have to realize that games and sports are among the most potent oppressive agents of our societies but that, paradoxically, they also are among the greatest liberators."[34]

Reformist tendencies regarding women as active participants in every sphere of society, including international athletic competition, have been partially accepted in Europe and North America longer than in other areas of the world. Yet, interestingly, the cry for greater female fairness in elite sport comes most strongly from many European countries, Canada, and the United States. The reason is a difference of priorities. Men and women living along the shores of Africa's Lake Chad have far more important things to think about than the challenge of a 2-meter high jump. In many African and third-world societies, there have been and continue to be clearly defined roles for young men and women, and sport training and athletic competition is simply not part of their cultures. In a very different society, such as that of the United States, some dimensions of social reform have moved faster and earlier, as witnessed to by Glenna Collet when, in 1924, she was acclaimed the world's best female golfer and exclaimed, "Winning at golf is keen, exhilarating happiness, so much velvet."[35] There were few voices like hers 70 years ago. From that very small number grew a more vocal and assertive larger minority calling for fairness in everything. Only when the international level of concern reaches a "critical mass" will change take place and accelerate.

Seeking and Developing Talented Women

There are people in the Tripartite who are concerned that women are underrepresented inside Olympic stadia and in every NOC and ISF worldwide. That community of concerned men and women must seek ways to find uniquely talented women and allow them to earn their place inside the athletic arena as athletes and officials, and also inside the athletic office as local, national, international, and Olympic administrators. All of us—myself included—must adopt the "new way of thinking,"[36] which is intent on discovering and nurturing talent in every form, in every person, everywhere, and putting it to work for the physical and spiritual uplifting of all humanity. Ever greater opportunity for women in the Olympic Games and within the Olympic Movement will be one of many outcomes of such collective thinking.

The 10 years of Samaranch's IOC presidency have seen more change, more radical reconstruction of Olympic tradition, rules, and regulations than any comparable decade of the 20th century. Most of the changes are good and benefit more people, especially athletes, than those of any previous Olympic era. But it can all be improved, and in the area of women's involvement in the Olympic Games and the national and international Olympic hierarchies, each nation must do its part. I know North America best, and concentrated activism is taking place on that privileged continent.

The March 1988 and February 1990 editions of the *Journal of Physical Education, Recreation and Dance*—all 100 pages—were devoted to "women and sport, women and the Olympic Games—women and leadership. A focused thinker, USOC and IOC member Anita DeFrantz reminded all readers, especially young women, that "there is room at the top" of the Olympic world.[37] Cooperative recreational activities and sane, competitive athletics can combat myths about women's capacities and alleged frailties precisely because such physical activities are "visible and valued, and so hold a place of importance and prominence."[38] Full participation in the construction of one's proper place and level of excellence must be the goal of every man and woman everywhere.

Victory for women (or men) on the Olympic Games battlefield is not what we should be about. Fairness, fitness, natural exhilaration, pride in self, and respect for all competitors are a thousand times more important than gold. When superstar and double medal-winner at the Seoul Olympic Games, Nino Salukvadze, was asked about her success, she answered, "I have never wanted to be always first. I have a different aim—to show what I am capable of doing."[39] The Olympic Games are like the larger world, a very dramatic and visible place where the genius and folly of humankind, his and her glory and meanness are on display. Full and equal opportunity for women must be an ongoing mandate of Olympic leadership. Somehow, in a manner impossible to predict, future Games will incorporate greater athletic democracy. It is no longer utopian to believe that women will find their way in greater numbers into Olympic stadia and Olympic board rooms, and before the year 2000.

In a peculiar book with insightful observations, realist author Frank Harris wrote that there are three manifestations of the divine in humankind; first, freedom for

> the millions of the toil-weary and dispossessed—each of them with a spark of the divine . . . [second] beauty in girls and boys, the bodily beauty and grace of youth; . . . [third] genius in men and women, which is for the most part wasted and spent in a sordid conflict with mediocrity, and which should be sought out and put to use as the rarest and most valuable of gifts.[40]

Praise be to all those around the globe who are working for and will continue to strive toward "a whole new universe"[41] for women—and for men—equally.

Notes

1. Monique Berlioux, "Women in the Promotion and Administration of Sport," 2 October 1980, presented in Dublin, Ireland.

2. Alice Wexler, *Emma Goldman in Exile* (Boston: Beacon Press, 1989), 137.

3. A "52 percent solution" is discussed in the report of the [Canadian] National Task Force on Young Females and Physical Activity, Ottawa: Task Force Canada, 1989, 35.

4. Rosalind Miles, *The Women's History of the World* (Topsfield, MA: Salem House, 1989), xvi.

5. Mary Wollstonecraft, *A Vindication of the Rights of Women* (New York: Norton, 1967; originally 1792), "Introduction."

6. Henry Muller, *Time, 136*, Fall 1990, 4. The phrase "at the edge of the 21st century" belongs to Alvin Toffler, in his *Power Shift: Knowledge, Wealth, and Violence at the Edge of the 21st Century* (New York: Bantam Books, 1990).

7. Nadia Lekarska, "Women in the Olympic Games and Movement," *Olympic Message, 12*, December 1985, 51-54. The entire 80-page issue is written by women. Also, Lekarska's "The Entry Marathon of the Second Sex," *Olympic Review, 275-276*, September-October 1990, 454-461.

8. The year 1991 opened with the IOC composed of 7 women and 89 men; "New IOC Members," *Olympic Review, 277*, November 1990, 504-506.

9. Toffler, *Power Shift*, 470.

10. Fani Kakridi-Enz, "Women and the Olympic Movement." Unpublished paper presented to the IOA, Olympia, Greece, June 1990. For a summary see "Female Competitors in the Early Years of the Olympic Games and a Modern Day 52% Solution," by John Lucas, *Proceedings IOA 1990*, 94-101.

11. Nancy Gibbs, "The Dreams of Youth," *Time, 136*, Fall 1990, 12.

12. Monique Berlioux, speech, "Le Femme Dans le Mouvement Olympique," in Portugal, 20 April 1990.

13. Margarita Papandreou, "Feminism and Political Power: Some Thoughts on a Strategy for the Future," in Ellen Boneparth and Emily Stoper, eds., *Women, Power and Policy Toward the Year 2000* (New York: Pergamon Press, 1988), xi.

14. Vertinsky, letter to author, 17 January 1990.

15. Anita L. DeFrantz, "The Challenge of the '90's," *New York City Sun*, 15-21 November 1989, Sports supplement, 19.

16. UNESCO, *Physical Education in the Cause of Humanism: Annex*, 21-25 November 1988, 2.

17. Mike Boit, "Where Are the Kenyan Women Runners?" *Olympic Review, 259*, May 1989, 208.

18. Ma Lizhen, "Women: The Debate on Jobs vs. Homemaking," *China Reconstructs, 38*, March 1989, 68; Sei-Wha Chung, "The Women's Movement in Contemporary Korea," *Korean Culture, 10*, Summer 1989, 39.

19. Ranha Kumar, "Contemporary Indian Feminism," *Feminist Review, 33*, Autumn 1989, 29; Amy Kaslow, "Low Living Standards Persist for Caribbeans and Latin Americans," *Christian Science Monitor*, 29 October 1990, 7; George D. Moffett, "Status of Women Evolves Slowly in Saudi Arabia," *Christian Science Monitor*, 6 November 1990, 7.

20. "IOC's Berlioux: Diffident, Powerful, Indispensable," *International Herald Tribune*, 22 December 1983, 17.

21. Venezuela's Flor Isava Fonseca was the first woman voted to the IOC's executive board. See *Olympic Review, 277*, November 1990, 489.

22. Patricia Vertinsky, "Evolution or Imposition: A Comparative Study of the Pursuit of Sexual Equality in Physical Education and Sport in the USA and Canada," *Proceedings*, Wingate Institute of Physical Education Annual Symposium, Israel, 1979, 163.

23. David Miller, "Women Argue for Greater Role in Sport," *London Times*, 3 November 1990, p. 28. Also *GAISF News, 60*, December 1990, 1-2, 4.

24. José Cagigal, "Women and Sport," *Olympic Review, 176*, June 1982, 354.

25. George Pallet, *Women's Athletics* (Dulwick, England: Normal Press, 1955), 254. Alice Milliat's accomplishments are discussed in M.H. Leigh and T. M. Bonin, "The Pioneering Role of Madame Alice Milliat and the FSFI in the Establishment of Track and Field Competition for Women," *Journal of Sport History, 4*(1), 1977, 72-83.

26. Nawal El Saadawi, *The Hidden Face of Eve*, trans. by Dr. Sherif Hetata (London: Zedd Press, 1980), xv. For something of the sexual and metaphysical ramifications, see Fatima Mernissi, *Beyond the Veil* (New York: Wiley & Sons, 1975), vii; and the homely but helpful article "For Women Only: A Train Car Safe From Men," *New York Times*, 15 January 1990, A4. That control over women must never be allowed to be the source of honor for Muslim men was pointed out by Mahnaz Ispahani in "Varities of Muslim Experience," *Wilson Quarterly, 13*, Autumn 1989, 71.

27. In the capacity of IOC secretary general, Françoise Zweifel serves as indispensable liaison with her native Swiss government officials, both city and state; she is contact person and chief protocol officer for the executive board and full IOC meetings in capitals around the world. The brilliant, intense 36-year-old Michèle Verdier is the IOC director of information and is frequently "on-stage" for the world media, born in Grenoble, France, she speaks seven languages, has a hidden sense of humor, and has become a fixture inside the Château de Vidy and at all Olympic committee meetings. Ann Beddow is the IOC's director of NOC relations and keeps in constant contact with all 168 committees around the world. As director of "Villa Olympique," Madeleine

Ricard's work continues to grow in importance; she is the guardian of valuable and historically important Olympic artifacts (e.g., books, Olympic memorabilia, and objets d'art) and serves as technical assistant in the construction of the new Olympic Museum. Myriam Gross is a Swiss and Deputy Director of Olympic Solidarity. Annie Inchauspé is the quietly efficient personal secretary to IOC President Samaranch, an indispensable aid to the president's extraordinary busyness. Fani Kakridi-Enz is from Greece, is wholly committed to the Olympic Movement, and serves it well as historian, archivist, and administrator of the Olympic Museum.

28. Toffler, *Power Shift* (New York: Bantam Books, 1990), 474.

29. *Official Report USOC: The 1984 Olympic Review Sarajevo-Los Angeles*, (Colorado Springs, Colorado: USOC, 1985), 237.

30. Frank Deford, "The Spirit of Olympism," *Sports Illustrated, 68*, 22 February 1988, 2-3.

31. Joan S. Hult, "The Female American Runner: A Modern Quest for Visibility," Barbara L. Drinkwater, ed., *Female Endurance Athletes* (Champaign, IL: Human Kinetics, 1986), 158.

32. K. K. Sklar, "A Call For Comparisons," *American Historical Review, 95*, October 1990, 1111.

33. Lia Manoliu, interview with author, at Olympia, Greece, 26 June 1990. World's greatest female gymnast of the 1960s, Vera Caslavska of Czechoslovakia, was selected president of the Czech Olympic committee in 1990; *Olympic Review, 274*, August 1990, 409.

34. Geneviève Rail, "Women's Sport in the Post-War Period," International Olympic Academy presentation, 1990. The entire 15-day session was devoted to "Women and the Olympic Movement."

35. Glenna Collet, quoted in *Literary Digest, 82*, 13 September 1924, 74.

36. "The New Way of Thinking," *Women of the Whole World, 2*, 1988, 7.

37. Anita DeFrantz, "Women and Leadership in Sport," *Journal of Physical Education, Recreation and Dance, 59*, March 1988, 47.

38. M. Deborah Bialeschki, "The Feminist Movement and Women's Participation in Physical Recreation," *Journal of Physical Education, Recreation and Dance, 61*, January 1990, 47; also "Women in the Olympic Games," *JPERD, 55*, May-June, 1984, 61-72.

39. Salukvadze won a gold medal in small-bore pistol shooting and a silver medal for air gun shooting. See *Soviet Woman*, December 1989, 40.

40. Frank Harris, *The Bomb* (Chicago: University of Chicago Press, 1963; originally 1909), 184-185.

41. Francene Sabin, *Women Who Win* (New York: Dell, 1979), 18.

C·H·A·P·T·E·R· 13

Samaranch's Presidency: A Hard Act to Follow

To be the president of the IOC is the most wonderful post one can ever hold. I would give up any assignment as a minister in my country to be the IOC president.

Juan Antonio Samaranch, *IOC president*

In fall 1986, in Lausanne, Switzerland, the IOC convened in a secret meeting inside the Palais de Beaulieu and chose Barcelona, Spain to be the site for the 1992 Summer Olympic Games. President Samaranch abstained from voting; after all, his home town was involved in the close competition. No one hinted that it would be easy, and Samaranch warned the committee that fiscal, ideological, and administrative concerns, and, above all, world politics would play a big part in the success or failure of the Spanish Games. Samaranch is a very private person, and he probably did not reveal his feelings, but an end-of-the-year 1990 headline in *El País* read, "The Pre-Olympic year for Barcelona has arrived and already the world abounds with unrest, an aperitif to the Olympic Games."[1]

Several years earlier, when he won the IOC presidency over Lance Cross, Willi Daume, Mark Hodler, and Canada's James Worrall, this former Spanish ambassador to the Soviet Union admitted to then IOC director, Monique Berlioux, that "to be the president of the IOC is the most wonderful post one can ever hold. I would give up any assignment as a minister in my country to be the IOC president. There is nothing like it."[2] Nearly a dozen years later, as the Summer Olympic Games approached in his Barcelona City, he felt exactly the same way, an attitude that made his routine 75-hour workweek somewhat less fatiguing.

Rise to the IOC

Juan Antonio Samaranch Torello was born in Barcelona on 17 July 1920, the son of upper middle-class parents, Francisco Samaranch and Juana Torello; his father was a textile industrialist and president of the province's legislative body, the Diputación.[3] As a boy, he played sports only moderately well, but passionately, especially field hockey and soccer with some boxing.

Then, like many boys, the teenaged Samaranch was caught up in the bloody Spanish Civil War (1936-1939) between the democratic, popular Loyalists and General Francisco Franco's conservative, monarchist, land-owner coalition. A recent writer in London's *Independent* said that the boy Samaranch, "undoubtedly right-wing in his instincts," fled to France in 1938 and soon "returned across the Pyrenees to enlist with the Nationalists" and the new Franco hegemony. After the war, he received an excellent education at the Higher Institute of Business Studies. The same writer noted that while working on an advanced degree in economics during World War II, Samaranch had been employed as a sportswriter by the Barcelona daily, *La Prensa*. He had been a lifelong supporter of the Real Madrid football team when he was assigned to cover a match between that club and the local Barcelona club—Madrid won, 11-1, "a triumph reported by Samaranch with such obvious glee that his credentials were withdrawn."[4]

In 1954, the young Samaranch became a member and eventually president of the Spanish Olympic Committee and served as team manager of his country's world-champion roller hockey team. More important, he was the Spanish Olympic team's *chef de mission* at the 1956 Winter Games in Cortina de'Ampezzo, Italy, and at the Summer Olympic Games in Rome (1960) and Tokyo (1964). During the years before his election to the IOC, Samaranch worked assiduously with his national football federation, in several substantial key roles with the Spanish national Olympic committee, was leader of the Mediterranean Games II, and still found time for the family textile business and his own banking interests.[5]

In December 1955, he married Maria Theresa Salisachs-Rowe, whose English mother accounts for "the second barrel of her surname." The slender and strikingly attractive Señora Samaranch came from a prominent Madrid family who had played a special role in the social life of the city. She's called "Bibis" by friends and has raised two children—Juan Antonio, an MBA-degree graduate of New York University, and Maria Teresa, an economist who lives in Barcelona.[6] Sra. Samaranch "has always been, and still is, at [her husband's] side . . . knows what's going on, and in fact remains his number one advisor," was Monique Berlioux's description.[7]

For more than 15 years, from 1955 to 1972, the young Samaranch was an unabashed admirer of IOC president Avery Brundage and exchanged more than 75 letters and other correspondence with the curmudgeonly American. Reading them, one learns more about Samaranch than about the much older Brundage, for the Spaniard's awkward English is filled with personal ambition, utter devotion to Olympic principles, and an almost boyish adulation of the president. "Congratulations on your reelection, Mr. President," wrote Samaranch in 1960. "None of us are surprised that know your intelligence, laboriousness, and love for Olympic ideals." After his election to the Spanish NOC presidency, Samaranch wrote on 14 February 1967, "My dear President and Friend, I shall now devote all my attention and enthusiasm in order to succeed in the diffusion of the Olympic movement and our mutual Olympic ideals." He sent a telegram to Brundage the next year, the Olympic year, as the official Olympic Torch passed through Spain from Olympia, Greece, and on its way to Mexico City. "The Torch is here," he almost shouted. On behalf of all Spanish sportsmen, "may I express to you our admiration and affection and respectfulness towards your person."[8]

As early as 1957, Samaranch's portfolio was marked "special." The president of the Comité Olimpico Español that year, José Antonio Elola-Olaso, wrote Brundage, "We beg you, Mr. President, that at the next Congress, which is about to open, it is desirable to nominate Mr. Juan Antonio Samaranch as a member of the CIO."[9] But Samaranch had to wait 9 more years before gaining IOC membership. A new IOC mandate stated that only nations having hosted either Winter or Summer Olympic Games could have two members on the committee. Spain did not qualify. IOC chancellor from Switzerland, Otto Mayer, was fully aware of the old practice of allowing multiple membership and of the restrictive new regulation, and in a letter to Brundage on 12 February 1957, he wrote,

Samaranch visited me today. He's about 35 years old, rich, an absolutely talented and devoted man. Samaranch requested consideration for IOC membership, but I told him that 2 from a nonsignificant country was impermissible, and besides, had not Spain just withdrawn from the Melbourne [Olympic] Games! 'Yes,' said Samaranch, 'it was a very big mistake by my country.'[10]

Samaranch went back to work and waited, while his country was served on the IOC by Pedro de Ybarra y Mac-Mahon, Barón de Güell.[11] But Brundage knew Samaranch, and the able, pugnacious, and puritanical Olympian wanted the Spaniard on his committee. Brundage saw in the neatly-dressed and unobtrusively small Catalonian a close-to-ideal member of the exclusive club: intense, taciturn, extremely upright in both sport and business, wealthy, and importantly, a strong supporter of the right wing—the king and General Franco. Without looking left or right, or at the newly-written Olympic Charter, Mr. Brundage selected the 46-year-old Samaranch to join the IOC. Samaranch remembered it this way:

> My election as a second member from Spain was quite impossible. But Avery Brundage wanted my election. And he got me elected. After lunch, I asked President Brundage why he was so interested in making sure I got elected. His answer: 'Because I am sure that one day you will be president of the International Olympic Committee.'[12]

Samaranch had prepared himself well for productive membership on the IOC, including gaining full command of three languages other than his native tongue. In a figurative way, he leapt at the chance to serve.

Nurturing Years on the IOC

Olympic watchers from the *London Times*, Norman Fox and David Miller, were sure that President Brundage was attracted by Señor Samaranch's reputation as a Franco supporter[13] and that the IOC executive board saw in the man "the capacity to listen and observe, together with a rare combination of determination and sensitivity to the mood of his colleagues."[14] Samaranch began working very hard on both the domestic and international fronts, and in a 7 January 1967 letter, Brundage complimented him not only for readying the Spanish Olympic team, but also for his efforts "in educating all the peoples in the high ideals of the Olympic movement."[15] It was a short move to Spanish NOC president (1967 to 1970), then to IOC executive board member (in 1970), and then to IOC vice president (1974 to 1978). Journalist John Rodda remembered the unquixotic Samaranch in 1968, when he was elevated to IOCs chief of protocol, which Rodda called an "electrifying promotion."[16]

Lord Killanin succeeded Brundage in 1972, in an IOC atmosphere as strained as at any time in its history. But the talented Samaranch continued to move ahead and in 1977, at King Juan Carlos's request, accepted the position of Spanish ambassador to the Soviet Union and Mongolia—the first such appointment in the postwar era. The Samaranchs received "high grades" for diplomacy and social and cultural activities while in the Soviet capital.

The undemonstrative Catalonian at no time forgot what he had written about his earlier, primary commitment to what idealized sport can do for youth. More important than winning athletic medals, he told Olympic Academy members in 1969, is the personal "spiritual summit." Protocol, ceremony, and pageantry are not peripheral to the Olympic Movement, but rather enhance the deeper message of Olympic philosophy, he told colleagues at the 1973 Olympic Congress in Varna, Bulgaria. IOC vice president in 1978, he again paid tribute to the real and spiritual leader of the Movement, "to the reviver of the Games, Baron de Coubertin." We are an army of peace, a missionary group without weapons, he told the IOA young people at Olympia, Greece, in 1978.[17]

Rarely had the IOC seen a member with so many skills. Equipped with "deceptive calm and considerable power," Samaranch knew well the rapidly growing Olympic Tripartite "engine" (i.e., IOC-NOCs-federations). Appearing almost obsequious in his willingness to accommodate any IOC operation, the quiet man from Barcelona was schooled in almost every aspect of the Olympic world. Almost 60, the soft-spoken Spanish ambassador was in the process of strengthening one of his several theses, the pragmatic admission that "sportsmen cannot rule the world as politicians do."[18] Samaranch knew politics; he had considerable executive skill; he could work with colleagues in an unchaffing manner—and he knew sport. In Moscow the summer of 1980, the Olympic world was in the first stages of chaos: The United States and several dozen nations had declined to participate, and the Olympic Games were about to begin without them. President Killanin had done his best, but stronger leadership was needed to save the Olympic "ship." The IOC, meeting as usual in private session, elected His Excellency Mr. Samaranch to be its next leader.

The IOC President: From Barcelona to Lausanne

The Olympic Games boycott of 1980 was so traumatic that the IOC presidential election that took place in Moscow seemed futile to journalist John Rodda, who wrote that "three men are prepared to become king of a crumbling castle": 66-year-old Olympian and Canadian circuit judge, James Worrall; 67-year-old head of New Zealand television, Lance Cross; and the utterly enigmatic 60-year-old Samaranch. Also on the ballot, though given little chance, were the giant intellect of the IOC, the patriarchal German, Willi Daume, and the veteran Swiss, Mark Hodler. "Samaranch will win narrowly," predicted Rodda, "and end up with an executive board that will have a strong old world influence which will match his every step."[19] An Olympic specialist, Rodda was half correct: Samaranch did win on the first ballot.

The Associated Press's Olympic expert, Geoffrey Miller, was of the opinion that the combined Latin American and Eastern bloc IOC members had "locked up" the vote for Samaranch.[20] When Killanin introduced Samaranch to the press (some of whom irreverently compared the occasion to the first appearance of a newly elected pope),[21] the new leader said candidly, "My election was very easy. I knew all the members very well, and they knew my situation.''[22] (Barry Lorge of the *The Washington Post* predicted, correctly it turned out, that Samaranch would resign his ambassadorial post by 1 November 1980 and move back to Barcelona.)

But Samaranch was self-effacing, too, and told Ken Reich of the *Los Angeles Times*: ''I hope I can do something for the Olympic movement. But I am not used to working alone.''[23] Rather than worry about who was watching him from the ''old world,'' like Rodda had suggested, Samaranch set out at a fast trot to surround himself with people of color, non-Europeans, ''youths'' under 40 years of age, and women. This man who seemed to have ''no special presence'' (though only to the most casual observer) looked forward eagerly to the next 8 years. Samaranch immediately warmed to his responsibility and announced plans to double the size of Olympic headquarters, adding a library and a photographic and film center—facilities ''worthy of our mission.''[24]

The problems ahead were immense, a ''mission impossible,'' wrote one journalist. The boycott was still in place in Moscow; rumors abounded of retaliation in Los Angeles 4 years hence; and yet the new president told CBS News, ''The 1984 Olympics must be the Games of reconciliation.''[25] Possessing the greatest prescience of all the journalists in Moscow that day was Chris Brasher of the *London Observer* who predicted that Samaranch would gradually become a superb IOC leader, ''but I would not put any money on my being able to attend a Games whose ideals I would recognize in 1992.''[26]

The immediate task ahead of Samaranch and his people was to prepare for the gathering of the entire Olympic family at the Congress in Baden-Baden, West Germany, and to decide what was to be done about the Los Angeles Olympic Games in 1984. The 1981 Baden-Baden Congress was very productive, because Samaranch insisted that every major issue be aired and encouraged suggestions of a progressive nature.[27]

So the restless, inquiring Samaranch began the first of his now legendary wanderings: Rome, Athens, Baden-Baden, Nairobi, Los Angeles, Monte Carlo, Milan, New York City, Oslo, Stockholm, Liechtenstein, and Paris—all in 1 year *flat!* Far-flung associations and consortiums of NOCs heard him and saw him. The international sport federations (ISFs) got the word: Big changes are on the horizon. The organizing committees for the next Olympic Games in Sarajevo and Los Angeles were uplifted by his quiet persistence and support. He visited 50 heads of state—from the White House, to the Elysée Palace, to the Kremlin, all in 6 months, prompting longtime IOC member Jean de Beaumont to call Samaranch ''the pope of sport.''[28] Such effort had never been seen from previous IOC presidents.

One source of unease for the new president, still living in Barcelona, was the power of a non-IOC member and IOC director since 1971, Monique Berlioux. She possessed an impressive intellect, a commanding physical and psychic presence, and a lifetime of experience in international sport and appeared in every way to be more than an employee of the IOC. Then President Samaranch moved to Lausanne and into a suite at the Palace Hotel;

he spent little time there, preferring to work a full dawn-to-dusk day at the Château de Vidy close to Berlioux.

Proximity made things worse between these two who loved the Olympic Movement and its ideals so passionately but in divergent ways. It was "tension city" inside the Château, recalled Richard Pound. Berlioux, when asked to compare IOC presidents, said diplomatically, "Killanin was more jovial than Brundage, and Samaranch is a hard worker, far more than I thought he could be." (According to David Miller, "Killanin had privately promised colleagues to reduce her power, but failed.")[29]

In July 1984, Samaranch was interviewed by Clive Gammon of *Sports Illustrated*, and their conversation suddenly became tense when the president spoke about administrative style. His way, he said, was "to work at headquarters, to put every man in his place in the organization. And I assure you also that the director is only the director, and the president is the president."[30] There was no need to mention Director Berlioux by name. The next year she was forced to resign her position of 14 years, and just about every major newspaper in Europe and North America carried the story. They were philosophical opposites, wrote Randy Harvey in the *Los Angeles Times*, she a Coubertin-Brundage traditionalist and Samaranch "pressing for change as dictated by today's economic and political realities."[31]

The year 1986 was a big one in the dazzling career of President Samaranch and for the 90-year-old IOC. Samaranch did not appear tired at the 91st IOC session, 12-18 October 1986—it was, after all, in Lausanne, his adopted home—but there was a surrealistic quality about the man. He had completed a dozen circumnavigations of the world and had visited more than 140 NOCs and heads of state. He had done the near impossible and visited every one of the 45 national Olympic committees on the African continent. David Miller of the *London Times* accompanied Samaranch on part of this extraordinary visit and sent articles back to the *Times*'s home office from Dakar, Senegal; Nouakchott, Mauritania; Freetown, Sierra Leone; Ouagadougou, Burkina Faso; Niamey, Niger; Accra, Ghana; Cotonu, Benin; Bangui, Central African Republic; Kampala, Uganda; and Djibouti.[32] No other IOC president had even envisioned such an effort. It strengthened Samaranch's hand and the health of the Olympic Movement for years.

Samaranch emerged from the 1986 IOC meeting as leader of a new Olympic age. He and his closest advisors had succeeded in inviting almost all professional athletes to the Olympic Games of the 1990s. The Olympic Tripartite was significantly strengthened. Business transactions with a dozen international networks and with the TOP-ISL (see chapter 7) cartels were consummated. Albertville, France and Barcelona, Spain were selected for the last Olympic Games to be held in the same calendar year (see chapter 14). Possibly, most important of all, the unimposing Samaranch had helped the Olympic Movement and the Olympic Games to become one of the great human enterprises of the late 20th century. It is no wonder that the Spanish journal *El País Semanel* wrote, "Juan Antonio Samaranch is the most international Spaniard of our time."[33]

The Aura Grows

Juan Antonio Samaranch possessed many skills, none more abundantly than diplomacy and patience. His way with the NOCs, the federations, the IOC, and business and political leaders was, an Olympic "watcher" of 40 years, Gaston Mayer, said, "not a question of force, but of persuasion and discussion ... Samaranch is the master of this form of diplomatic exercise."[34] By 1987, master of the Château de Vidy, President Samaranch had expressed many times his deep-seated belief in contrasting idealistic and realistic tenets: "Sport is the most important social activity and force in the second half of the 20th century," and "sportsmen have no power; politicians rule the world;" therefore, the IOC must be constantly engaged in dialogue.

In his own Olympic house, Samaranch had to work closely with some formidable figures, men and women of special presence and ambition: Marat Gramov, German Rieckehoff, Mario Vázquez Raña, Robert Helmick, Anita DeFrantz, Louis Guirandou-N'Diaye, Kevan Gosper, Richard Pound, Philippe Chartrier, Jean-Claude Ganga, Flor Isava Fonseca, Un Yong Kim, Kéba Mbaye, and Walther Tröger. There are others, of course, but the next IOC president (to be elected in 1993 or 1997) must surely come from this group of 14. When Samaranch, "the don of the Olympic Movement,"[35] took quiet charge of the 92nd IOC meeting in Istanbul, his demeanor was such that one journalist quipped, "This can be a better show than the Olympics. This is politics, enormous ego, and huge amounts of money."[36] The observation was only half correct, for intrinsic to every Olympic family meeting, and especially part of the Winter and Summer Games themselves, are elements and mixtures of ultimate athleticism, high drama, fair play, the personification of physical skills, comradeship, and the mysterious glue of internationalism.

The Olympic Movement has grown stronger in spite of boycotts, said Samaranch on the eve of the Calgary-Seoul Olympic Games; in a sense, these same crises have strengthened our resolve and tested our mettle, and we are the better for it. Samaranch's 2 years of diplomacy with contentious politicians and sport leaders from North and South Korea were his finest hours, and the double Olympic Games of 1988 were the most successful combined Games of the century. Samaranch might agree with the scholar who wrote that the "Olympic system" must work like a powerful world entity, not to defeat the forces of international politics, but to keep alive, vibrant, and meaningful "the ideals of the Games."[37]

The former textile manufacturer, after completing his first 8 years in office, had radically reformed the Movement within and without; he had increased financial aid to the economically underdeveloped nations; he had surrounded himself with an IOC comprised of men and women, poor and rich, socialist, communist, and capitalist, from every geographic area of the world. More important, he had helped the Olympic Games become significantly more representative by opening them to the professional athlete.

Along with these flood tides of athletic democracy came the flotsam and jetsam of drugs, commercialism, the vulgar, uneducated, athletic gladiator, and a mind-numbing gigantism that sometimes made men and women, inside and outside the Olympic stadium, "behave selfishly, coarsely, indecently,"[38] divorcing themselves from the well-mannered family of Olympic camaraderie.

Diplomacy works to avert confrontation. Samaranch and his most intimate cadre lived by this code. But it took a great deal of time and effort, reminding John Rodda that the man on the second floor of Olympic headquarters was indeed "a disciplined workaholic."[39] Samaranch, himself, metaphorically shrugged his shoulders and answered,

> What I do is to conduct the orchestra which has excellent soloists; they are so good that in some cases the conductor can sit down and the Olympic symphony will still go on.[40]

Samaranch disliked direct confrontation, not only as ambassador of Spain to the Soviet Union (in the 1970s), but throughout his IOC tenure. Lengthy negotiations, discussions, and frequent compromises were more his style and more to his liking. "To see that each day brings an improvement" was how he expressed his work ethic to a Soviet journalist at the Second International Conference of Ministers and Senior Officials Responsible for Physical Education and Sport.[41] Always a practical man, he indulged nevertheless in the hope that his own 40 years in sport, surrounded by the most talented and diverse tapestry of Olympic bureaucrats around the world, plus his personal ties with France and Spain, would result in "the best Olympic Games of all time" in Albertville and Barcelona.[42]

Samaranch's Move Into the 1990s

President Samaranch seemed serene amidst the organized cacophony of the Tokyo IOC meeting in September and October 1990 (see chapter 3). Surrounded by his ever-moving entourage, Samaranch paused a moment, his hand extended as our eyes met. "Welcome to Tokyo, Professor, the Olympic family is ever in need of people with an intellectual bent. Don't stop," he said and moved on to another meeting. Several months earlier, in his art-filled office in Lausanne, he shared several revealing hopes for the 1990s:

> We must maintain impetus and at the same time reduce any negative images of our movement, deserved or undeserved. We have such plans—cultural, educational—humanely, as well as athletically. Our task, yours and mine, is now to turn these promises into action.[43]

The "great person" theory persists. Of course, such people are shaped by both heredity and circumstance. But for one historian, "the power of the individual is self-evident out there in the battlefield." Dr. Gabor S. Boritt of Gettysburg College was talking in 1863 about the level plain near his campus.[44] Samaranch's innate talents were never submerged, but his elevation to the IOC presidency—the ultimate and perpetual sport-crises post— accelerated the development of his administrative skills. He has but a short time to fall or rise even further. There is no middle road, no Olympian homeostasis for this man, and his reelection to the presidency for an additional 4 years (until 1993) was a mere formality, a public acknowledgment of a job very well done—thus far.[45]

Notes

1. *El País*, 24 December 1990, 4. (Author's translation).

2. Monique Berlioux, "The IOC and Its Presidents," keynote address at the United States Olympic Academy (USOA) 1988, *Proceedings USOA 1988*, 130-150.

3. Bill Shirley, "He's in Charge of Games Others Play," *Los Angeles Times*, 2 February 1983; part 3, p. 10; "Xavier Ventura Interviews Juan Antonio Samaranch," *Catalònia Cultura, 8*, March 1988, 29; *Le Comité International Olympique* (Lausanne: CIO, 1981), 134.

4. "Gamesman of the Olympics," *London Independent*, 27 August 1988, 12.

5. Samaranch, who grew up with two brothers and two sisters, eventually sold his share of the family textile business to his brothers. When his banking interests got him into trouble in 1959, IOC chancellor Otto Mayer wrote in alarm to President Brundage, "Our friend Samaranch is also in the scandal of finance in Spain. About 400 million *dollars* have been placed in Switzerland and in the USA. Important political personalities are also in it!" (*Avery Brundage Collection* [ABC], box 62, reel 36) Thirty years later, in 1989, Samaranch became a powerful banker and "presidente de la Caixa de Pensions" (*Cambio 16, 275*, 26 June 1989, 58).

6. Mark McDonald, "Samaranch's Undying Flame," *Dallas Morning News*, 13 December 1987, 12; Clive Gammon, "Still Carrying the Torch," *Sports Illustrated, 63*, 16 July 1984, 59.

7. Berlioux, *Proceedings USOA 1988*, 146.

8. These three correspondences are recorded in the *ABC*, box 62, reel 36; the originals are at the University of Illinois, and copies at Cologne's Sporthochschule, Western Ontario University, and The Pennsylvania State University.

9. Elola-Olaso, letter to Brundage, 1957 (*ABC*, box 62, reel 36). The IOC meeting took place in Sofia, 2-5 June 1957; therefore, his letter was probably written in May of that year. The Barón de Güell wrote Brundage

on 22 March 1966, strongly urging that "Samaranch be the second member of the IOC from Spain—a practice we have had for 40 years" (*ABC*, box 62, reel 36).

10. Mayer, letter to Brundage, 12 February 1957 (*ABC*, box 62, reel 36).

11. Mac-Mahon was appointed to the IOC in 1952; his father-in-law, Santiago Güell y Lopéz, Barón de Güell, also served the IOC from 1922 to 1954. Thus for a brief time, 1952 to 1954, there were *two* IOC members from Spain ("IOC Members in Spain," *Olympic Review, 107-108*, September-October 1976, 516).

12. David Rosner, "The Most Powerful Man in Sports," *Sports inc, 11*, 13 March 1989, 16. A few IOC members objected to the irregular method of Samaranch's election, "but Brundage was adamant," remembered Monique Berlioux (*Proceedings USOA 1988*), 146.

13. Norman Fox, "The Diplomat Treading Warily at the IOC," *London Times*, 23 September 1981, 16.

14. David Miller, "Profile of Antonio Samaranch," *London Times*, 15 September 1988, 10.

15. Brundage, letter to Samaranch, 7 January 1967 (in *Olympic Review, 107-108*, September-October 1976, 513.

16. John Rodda, "Making of an IOC President," *Manchester Guardian*, 17 July 1980, 22.

17. Samaranch, "The Olympic Spirit in the Modern World," *Proceedings IOA 1969*, 49; *Proceedings Olympic Congress Varna 1973*, 133-134; "Protocol and Olympism," *Olympic Review, 124*, February 1978, 92; "Olympism in the Various Sectors of Society," *Proceedings IOA 1978*, 42-48.

18. David Miller, paraphrasing Samaranch, in the former's essay "Samaranch the Ringmaster Keeps His Horses Under Control," *London Times*, 3 December 1984, 21. Several years earlier, a Spanish newspaper noted that "Don Juan Samaranch swims in a swift current of athletic reform and in the direction of intellectual leadership of the Olympic Movement" (*La Vanguardia Española*, 22 January 1972, 5.).

19. John Rodda, "Picking a President," *Manchester Guardian*, 15 July 1980, 22; John Hennessy, "Diplomatic Who Became Sporting World's Most Influential Ambassador," *London Times*, 17 July 1980, 20.

20. Geoffrey Miller, "Spain's Samaranch," AP release, 14 July 1980.

21. Barry Lorge, "Spaniard Named," *Washington Post*, 17 July 1980, F1, F4.

22. Samaranch, quoted in Mark McDonald, "Samaranch's Undying Flame," *Dallas Morning News*, 13 December 1987, 12.

23. Kenneth Reich, "Samaranch: Careful Planner to Lead Olympic Body," *Los Angeles Times*, 17 July 1980, part 1, 12.

24. Samaranch, quoted in *Olympic Review, 155*, September 1980, 478.

25. "An Olympic About Face," *San Francisco Chronicle*, 17 July 1980, 49; CBS News, 4 August 1980.

26. Christopher Brasher, "Don't Bet on 1992," *London Observer*, 20 July 1980, p. 22. Neil Amdur predicted "a shift from West to East" in *New York Times*, 17 July 1980, D17, D19.

27. John Lucas, "The Impact of the 1991 Olympic Congress in Baden-Baden," *Proceedings USOA 1982*, 103-109. Also *London Times*, 1 October 1981, 24; *International Herald Tribune*, 1 October 1981, 13; *London Times*, 2 October 1981, 16; *International Herald Tribune*, 3-4 October 1981; and John Lucas, "Out at Home," *New York Times*, 2 November 1981, 25.

28. Beaumont, "Welcome," *Olympic Review, 177*, July 1982, 412.

29. Pound, quoted in *Sport inc, 11*, 13 March 1989, 19; Berlioux, quoted in *Los Angeles Times*, 2 February 1983, part 3, 10; Miller, quoted in *London Times*, 15 September 1988, 10.

30. Samaranch, quoted in Clive Gammon, *Sports Illustrated, 63*, 16 July 1984, 62. David Miller wrote, "A necessary change in the mechanics and streamlining of the IOC office involved the position of Madame Monique Berlioux, a redoubtable Frenchwoman, who, during the prolonged absenses of past presidents Avery Brundage and Lord Killanin," had functioned as the nontitled director of IOC business (*Olympic Message, 23*, March 1989, 22-23).

31. Randy Harvey, "I.O.C. Takes Cue From Its Leader," *Los Angeles Times*, 21 October 1986, sec. 3, 1.

    Interesting and occasionally lurid details of the Berlioux resignation can be found in *Washington Post*, 3 June and 6 June 1985, D2; *Los Angeles Times*, 3 June 1985, part 3, 1, 3; *New York Times*, 5 June 1985, B8; *London Times*, 5 June and 6 June 1985, 23; *Toronto Globe and Mail*, 6 June 1985, 17.

    Sports Illustrated wrote, "The IOC loses a righthand man . . . ," 17 June 1985, 17; Simon Barnes called Berlioux the "Martin Luther King of the Olympics," after quoting her comment, "I have a dream" (*London Times*, 13 May 1986, 28). Chris Brasher's 1-inch headline, "Olympic Idealism Stabbed in the Back," unambiguously stated how he felt about Mme. Berlioux being "fired" (*London Observer*, 9 June 1985, 42). French sport organizer Alaiin Danet told Randy Roberts, "You can't imagine how much Samaranch and Monique Berlioux hate one another" (*Los Angeles Times*, 24 August 1987, 14).

32. The following articles by David Miller appeared in the *London Times*: "Proudest Moment for Mauritania," 29 October 1985, 29; "Olympic Tour Tends the Roots," 30 October 1985, 22; "A Nation Yet to Get on its Bike," 31 October 1985, 27; "Bags of Talent but Little Money,"

2 November 1985, 23; "Legion of Smiles in Nation at War," 5 November 1985, 20; "Machine Guns and Hot Shots," 6 November 1985, 23; "Inspiration Flickers in the Heart of Darkness," 9 November 1985, 34.

33. *El País Semanel*, 4 December 1988, 24.

34. Gaston Mayer, "Updating the Olympic Programme," *Olympic Review, 177*, July 1982, 402.

35. Steve Woodward of *USA Today* wrote an essay by this title and commented that "the diminutive Spaniard has guided the Olympic Movement through troubled times into a unity that encompasses the nations of the earth" *Olympian, 15*, April 1989, 28.

36. Unnamed journalist, quoted in Michael Precker, "Mighty IOC Tries to Steer Sound Course," *Dallas Morning News*, 10 May 1987, 1B.

37. Barbara Ann O'Neill, "International Sports: Have States Succeeded Athletes as the Players?" *Dickinson Journal of International Law, 6*, Spring 1988, 436.

38. George William Curtis, the brilliant editor of the 19th-century *Harper's Monthly*, used this phrase in his little book, *Ars Recte Vivendi* (New York: Harper & Bros., 1898), 30.

39. John Rodda, "The IOC Since 1972," *Olympic Message, 23*, March 1989, 15.

40. Samaranch, letter to author, 5 March 1990.

41. Samaranch, quoted in *Sport in the USSR, 311*, February 1989, 23.

42. Samaranch, quoted in *Catalònia Cultura, 12*, January 1989, 7. Always the tongue-in-cheek, cynical surveyor of the Olympic Games, Simon Barnes called Samaranch the mysterious man-in-the-middle who makes things happen, the "image-broker for the world," and "probably the only man in the world who looks like his passport photograph" (Barnes, "Creator of the Olympic Image," *London Times*, 16 December 1988, 40).

43. Samaranch, interview with author, at Lausanne, 26 February 1990.

44. Andrew Rosenthal, "The Historical 'I': More Than Ever Personality Drives World Events," *New York Times*, 31 December 1990, E3.

45. At San Juan, Puerto Rico, on 30 August 1989, Samaranch, having retired after completing his 8-year tenure, was unanimously elected to an additional 4-year term, the IOC's first such happening; *New York Times*, 31 August 1989, D22.

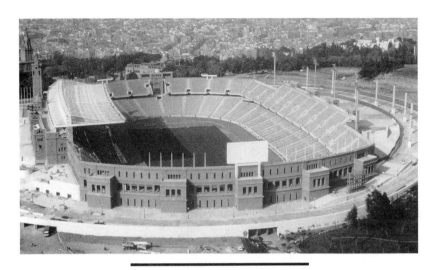

C·H·A·P·T·E·R·14

Albertville and Barcelona Beckon: The 1992 Olympic Games

The name of Barcelona, of Catalonia, and of Spain will be pronounced millions of times; they'll attract the attention of the whole world.

Carlos Ferrer Salat, *president of Comité Olímpic Español (COE)*

In one grand act combining showmanship, symbolism, and genuine sincerity, President Samaranch, on receiving a gift of doves of peace in a cage, "immediately opened the prison and released the Olympic birds." Samaranch kept the bronze plaque given him with affection by the staff of the Princess Sofia Hotel in Barcelona during the Association of National Olympic Committees (ANOC) meeting in June 1990. "Your words and acts, like the dove, symbolize yours and your movement's devotion to peace and freedom,'' it read.[1] Through all the unrestrained hoop-la surrounding the Albertville and Barcelona Games of '92, these doves were meant to remind any who would listen that the old, time-honored, tired but still meaningful song of Coubertin—peace on earth through sport—was still alive, although not fashionable. Vice president of the USOC, William B. Tutt, told me in the most fervent tones that if the bureaucrats of the international Olympic Movement do their job supremely well, then the athletes of the world will be released to soar and sing—''to achieve monumental accomplishments.''[2] The double Olympic Games of 1992, and the separate international festivals of 1994, 1996, and 1998 will decide the fate of the Games and determine if they will continue into the 21st century. IOC member from Greece, Nikos Filaretos (he's also president of the International Olympic Academy) told me, in hushed tones, ''I'm uneasy; things have been going almost too well. It could be the calm before the storm and if so, then we must be ever-vigilant.''[3] The Olympic Games are not the planet's last great hope, but they are a recurring event of some durability that allows thousands of young men and women the opportunity to become what philosopher Michael Novak called ''a good person . . . to play well, and thus go beyond the rules . . . to hit the mark exactly.''[4] All of this puts almost too much burden on the '92 Games, which are after all, looking at the Games' other face, festivals of drama, spectacular physical and psychic power, and fun. Albertville and Barcelona seem capable of evoking this whole range of human emotions.

The Albertville Equation: February 1992

For 135 days, from 6 December 1990 to 21 April 1991, the Albertville, France, Winter Olympic Games site was engaged in a dress rehearsal, pre-Olympic competition program. ''We hope the actual games will go off in impeccable fashion 430 days from now,'' declared comanagers M. Michel Barnier and Jean-Claude Killy. [5] Of course the Comité D'Organisation Des XVIe Jeux Olympiques (COJO) D'Hiver D'Albertville et de la Savoie made every effort to get the world's best athletes to this pre-Olympic ''summit.'' Every venue was tested as were all aspects of the Games' organization: transport, telecommunication, accommodations, security, accreditation, translation, results system, television coverage, medical services, weather-forecasting, sound effects, catering, reception, protocol, volunteer efficiency, ticket sales, and the important Opening and Closing Ceremonies. Choreographic and management experts were brought in to orchestrate the ceremonies and watch over the seven separate mini-Olympic Villages.

COJO, formed on 24 February 1987, immediately began developing the administrative and venue infrastructures, marketing, advertising, logistics, pre-Olympic trials, and the selection of 6,000 qualified volunteers. An ambitious Olympic Arts Festival concept and everything else were carefully outlined to IOC President Samaranch during the last days of April 1990. Optimistic projections 500 days before the Games talked about 3 billion francs expense and 3 billion francs in revenue.[6] Thirteen venues would accommodate 2,000 athletes, 40,000 accredited persons, "a million spectators . . . and 2 billion television viewers."[7] The IOC, the "Savoie '92" government-business association, and the Albertville municipality supplied hundreds of millions of francs, not including the $400 million from worldwide television companies, notably CBS in the United States.[8] President of the French Republic, François Mitterrand, pledged nearly 1 billion francs and envisioned a truly great Olympic Games in Savoie, a tribute to French greatness and "a symbol of a European renaissance."[9] Of course, the massive environmental intrusion that occurs at every Winter Olympic Games brought out critics in great numbers, and one especially colorful writer called it "a kind of Faustian pact with the 20th century." The same observer claimed that the Reverend Marcel Charvin from the French Alps town of Val d'Isère mourned that "since coming here in 1939, I've seen a village of shepherds transformed into a village of businessmen."[10]

In a most provocative and possibly prophetic way, many European economists and politicians saw in these double Olympic Games in France and Spain 1992 a great boon for the European Community's (EC) 12 nations' efforts to merge into a Common Market—a recognition that sport and economics form a kind of cultural and financial symbiosis. In economic terms, the French finally have reached a point where they need no longer look enviously at the Germans. At least in the early 1990s, France "displays an attractive stability in its currency, prices, and politics."[11] Some predicted a financial "super-Europe" and near the front of the parade were France and Spain, both of them among the sturdiest economies in the free world. In a kind of French Olympic euphoria, COJO and the national electric company (EDF) paid eight artists to paint a 250-meter portrait of Hercules on the face of the Tignes Dam near Albertville. The project took 60 days "using a process similar to the Renaissance tradition of fresco painting," and Jean-Marie Pierret and his team were paid $480,000. [12] Everything about Albertville was planned to be big, very big.

Catalonian Complexities for the Summer of 1992

Twenty-seven nations participated in the 1986 Asian Games, using the fully completed, awesome congregation of stadia in Seoul, Korea, exactly 2 years before the Olympic Games in that city. President of the Asian Olympic Council, Sheikh Fahad al-Ahmad al-Sabah, obviously pleased, said "Our friends in Korea have given an example to the whole world that they will be capable of holding a 1988 international games which will be one of the best in the world." Of course, South Korean president, Chun Doo Hwan, called them an "unqualified success" and urged their North Korean cousins to join them in exactly 2 years "onto the path of national reconciliation."[13]

A similar celebration in Barcelona 2 years before their own Summer Olympic Games was not possible, for thousands of construction workers were laboring in around-the-clock shifts to complete (and in some cases to just *begin*) building venues, the Olympic Village, hotels, and airport expansion. There was concern mixed with determination in the headquarters of the Comité Olimpico Organizador de Barcelona '92 (COOB '92). Samaranch flew from Lausanne to his home town, and his visits were more than social calls. "Bienvenido, Mister Samaranch, all is progressing satisfactorily," he was told by chief executive officer Miquel Abad; COOB '92 president and the mayor of Barcelona, Pasqual Maragall; NOC president, Carlos Ferrer Salat; the Prime Minister of Spain, Felipe González; Jordi Pujol, leader of the Generalitat; and the King of Spain himself, His Majesty Juan Carlos. Always the diplomat, Samaranch's coded message was understood by all: "I wish to work more closely with the Barcelona Committee."[14] The association of NOC's June 1990 meeting in Barcelona gave enormous motivation to the Games committee to work "around the clock" for the next 2 years. (I was there, and during the all-day inspection tour of venues I was alternately discouraged and exhilarated by the Olympic panorama.) The local people were undaunted, one of them writing an anticipatory panegyric of his city: "Finally, after three quarters of a century made of illusions, hopes and sacrifices, Barcelona will be part of the great modern cities, thanks to Olympism and Sport."[15] As always with Olympic Games host city spokespeople who talk in this vein, it was putting a heavy burden on both the Olympic concept and the quadrennial festival.

Spain and the Mediterranean city of Barcelona have a great deal going for them: a prideful history, a 70-year-old effort to host an Olympic Games, and a 1990s-strong economy that has all the earmarks of continuing. After World War I, Barcelona organizers attempted to host the 1924 Summer Olympic Games, and in spite of Pierre de Coubertin's famous 1926 comment, "Before I came to Barcelona, I didn't know what a sporting city was,"[16] the Games went to Paris and then Amsterdam. Barcelona tried again, unsuccessfully, in 1936 and again in 1972.[17] Then, in the 1980s and 1990s, having overcome some of its political and economic encumbrances, modern Spain entered a new era of optimism and relative prosperity, one manifestation being its 1986 acceptance of the Olympic Games responsibilities.

The profit motive was most assuredly not our reason for hosting the Games in '92, was Abad's emphatic answer to a journalist's inquiry. The whole Barcelona infrastructure, everything about the city, was being upgraded, and that included "our country and its image around the world," he said.[18] The *New York Times* travel section headline proclaimed, "Spain: New Vitality Amid Old Traditions." *Business America* was sure that the Barcelona Olympic Games "will open doors for U.S. business," whereas a *Building* magazine writer saw in Barcelona's "fever of construction" a kind of urban renaissance.[19] "The country is changing gears," argued Merril Stevenson in a lengthy scholarly piece in the *Economist*. Rags to riches, new freedoms, and vulgar license abounded everywhere, he said. Provincial pride, national pride, and sometimes a lack of civic responsibility mark these new Spaniards, he wrote:

> For Spaniards seem to have in their bones another quality rare in Europe: an utter lack of servility that at its worst comes close to anarchy and at its best is the essence of democracy.[20]

Barcelona is a pulsating, vibrant city, wrote Edward Schumacher in the *New York Times*, a community "that out of its cultural implosion and assertiveness has produced a robust creativity."[21] In other words, it is a place and time and people wholly capable of hosting the Olympic Games.

Unable to match Seoul in size and grandiosity, the Barcelona Olympic Games organizers planned for a great, error-free sport spectacle plus a most ambitious cultural festival. The 4-year cultural master plan called for the Year of Culture and Sport (1989); the Year of the Arts (1990); the Year of the Future (1991); and finally, the Year of the Games—1992. Concerts, exhibitions, festivals, and performances took place within the grand scheme or "Marco de la Olímpiada Cultura." *Architectural Review*'s Peter Buchanan called Barcelona "Europe's most exhilarating city" and predicted that the waterfront Olympic Village itself would be a work of art.[22] New, handsome buildings are going up everywhere, said a *New Leader* writer, a "special magic" pervades Barcelona, which, artistically, ranks behind only Paris, London, and Rome.[23] COOB '92 organizers trumpeted that the origins of European "Modernismo" were Catalonian and Barcelonian, that startling avant-garde art, architecture, and graphics whose characteristics are "sinuous and asymmetrical lines, vivid floral ornamentation, the use of new materials such as sheet iron and concrete and the obsessive reproduction of Wagnerian iconography."[24] Even the Catalán language, for so long forbidden by Franco, is in the midst of a renaissance and was selected as the fourth official language (with French, English, and Spanish) at the 1992 Games of the XXVth Olympiad. Barcelona, awash in sport, culture, and amiable ambiance, found itself standing shoulder-to-shoulder with the other great Olympic Games host cities. "Head down and sprinting for the line," is how a *London Times* reporter described Barcelona's Olympic preparations.[25]

Barcelona Sets Its Plans

History suggests that general secretary of the European NOCs (AENOC), Mario Pescante, cannot have been correct but only indulged in wishful thinking when he predicted that in Barcelona, the Games "for the first time in modern Olympic history, will be free of tensions and preoccupations."[26] As was true in Seoul, Los Angeles, and Moscow, every conceivable natural or human aberration could have visited these Olympic cities. Barcelona in the summer of 1992 is no different. The potential for a monumentally positive way to close the century is there in Barcelona, but lurking everywhere in Spanish life are forces capable of derailing the best laid plans of COOB '92 organizers. Among them are

1. resumption of the Persian Gulf War or other confrontations;[27]
2. the drain on governmental resources of funding both Expo '92 and the 1992 Olympic Games;[28]
3. terrorism, external and domestic;[29]
4. an acceleration of longstanding, virulent separatist movements in the Catalonia region and in the micronationalist Basque country;[30]
5. threats to the less than deep-rooted tradition of Spain's democratic governance (its constitutional monarchy);[31] and
6. malaise and excessive consumption that sometimes accompany sudden spurts of prosperity.[32]

Possibly these problems are no greater than those any other modern society has faced, and the resilient Spanish are certainly up to the task. I'm reminded of the true story that when America's "founding fathers" labored through the hot Philadelphia extended spring and summer (18 May-18 September) of 1787, pounding out with greatest difficulty the nation's Constitution, a lady asked Dr. Benjamin Franklin whether America had a republic or a monarchy. "A Republic," he replied, "if you can keep it."[33] The Spanish worked to resolve their political uncertainties, not just because the Olympic Games were scheduled to begin on 25 July 1992, but despite disconcerting political vacillations, these people have set sail on a course of enlightened democratic reform, hoping for a general rise in living standards. Spain is a leader in making the 1986 Single European Act a reality, an exciting economic concept signed by members of the European Community Act. "The intention was to create a region in Europe that would include 12 countries with no internal barriers to free trade by 1992."[34] Complete freedom of movement would be guaranteed for services, goods, people, and capital. Spanish prime minister Felipe Gonzáles led the way with a call for a "common European citizenship."[35] Barcelona is special in so many ways, not the least of which is its prosperity, some "20% higher than the rest of Spain," wrote Dr. Thomas P. Rosandich, president of the United States Sports Academy, a visitor to the 2,000-year-old seaport city.[36]

History has a way of repeating itself, though never exactly. Five hundred days before the 1932 Summer Olympic Games in Los Angeles, there was a pervasive lack of interest among city dwellers, Californians, and Americans in general regarding the upcoming Olympian festival. The whole organizing committee found itself in a trough of depression. The worldwide economic catastrophe had defeated them, they thought. Interest began to pick up measurably in the spring of '32, and by summer, with the Olympic Games "just over the next hill," the city was awash with people. The Games had unprecedented high attendance, record-breaking crowds. Half a generation later, the IOC chose a war-shattered London to be the site of the postwar Olympic Games. Shell-shocked English men and women could not have cared less and showed no interest in a second Olympic Games in their capital city all through 1947 and most of 1948. There was great concern in the minds of Lord Burghley and his organizing committee. But then, despite abysmal weather, hundreds of thousands of spectators attended a necessarily Spartan but dignified Olympic festival.

I was in Rome during the furnace-hot summer of 1960. Much of the population had abandoned the city, seeking cooler waters, and apathy about the Olympic Games seemed as widespread as it had been during the entire previous year. Yet most people returned home for the Olympic Games, and "SRO" (standing room only) was the rule rather than the exception—despite "the hottest Rome August in memory," with 10 consecutive days of above 100 degrees Fahrenheit (39 degrees Celsius). Olympic historians noted exactly the same thing in Los Angeles 1984. Five hundred days before the Games there was not a ripple of interest among Americans, not even in the "City of Angels." Peter Ueberroth and his hard-driven LAOOC crew, not especially sensitive to Olympic history, could not understand why, all through 1983 and much of 1984, the millions of Californians were shockingly uninterested in the pending great festival. But they showed up in hundreds of thousands on July 28th, and their numbers increased over the next 2 weeks.

It has always been so; it was so in Barcelona in 1991, and there is no reason to expect a different scenario in the summer of 1992. Record crowds will be there in Barcelona on the afternoon of the Opening Ceremony. Barcelona's COOB '92 organization announced in overt and subtle ways that it was not their intent to match, let alone out-do, Seoul in size and pomp. The Catalonian organizers envisioned a great but not gargantuan Olympic Games, a festival to bedazzle and be remembered in positive ways, athletically, culturally, and visually. "My dream is to film the Barcelona '92 Olympics," said king of Olympic Games filmmakers, Bud Greenspan.[37] It was his second exhortation about the anticipated specialness of an Olympic Games in a city that had waited 70 long and often hard years before actually playing the host. Quality, always quality, is our aim, repeated Carlos Ferrer Salat, president del Comité Olímpic Español (COE), echoing everyone on Barcelona's organizing committee.[38] An absolutely stunning Olympic Games in Barcelona will have immense physical benefits to the city, said Samaranch, but the spiritual benefits will be even greater:

> The name of Barcelona, of Catalonia and of Spain will be pronounced millions of times; they'll attract the attention of the whole world. We must . . . sell the image of the city and of Catalonia, sell our culture and our national character, explain what Barcelona and Catalonia are now and what they want to be in the next few years.[39]

The most passionate though cautiously optimistic of those in the host city hoped for and worked toward making Olympic Barcelona a focus for the finest expressions of Catalonian, Spanish, and *human* culture. Barcelona is on the edge of a future similar to several immediately preceding Summer Olympic Games sites, and at the same time that Spanish city's inhabitants have had the privilege to plan and anticipate a rare festival, precious, even exotic, and very exciting. And thus, COOB '92 Barcelona, Catalonia, and Spain—slow out of the starting gate of Olympic Games preparation—moved rapidly in the early months of 1991, some 500 days before the opening of the Games. David Miller's essay, "Barcelona Blossoms Under the Olympic Dream," underscores this theme of accelerated progress. Transfixed by the new venues, especially the new Olympic diving pool on the open cliff face of Mont Juic, Miller was "thrilled with expectation. And it is not even my home."[40] Amidst ineffable sadnesses, wrote novelist Edith Wharton in 1933, there are "a thousand little daily wonders to marvel at and rejoice in."[41] If all goes well, these different Olympic Games in Barcelona will become one of those "wonders," the accompanying sadnesses giving way to a larger sense of rejoicing.

Notes

1. "Juan Antonio Samaranch, el embajador de la paz," *Sport Diaro del Mundial* [Barcelona], 6 June 1990, 53.

2. Tutt, letter to author, 4 January 1991.

3. Filaretos, interview with author, at Olympia, Greece, 22 June 1990.

4. Michael Novak, "Sports and the Moral Life," *Creative Living, 13*, Spring 1984, 2, 4. This is the second time I have used this phrase—no apology (see chapter 10).

5. Their quotes found in *Flash, 38*, (COJO) 10 December 1990, p. 1. "There is nothing that will escape our scrutiny," declared the Barnier and Killy team. See *Madrid El País*, 14 February 1990, 56.

6. *Flash 36*, 28 September 1990.

7. *Flash 37*, 30 October 1990. Also *The Olympic Challenge Bulletin No. 4* (1987) and the 20-page brochure *Jeunesse Du Monde En Savoie 1992*.

8. A most informative document was *The Challenge/The Team* (COJO, 1989; 35 pages). Also the bulletins "Actions Carried Out By the COJO," "Olympic Site and Games Calendar," "Organizing Committee For the XVIth Winter Olympic Games in Albertville and Savoie," and "Other Actions Related to the Games" (all 1989).

9. Mitterrand, quoted in *A 1000 Jours Deux*, (COJO) June 1989, 17.

10. James M. Markham, "On to Olympian Glory, but at Too Steep a Price?" *New York Times*, 2 January 1989, 4.

11. Howard La Franchi, "Socialists Bring France Prosperity," *Christian Science Monitor*, 26 April 1990, 8. Other essays on France's business

strength are found in *Export Today, 6*, May-June 1990, 16; "Europhoria," *Wilson Quarterly, 14*, Winter 1990, 57-69; *Business America, 110*, 3 July 1989, 2-4.

12. "Albertville's Hercules," *New York Times Magazine*, 5 November 1989, 130.

13. "Praise for Koreans," *New York Times*, 28 September 1986, 10S; "Success of Asias Illustrates Koreans' True Worth: Chun," *Korea Herald*, 4 October 1986, 1.

14. *New York Times*, 10 December 1989, 6S; "COOB Hopes Samaranch Will Stop his Criticisms," *El País*, 14 March 1990, Sport sec., 1. "Political Disagreements Hurting Spain's Olympic Preparation," said a headline in the *Wall Street Journal*, 3 April 1990, 17; also see *El País*, 1 April 1990, 50. *El País*, 3 April 1990, 59, reported what appears to have been a crisis in COOB '92 progress. The *Atlanta Journal*'s Bert Roughton observed that "everyone's a little jittery" in Barcelona (17 June 1990, C2). Mr. Samaranch's emissary to Barcelona, Gunnar Ericson, was very concerned about venue and hotel construction delays and that little had been done about solving the city's traffic nightmares (*El País*, 27 July 1990, 31). Samaranch's strongest words came in a public statement: "I believe that the city of Seville is making better progress toward its 500th year celebration than is Barcelona in its Olympic efforts" (*Cambio 16, 922*, 31 July 1989, 12). On pages 15-17 in the same issue, *Cambio*'s editor wrote a discouraging essay: "El gran atasco de la capital olímpica del 92" (Barcelona's grand Olympic plans grinding to a halt)." "The Pain in Spain" (*Sports Travel, 2*, February 1990, 74-75) said that Barcelona's "facelift" was moving very slowly.

15. Andrés Merce Varela, "Barcelona '92: It Was Just a Matter of Time," *Sport Europe. AENOC Official Magazine, 1*, 1990, 49.

16. "Coubertin Was Right," *Olympic Panorama, 1*, 1989, 8, 22. This article has an interesting photo of Coubertin in Barcelona in 1926.

17. "Barcelona, Host City," *COOB '92 Press Dossier*.

18. Abad, "Two Years Before the Olympic Games: 'They will be the best in history'," *Barcelona Olímpica, 17*, 1990, 74.

19. *New York Times*, 22 October 1989; sec. 5, p. 1; *Business America, 110*, 28 August 1989, 1; *Building*, 27 January 1989, 39.

20. Merril Stevenson, "The Next Transition," *Economist, 310*, 11 March 1989, Survey section, 22.

21. Edward Schumacher, in *New York Times*, 14 January 1990, Travel section, p. 10. Nearly 700 billion pesetas are being invested in Barcelona infrastructure, and it's just the beginning, wrote *España 90*, in the August-September 1990 issue.

22. Peter Buchanan, "Boost for Barcelona," *Architectural Review, 185*, April 1989, 74.

23. Janice Valls-Russell, "Getting Ready for the Olympics, Welcome to Barcelona," *New Leader, 72*, 9 January 1989, 9-10. COOB '92 Divisió de Cultura has published several extremely handsome brochures titled *Olímpiada Cultural*.

24. Joana Bonet and Paco Elvira, "Barcelona, Capital Del Modernismo," *Ronda Iberia* [airline magazine], June 1990, 41-42. Schumacher (see Note 21) called Catalan Nationalism and Catalan Art Nouveau, or "Modernismo," nearly synonymous.

25. Peter Strafford, "New Confidence in a Proud Land," *London Times*, 9 September 1989, 54.

26. *Sport Europe. AENOC Official Magazine, 2*, August 1990, 7.

27. IOC vice president Richard Pound said that his committee would wait a year before considering whether the hostilities in the Persian Gulf necessitate a cancellation or change of site for the Albertville or Barcelona Games. "A year would have to go by with the situation still unresolved before any move is made," said Pound (James Christie, "No Rush for IOC on Iraq," *Toronto Globe and Mail*, 19 January 1991, A21.

28. "Expo '92 in Seville," *Business America, 110*, 28 August 1989, 6-7; "World's Fair Is Boost to Seville," *Christian Science Monitor*, 1 November 1989, 4; Alan Riding, "With Spain's Prosperity Comes a Measure of Pain," *New York Times*, 15 October 1989, 1, 18; "Blocked Funds Put U.S. Role in Seville World Fair in Doubt," *New York Times*, 17 April 1990, A8; Nigel M. Healey, "Completing the Internal Market in Europe: The Road to 1992," *Contemporary Review, 254*, June 1989, 281; "Llegar a la EXPO, el Gran Problema," *España Económica*, June 1990, 30-33.

29. The three desolate miles of Mediterranean coastline next to the Olympic Village are "a security officer's nightmare" (*New York Times*, 15 September 1989, G3); "Olympic Security Called "Flexible," *Newark Star-Ledger*, 4 December 1990, n.p.

30. Richard Gunther, *Spain After Franco* (Berkeley: University of California Press, 1988), 389; P.N. Gómez, "Bilingualism or the Death of a Language," *Catalònia Cultura, 10*, September 1988, 44-45. Devoted entirely to the Olympic Games, *Catalònia Cultura, 12*, January 1989, has a powerful nationalistic flavor. Regarding the underground Popular Liberation Front (FLP) in Catalonia, see Donald Shane, *Dilemmas of Social Democracy* (New York: Greenwood Press, 1989), 26; "Catalonian Radicals Agree to an Uneasy Peace During the Olympic Games," *Cambio 16, 931*, 2 October 1989, 32.

31. "Radical Groups in Barcelona Strain for Power," *El País*, 23 August 1989, 25; "Catalonian Parliament Demands Self-Determination,"

Catalònia Cultura, 18, March 1990, 3; "There is constant political warfare between Barcelona and Madrid," said *London Times* journalist, Peter Strafford in an essay called "New Confidence in a Proud Land," 54.

32. "Drug Trade . . . Is Overwhelming Spain," *New York Times*, 9 November 1988, A6; "Crime Wave Alarms Spaniards," *New York Times*, 15 January 1989, 13; "Gaudy, Bawdy Barcelona," *New York Times*, 4 March 1990, Sophisticated Traveler sec., 60-72.

33. Franklin's quote may be found in Jeffrey St. John, *A Correspondent's Report From the Convention of 1789* (Ottawa, IL: Jameson Books, 1987), 225.

34. John P. Dessauer, "The Global Wave That Europe Is Catching," *World Monitor; 2*, September 1989, 16.

35. González, quoted in *España 90*, August-September 1990, 2.

36. "Spain, 1992: A Vintage Year," *USSA News, 12*, Fall 1990, 2.

37. "Bud Greenspan: 'My Dream is to Film the Barcelona '92 Olympics'," *Barcelona Olímpica, 3*(15), 1990, 76.

38. Salat's comments in "Accés Limitat als Jocs del 92," *El País*, 5 June 1990, 10.

39. Samaranch, quoted in Xavier Ventura, "Juan Antonio Samaranch," *Catalònia Cultura, 8*, March 1988, 32.

40. David Miller, *London Times*, 24 January 1991, 34.

41. Edith Wharton, *A Backward Glance: An Autobiography* (New York: Scribner's Sons, 1985; originally 1933), 379.

C·H·A·P·T·E·R· 15

The International
Olympic Academy

Olympic ideology, through the combined voices of all the
academies make a small contribution to world peace.

Horst Ueberhorst, *sport historian*

IOC member from Finland, Peter Tallberg, in a 1982 letter praised the
mission of the Greek-based International Olympic Academy (IOA) as
fraternal, philanthropic, and with absolutely no other raison d'être than that
of succor for all youth everywhere. He reminded me of the Tallberg
allegiance to the Coubertin ideology and philosophy of Olympism:

> My grandfather won an Olympic bronze medal in yachting in Stockholm
> 1912, and my cousin achieved also bronze in Moscow. I myself have
> participated 5 times as an athlete and once as a team leader; my brother
> Henrik twice and my brother Johan once. My eldest son Mathias took
> part in the Moscow Games and is now seriously training for the L.A.
> races.[1]

No wonder Tallberg accepted invitations to attend and lecture at the IOA, nestled against the Kronian Hill no more than 800 meters from the ancient ruins at Olympia, Greece. My own reason for an abiding interest in this part of the world is that my parents were born in central Macedonia, now Albania. I grew up in a home rich in Balkan myth and story-telling.

Modern-day archaeological diggings began in Olympia in 1961, the same year that the Academy opened. The former great president of the Academy, Professor Doctor Nikolaos Nissiotis (1925-1986), was convinced that these two events did not overlap by chance, but rather that "their coincidence is a symbol of the symbiosis of time and space and an expression of the timelessness of the Olympic Idea."[2] From the beginning, "believers" like Nissiotis declared that the IOA was the philosophical center of the Olympic Movement, the metaphysical and spiritual repository for those invisible and precious ideas that transcend stadium activities, that can enlarge upon the deeper meaning of 100-meter races that should be won with hard work, honesty, honor, and dignity. (If such language offends, then this chapter is not for you, for it is the vernacular of the Academy during its 15-day course).

I cannot say for sure, but I believe that Nissiotis, the longtime and revered dean of the Academy Otto Szymiczek (1910-1990), Cleanthis Talaelogos (1902-1990), Nicolaos Yalouris, and Epaminodas Pertalias would have agreed with futurists John Naisbitt and Patricia Aburdene that the modern worship of science and the rational has been excessive, possessive, and therefore, in part, damaging. The millenial year 2000 will be a metaphor for the future, a future "that specifically values the emotional and the nonrational."[3] Closer to home, IOC executive board member Flor Isava Fonseca told me in a most forceful way that "no less than a spiritual revival is necessary *within* the Olympic Tripartite to save our movement . . . And the IOA, in concert with a dramatically enlarged number of national Olympic academies on every continent, must be one way to engender these reforms."[4] Brilliant education and love (those were her words), a kind of holistic ambiance so reminiscent of Olympic Academy education, must rule future IOC members' "minds and souls" and in so doing help them deliver the "good news" to all the world's youth.[5] Many may be turned off by her Olympian messianic message, but I know the lady well enough to know that she will retract not one word.

Most of the hundreds of lecturers over the 31-year history of the IOA have emphasized a refusal to worship the god of modern-day technology in order to experience a very personal rebirth of the Renaissance spirit. Two-time American Olympic marathoner, John J. Kelley (who has never been to the Academy), was convinced that some athletes and leaders at the fore of the Olympic movement have turned the traditional philosophy "on its head . . . as in Bob Dylan's song *Idiot Winds*: 'What's good is bad, what's bad is good.'"[6] This does not imply that attendance at the IOA will measurably melt international collective malaise, though most who testify about their

Olympia experience use words like *important, unique, meaningful, ethereal,* and *informative.*

An Historical Perspective

Professor Marvin H. Eyler of the University of Maryland, searching for a simple and honest definition of the elusive Olympic philosophy, called it "the Right Stuff," and it seemed that the delegates at the 1980 IOA understood his reference to the best-selling book by Tom Wolfe that described America's astronauts as having the "right stuff," or desirable physical, intellectual, and moral ingredients.[7] Baron de Coubertin, even in his last year of life (1937), was never fully satisfied with the concept he called Olympism, and he continued to struggle for a plain and unambiguous Olympic message that he could deliver to the whole world. He was unable to do so, but before he died, he called for the establishment of an Olympic school of philosophy, a place and academic atmosphere of inspiration and scholarship, a symposium setting in which to analyze and synthesize the deeper meanings of sport, competitive athletics, and the Olympic Games.

The dreamer-innovator Coubertin visited "sacred Olympia" in spring 1927 and in the stillness of that "holy place" envisioned a philosophical school of sport.[8] A month earlier, on 16 March 1937 (according to Coubertin's corresponding friend, Dr. Carl Diem), the baron had written "to the German Government, . . . [proposing] that it should found an International Olympic Institute, a Centre d'Etudes Olympiques."[9] He lamented that

> I have not been able to carry out to the end what I wanted to perfect . . . I believe that a Centre of Olympic Studies would aid the preservation and progress of my work more than anything else, and would keep it from the false paths which I fear.[10]

Historian Nina Pappas presented credible evidence that while at Olympia, Coubertin shared his dream and concern with his Greek colleague Jean Ketseas, who in turn discussed the provocative idea of an Olympic school with his own teacher, Professor Chryssafis, the Greek minister of education.[11] Conversely, Norbert Müller, in his 1975 doctoral dissertation and later in his 1987 *Internationale Olympische Akademie IOA—25 Jahre im Spiegel der Vorträge 1961-1986,* suggested that Ketseas did not precisely remember these 1927 events.[12]

In any case, all agree that after the war, IOC member Ketseas and Carl Diem, rector of the Cologne Sporthochschule, worked together to make the vision real, and in 1945 (Diem) and 1946 (Ketseas), they took action. Their combined proposal was forwarded to the IOC by member Ketseas and approved in 1949. Very hard work by the Hellenic Olympic Committee to create a center for education at Olympia, Greece, was matched by the labors of Professors Diem and Ketseas. On 19 June 1947, at the Stockholm IOC meeting, Ketseas made the formal request for permission to begin an Academy. The proposal was immediately seconded by Vice President Avery Brundage. After still more work by Diem and Ketseas—the task equally divided—on 28 April 1949, in Rome, the IOC voted for the enterprise, resulting in an additional 10 years and more effort before the concept was realized.

Finally, at the IOC's 58th meeting, June 1961, in Athens and Olympia, the excavations began, and the rudimentary academy convened only a kilometer away. Somehow, recalled Dean Szymiczek, delegates from 24 nations were there to hear 12 speakers discuss the historical and philosophical aspects of the ancient and the modern Olympic Games.[13] News of the IOA's existence spread rapidly, and in 1990, half of the world's countries sent delegates to Olympia for the IOA's 30th session, "Women and the Olympic Movement." It took a while before we sent anyone, said the Saudi Arabian NOC president, Faisal Fahd Abdul Aziz, "but once done, our delegates gained so much from the Academy experience."[14] It was a theme echoed by most who have attended academy sessions organized by the Hellenic Olympic Committee, the Greek government, and the IOC.

National Olympic Academies: Not a Universal Reality

Combining the most scrupulous scholarship with a very handsome, fully-illustrated book, Conrado Durántez published in the Spanish language *La Academia Olímpica Internacional*. It surpasses every other IOA history printed before 1988 and is most revealing about the author, about some of the major figures in the nearly 100-year history of the IOC, and about the major actors in and origins of the IOA; and it also details the 20-year history of the Spanish Olympic Academy.[15] Only the German Olympic Academy founded in 1961 is older, and it did not use the word *Academy* in its title but was called the Germany Sports Federation Annual Intellectual Symposium.[16]

Conrado Durántez was a young man in attendance at the 1961 beginnings of the IOA, but he was the main architect in the 1968 creation of the Spanish Olympic Academy. (Dr. Juan Antonio Samaranch also attended the 26 November 1968 Sesión Inaugural de la Academia Olímpica Española.)[17] The Spanish Academy became a model school of Olympic sport, history, philosophy, and pedagogy, having awarded "350 diplomas in its first 5 years of existence." José Maria Cagigal, Franz Lotz, and Monique Berlioux—all giants in the world of Olympic ideology—were guests of the Spanish academy, which was frequently referred to as a Centre of Olympic Studies. The passionate jurist Durántez reminded a special audience in 1976 that the Olympic idea of fairness for all, of cosmopolitanism, internationalism, and peace through sport "is today the most important sociological phenomenon in the world."[18]

The integral strength of the Academy (and Durántez's devotion to Olympic principles) attracted other "big name" guests and lecturers: Samaranch, Otto Szymiczek, historian Walter Umminger, Prince Juan Carlos of Spain, Prince George of Hanover (IOA president in 1970), IOC president Avery Brundage, and presidents of all the "Iberoamericanas" academies.[19] But not only famous speakers came. At the 16th Session (1984), several of Spain's veteran journalists, politicians, and sport and Olympic administrators joined Durántez and *more than 200 young people* from all over the nation.[20]

The Chinese Taipei Olympic Committee has fully supported the R.O.C. National Olympic Academy since 1978 and for a decade before that date sent bright and energetic delegates to the International Olympic Academy. Their most venerable IOC member, Henry H. Hsu, spoke to a large group at the 10th anniversary academy gathering in 1987 reminding them that Western Olympic ideology, when melded to ancient Chinese philosophy is truly the way of wisdom, for, as *The Book of the Mean* tells us, he said, all truth can be summed up in singleness in purpose, total sincerity, and the concept of "lasting, which becomes manifest. Manifest becomes perpetual. Perpetual generates wisdom and enlightenment."[21] An all-star group of lecturers shared ideas with the 150 delegates. Otto Szymiczek was there from Greece; Wayne Osness, George Killian, and Lisa Delpy from the USA; Vassos Constantinous from Cyprus; and some of Taiwan's most distinguished educators, sport scientists, and athletes volunteered to spend time with the young people. It was a new, yet very ancient kind of education that they received.

Half a world away, in Budapest, Hungary, the Magyar Olimpiai Akadémia met that same year, 1987. I was there as a guest, lecturing on the bewildering (to the audience) history of American athletic organizations, the AAU, NCAA, USOC, and USOA. Few, if any, European nations have more scholars studying the Olympic Movement and Games than does Hungary. Most of them were present in that exquisite city at their permanent headquarters in Alkotás. The dean of the Academy, Dr. László Kutassi was joined by a score of extremely well-versed Olympic scholars who led sessions on "Ancient Egyptian Sport," "Letters From Coubertin," "Marxism and the Olympic Idea"—a whole spectrum of topics.[22] Today, the *Hungarian Olympic Bulletin* reserves a "News and Information" section about its academy business and projected programs.[23]

Norway, in the midst of organizing Winter Olympic Games in 1994, still found time and energy to institute its own academy in Lillehammer. The indefatigable Samaranch was there on 26 June 1988, and the Nansen School, Norway's Humanistic Academy, hummed with excitement for 60 students and guests from the nation's ministry of culture.[24]

No IOC president has ever visited a United States Olympic Academy (USOA), but that has not diminished the enthusiasm for and devotion to Olympic principles of the 3,300 registered delegates who attended annual meetings 1977 through 1991.[25] Dr. Harold Friermood, for 55 years a national officer in the YMCA movement, created the USOA in 1977, after several years of hard work and 6 years after (he told me) "my extraordinary and illuminating 1971 IOA experience."[26] Early on, it was decided to rotate the sites of this American academy in order that young people from every geographic area of the vast country could attend. It worked, and the rotating of sites together with a small army of carefully selected speakers were the main reasons for its success. In a country not generally perceived to be filled with high-minded young people deeply concerned with the historic, philosophic, political, and technical aspects of the Olympic Movement, several thousand of them poured through the registration desks of USOA I through USOA XV, from Chicago, IL, to Colorado Springs, CO.[27] At Atlanta's splendid Emory University, USOC XIV hosted 400 young men and women from every quarter of the nation and 16 other countries, and 50 senior lecturers, who spoke on subjects ranging from Olympism to TOP-ISL to the Olympic Job Opportunities Program.[28] There are optimists, like myself, who say that the national Olympic Academy idea is so interesting, so appealing, and so important, that attendance will double by the Summer and Winter Olympic Games of 1996 and 1998.

The Future of Olympic Academies

The International Olympic Academy and the increasing number of national Olympic academies ("There are 40 of them, worldwide")[29] are opportunities for young intellectuals to discuss at length and in nontechnical language a kind of historic-philosophic, vernacular that might bestir a universal Olympian spirit in each delegate, a sense of fair play—a humanistic message to be carried home and shared with even younger men and women, boys and girls. But nothing comes "out of the blue," and if national Olympic academies are to proliferate and so aid the IOA and the IOC in their global mission, some practical steps must be taken. The two great architects of Ketseas and Diem's Olympia-based first academy, Cleanthis Talaelogos and Otto Szymiczek, died within days of one another in summer 1990. Vigorous old men to the very end, they were mourned and praised in a hundred NOCs and by 5,000 former IOA delegates on all six continents.[30] They did good, good work, but it was not enough. Those who understand, live by, and make every effort to share the message of Olympic philosophers must increase their numbers to hundreds of thousands. Only then, wrote sport historian, Horst Ueberhorst, can the "Olympic ideology, through the combined voices of all the academies make a small contribution to world peace."[31] The great teacher of IOA, John Powell of Canada, looked beyond his unabiding enthusiasm and optimism for the academy concept and admitted that "the Olympic movement is more important than the games, its objectives of putting principles into practice only possible if model national Olympic academies like the two in North America are duplicated and surpassed all over the world."[32]

Because this book is essentially futurist, I make seven suggestions for more effective dissemination of these "principles," the Olympic message. I believe with every fiber of my being that the undefiled concept of lofty, cooperatively competitive sport from kindergarten to the Olympic arena can contribute to the revelation of the highest, purest instincts hiding within each person. If enough people understand and practice the Olympic idea of fairness in every aspect of their lives, then the Olympic Games will become more than spectator diversion. "Time passes, but old values remain the same," said the young idealist and member of the IOC secretariat, Marie-Hélène Roukhadzé.[33] Despite their many successes, the Olympic Games are presently in a crisis. Clouds of doubt exist as to their mission, and as long as doubts persist, there will be tribulation. Athletes, coaches, judges, and administrators must either respect their own Olympic legislation or change it. If they do not, there will be more suffering and indignation, especially for the young men and women inside the stadium. British historian and diplomat James Bryce said in *The American Commonwealth*, "Suffering, and nothing else, will implant that sentiment of responsibility which is the first step to reform."[34] But enough suffering. The widespread promulgation of "soothing" Olympian ideas cannot be accomplished by only one international academy in Greece and 40 national academies. Much more is needed, and these seven reform suggestions are my own "sentiment of responsibility":

1. *The Olympic Adventure* volumes for children and young adults, an IOC project, should be made available to all officially registered delegates to the IOA and at every national Olympic Academy, worldwide. Doing so will fill a vast educational vacuum.
2. The IOC executive board, after consultation with its membership, the NOCs, and the sport federations, should select six "roving ambassadors" (one for each continent) to lecture full time and without salary on the subjects of Olympic history and philosophy; on Olympism, the Olympic idea, sportsmanship, and fair play; on heroes and heroines of the Olympic Games; and on the larger message of the international movement. Schools, universities, institutes, industry, business, media, and philanthropic and political groups would all qualify for "ambassadorial visits."
3. The Olympic organizing committees for the Winter and Summer Games should be urged to coordinate Olympic Solidarity youth camps on the site and invite all young people attending the Games to participate in appropriate gatherings, rallies, symposia, songfests, Olympic orientation sessions—all of them visionary and complementary to the competitions. These camp gatherings would be, as Robert Jungk said in 1981, "periodically recurring demonstrations of hope against despair, of affection against hatred, of warmth against cold, of softness against hardness."[35]
4. The United States Olympic Committee and American corporations (both commercial and grant-issuing) should commit monies to allow the United

States Olympic Academy (USOA) to expand its schedule from 3 days to 5, which would allow investigation of almost all important facets of the Olympic Movement. Even greater numbers of young adults would be encouraged to attend. The Olympic ideal still exists and, if it is nearly moribund, then these youthful, 21st-century leaders are "just what the doctor ordered" to breathe life back into it.

5. Expand the IOA vision to incorporate a multiplicity of symposia for 40 weeks a year. Few places on earth are more beautiful than the IOA and its environs; few places on earth surpass the IOA "sacred village" as a place to talk about . . . everything. Olympic family largess, international corporations, and private donations can make this academy in the shadow of the Kronian Hill the ultimate complement to the Baron de Coubertin and to all that most Greeks, old and new, hold sacred.

6. The Olympic Scientific Congress is held 1 year before the summer Olympic Games and is wholly funded by the IOC. I strongly urge that Congress organizers not only allow but encourage a 3-hour academy session devoted to issues of sporting ethics, sport history and philosophy, as well as elucidations on the binding cord between science and metaphysics. So many professionals in both "camps" would benefit.

7. Lastly, and to me stunningly provocative, would be to organize and initiate by Year One of the 21st century Olympic academies in every single one of the world's 175 countries, and thereby run the risk of engendering a new, heady—and yet very practical—one-world, Olympian consciousness. The topics discussed would not be "hard science," as in a comparison of fast twitch and slow twitch muscles in female Olympic sprint champions, but speculative, imaginative forays into human possibilities. I agree with philosopher Sam Keen that "if educators refuse to consider any future but one that's highly corporate, highly technological, and highly consumptive, then they betray the future."[36]

My sole reason for writing this book was to underscore the wholeness of the Olympic athlete beneath the umbrella of an Olympic bureaucracy that must increase and improve its specialized nature, but at the same time, in some kind of spiritual wrestling match, must become more integrated, less compartmentalized, more holistically *whole* while, as historian Roberta Park wrote, "forging logical links between practitioner and researcher."[37] I share this vision, and this chapter on Olympic academies is testimony not to my futurist perspicacity but to my belief in the limitless capacity for good in each of us, in all of us.

Notes

1. Peter Tallberg, letter to author, 9 February 1982.
2. Nissiotis, "In Olympia, Thinking for Olympia," *Bulletin 8 Baden-Baden Olympic Congress 1981*, 58.

3. Naisbitt and Aburdene, *Megatrends 2000*, (William Morrow and Company, Inc., New York, 1990) 295.

4. Flor Isava Fonseca, interview with author, in Quebec City, Canada, 24 May 1990.

5. The 69-year-old Venezuelan Fonseca represented her country in international equestrian competition, and during our 2-hour interview, she emphasized many times that it is *not* a retrogressive step for everyone within the Olympic family to come to grips with and share old-new perceptions of civility, morality, unmateriality, and balanced religiosity. Only then can we in the Olympic Movement, she concluded, aid in the dispersion of numbing universal loneliness and replace it with athletic good news.

6. John J. Kelley, letter to author, 9 November 1990.

7. Marvin H. Eyler, "The Right Stuff," *Proceedings IOA 1980*, 159-167.

8. Coubertin stood amidst Olympia's ruins and theorized about a modern "school of moral nobility and purity (une école de noblesse et de pureté morales)" in his *Mémoires Olympiques*, 208.

9. Carl Diem, "An 'Elis' of Our Times," *Proceedings IOA 1961*, 19. Diem cited a Coubertin letter reprinted in *Revue Olympique*, No. 1, 1938, 3.

10. Coubertin, quoted in Carl Diem's "Introduction," *Proceedings IOA 1961*, 7; also C. Robert Paul, "Spreading the Olympic Idea," *Olympian, 1*, October 1974, 8-9.

11. Nina K. Pappas, "History and Development of the International Olympic Academy 1927-1977," PhD dissertation, University of Illinois, 1978, pp. 15-16. Also John Powell, "The Contribution of the IOA to International Understanding," *Track and Field Quarterly Review, 87*, Spring 1987, 8.

12. Norbert Müller, "Die Olympische Idee Pierre de Coubertin und Carl Diems in ihrer Auswirkung auf die Internationale Olympische Akademie," PhD dissertation, University of Graz, Austria, 1975, p. 115. Also Müller's *IOA History* (Sehors-Verlag Niedemhausen-Taunus, 1987), vi, vii.

13. Dr. Szymiczek's essay on the IOA and the national Olympic academies in *Proceedings IOA 1983*, 62-69; Franz Lotz's unpublished paper on the Olympic Movement and the IOA (in the author's possession); also Szymiczek, "The International Olympic Academy, Its History, Achievements, Objectives," *Proceedings IOA 1964*, 45-60. Essentially confirming data can be found in Conrado Durántez, "The International Olympic Academy and the Centres of Olympic Studies" and Norbert Müller, "The Olympic Idea of Pierre de Coubertin and Carl Diem", both in *Proceedings IOA 1976*, 80-93 and 94-100, respectively.

14. Aziz, letter to author, 16 October 1989.

15. Conrado Durántez, *La Academia Olímpica Internacional* (Comité Olímpico Español, 1988).

16. Several German scholars assured me that only shortly *after* the establishment of the IOA did they come together on a *regular* basis to talk about and debate Olympic issues. I have no ''hard evidence'' about these meetings.

17. Durántez, *La Academia*, 42-44.

18. Conrado Durántez, ''The International Olympic Academy and the Centres of Olympic Studies,'' *Proceedings IOA 1976*, 92.

19. Durántez, *La Academia*, Photographs following 16.

20. *Academia Olímpica Española XVI* (Madrid: COE, 1984).

21. Henry H. Hsu, in *Report of the R.O.C. National Olympic Academy 10*, 1987, 13-14.

22. *A Magyar Olimpiai Akadémia Évkönyve*, 1987.

23. *Hungarian Olympic Bulletin*, 1989-1990, *36*, 26-27; *37*, 30; *38*, 24.

24. *Newsflash, 3*, December 1990, 7 (Newsletter of the Lillehammer [Norway] Winter Olympic Games Organizing Committee 1994). New academies emerge every year; ''Creation of an Olympic Academy in Tunis,'' *Olympic Review, 280*, February, 1991, 92.

25. I have in my possession all 15 *USOA Proceedings*, with the names of all delegates, lecturers, and guests.

26. Dr. Friermood, conversation with author, at USOA I, in Chicago, 19 June 1977.

27. 1977—University of Illinois—at Chicago; 1978—Illinois State University; 1979—Brigham Young University (Utah); 1980—Indiana University; 1981—United States Olympic Training Center at Colorado Springs; 1982—Pepperdine University (California); 1983—Texas Tech University; 1984—University of Oregon; 1985—State University of New York at Plattsburgh; 1986—Colorado Springs; 1987—University of Indiana at Indianapolis; 1988—Pennsylvania State University; 1989—Evergreen State College (Olympia, Washington); 1990—Emory University (Georgia); 1991—Colorado State University; 1992—Colorado Springs, Colorado.

28. *Proceedings USOA XIV*, 1990.

29. *Newsflash, 3*, ibid.

30. ''The Academy Mourns Its Masters,'' *Olympic Review, 278*, December 1990, 552-553.

31. Horst Ueberhorst, letter to author, January 1991.

32. John Powell, letter to author, September 1989.

33. See her essay in the *Olympic Review, 190-191*, August-September 1983, 551-552.

34. James Bryce (1838-1922), *The American Commonwealth, Volume I* (London: Macmillan, 1888), 352.

35. Robert Jungk, " 'Soft' Games: The Vision of an Alternative Concept,"
    Bulletin 6 Olympic Congress Baden-Baden 1981, 10.

36. Sam Keen, quoted in Scott Willis, "On Education for Alternative Futures:
    A Conversation With Sam Keen," *Educational Leadership, 47*, September
    1989, 73.

37. Roberta J. Park, "The Second 100 Years: Or Can Physical Education
    Become the Renaissance Field of the Twenty-First Century?" *Quest, 41*,
    April 1989, 20.

OLYMPIA
Olympic Sports illustrated by Hans Erni

C·H·A·P·T·E·R·16

The Preservation of the Olympic Heritage

> For too long the world has failed to recognize that the Olympic Games and the Olympic Movement are about fine athletics and fine art.
>
> Avery Brundage, *former IOC president*

In 1928, enjoying his retirement as much as he could, the always unsettled Pierre de Coubertin was unable to attend the Summer Olympic Games in Amsterdam, contenting himself with reading the official reports of several participating nations. He was displeased with what was missing from the *Official Report* of the British Olympic Association (BOA). Only technical, business, and athletic matters appeared in the report, he noted with distress. Where were the cultural, artistic, musical, and literary aspects of the Games? "I find no mention of them in the report; they are everything to the Olympic Movement."[1] Following the nightmare of World War I, Coubertin wrote to the president of Stanford University, Ray Lyman Wilbur, asking for funds to strengthen the new Institut Olympique de Lausanne, to enrich the 1920

Olympic Games with Greek-like art, learning, books, and pamphlets, and to build an Olympic library and museum. Berry I. Wheeler wrote President Wilbur on 18 January 1919, reminding him that young Coubertin had visited Stanford in the 19th century and had established the Carnot-Joffre literary prize. "I have had long experience with Pierre de Coubertin," wrote Wheeler, "and I regard him as an idealistic right sort."[2] A few years earlier, in spring 1906 at the Paris Comédie-Français, the baron organized and carried out an elaborate "Arts et Lettres" conference to aid the inculcation of all forms of culture into the Olympic Games, "et, un général, s'associer à la pratique des sports pour en bénéficier et les ennoblir."[3] Coubertin failed in this his favorite project and had failed in other endeavors, not because the concepts were wrong, but because his aim was often too high. His passion for the marriage of sport and art manifested itself in the Olympic Games art competition, which languished in relative obscurity from 1912 through 1948.[4] Two modern IOC presidents followed Coubertin's lead in perceiving sport and art as distinctly different domains, but still related. Avery Brundage (1887-1975) collected art treasures (and almost everything else), whereas Juan Antonio Samaranch accumulated several fortunes of art works, most of which are housed in Olympic museums.

The Austrian educator and Olympic specialist, Herman Andreas, wrote me of his concern about the negative public perception of the Olympic Games. People have not been told of the encompassing Coubertin vision, which is still part of the Movement, he said. "We must educate vast numbers that the Olympic Games includes elite athletics, politics, commerce, but also a great deal more." Dr. Andreas continued, "Olympic philosophy and education deals with universal fair play, cultural pluralism, dynamic democracy, art, music, dance, as well as elite sport."[5] Brundage did his part, and Samaranch contributed even more toward making Andreas's (and Coubertin's) dream a reality. Their collective hope is that millions of people will find excitement and revelation in Olympic art to no lesser degree than they do in an Olympic Games final heat.

Olympic Doyens of Art: Brundage and Samaranch

Poor-born Brundage grew up to become a millionaire before he was 35 years old. His eventful trip to Stockholm in 1912 brought no medals, but his post-Olympic "barnstorming" trip to Russia fired within him a love of fine art objects. Until his death in 1975, he constantly refined and enhanced his collection of precious objets d'art, discarding almost nothing. In his will, Brundage left to the University of Illinois an enormous cache of 300 crates filled with letters and reports plus several score of oversized scrapbooks jammed with 50 years of Olympic newspaper clippings. Close to the university archives, which house this collection, are the Brundage books and Brundage Museum.

His magnificent Oriental art collection, estimated in 1959 to be worth $35 million, had already been donated to the new Brundage wing of San Francisco's M.D. de Young Memorial Museum. It's a nearly priceless treasure, "a really excellent collection," said famous Orientalist Lawrence Hickman.[6] Brundage had pulled it all together from museums, galleries, warehouses, and his homes in Chicago and Santa Barbara. "Collecting is a disease from which you never quite recover," he once said, fondling some of his 3,000 exquisitely carved ivory Japanese *netsuke*.[7] Some were less perfect than machine-made netsukes, Brundage once told author Robert Shaplen, who wrote that it was, of course, an amateur carving of exquisite beauty that Brundage clutched in his large hand that day.[8] Brundage's lifelong espousal of absolutely pure amateur sport and pursuit of matchless works of art were equally precious to him. One art expert who recognized his passion said, "Few know more about Oriental art than Mr. Brundage."[9] His two interests were "poles apart: Asian art and the Olympic Games," said another interviewer.[10] Not so to Brundage, for his brand of athletics, as well as the original netsuke hand-carved ivories, was personal, amateur, and created with absolutely no profit motive in mind.

"For too long the world has failed to recognize that the Olympic Games and the Olympic Movement are about fine athletics and about fine art," President Brundage told a newspaper reporter in 1966.[11] Brundage was a strange man, to be sure. Early in his undergraduate studies in structural engineering and amidst the demands of his varsity athletic career (football and track), he took courses in Oriental art and philosophy. A lifetime later, one filled with extraordinary high and low points,[12] Brundage's art treasures lay safe in a San Francisco museum—nearly 3,000 precious objects, religious symbols, insignia of rank, ceremonial weapons, pendants, ornaments, figurines, miniatures, containers from the Neolithic period to modern times, pillows, ceramics, carved jade pieces, vases, and paintings. "The continuing generosity of Mr. Avery Brundage," we are told, "is achieving wonders even today when the acquisition of important Oriental objet d'art has become a formidable task."[13] Just such a "formidable task," at least for a sportsman, was left for another Olympic committee president, Juan Antonio Samaranch.

The privileged life, never knowing poverty, is not necessarily one in which appreciation for the arts flourish. Somehow, somewhere in Samaranch's affluent background, he found that a well-focused personal commitment to the work ethic brought him even greater joy than being surrounded by fine things and art objects. The intense Spaniard was the very model of the German saying, "Arbeit Macht Glücklich"—Work makes you happy. Thus, Samaranch's family and his dual passions for sport and art dominated his life, especially following his inauguration as IOC president. On the 67th anniversary of Coubertin's residency in Lausanne, the city and the IOC, led by Samaranch, celebrated the first Olympic Week. Films, speeches, poster exhibitions, erudite lectures, museum displays of sport antiquity, and the awarding of medals, trophies, and special presentations of the Olympic Order marked the February 1982 occasion. No one was more pleased than the president for, as he said, this form of Olympic culture represents "the ideal reflection of an epoch, of a civilization, of an idea."[14] And so, for the next decade, as a much needed enriching intellectual and cultural surcease from hard work, Samaranch threw himself into a hundred and then another hundred excursions into the familiar world of art, music, and *haute culture*. Paintings, icons, sculptures, shelves full of leather-bound volumes, scores of gold and silver gifts, and even drawings by Picasso and Dali—"paintings that are too expensive for me"[15]—were all transferred from President Samaranch's office and hotel suite in the *Palace* to the Ville Olympique, on the shore of Lake Geneva and 2 kilometers from the Château de Vidy. In 5 years from its opening in 1986, this Olympic House is filling rapidly with treasures from every corner of the globe. Mr. Samaranch has an office in the handsome 18th-century building. (I have no idea how often he visits it, but knowing something of his disposition, I suspect he would like to be there frequently.) Somewhat in vain, but always unflaggingly, Samaranch's 12-year effort to show in dramatic fashion that the Olympic Games are cultural "happenings" as well as grand sporting championships is a tribute to his persistence as well as to his personal taste. I suspect that he will continue in this vein.

Olympic Games Ceremonies and the Cultural Olympics

At the Closing Ceremony of the Games of the XVIth Olympiad, on Saturday, 8 December 1956, the 103,000 spectators packed into the Melbourne Cricket Ground were surprised to see the athletes enter the stadium as they wished, with whom they wished, "in a single cavalcade . . . symbolizing the spirit of international friendship." The idea was suggested to President Brundage by a 17-year-old Chinese boy whose signature was undecipherable but whose request was clear—internationalism is superior to nationalism.[16] The ultra-conservative Brundage, for his entire life a prisoner of tradition, surprised many by accepting the youngster's suggestion and allowing the Olympic Closing Ceremony tradition to be altered. It was revealed several days later that the IOC had been recommended for the Nobel Peace Prize.[17]

The Opening Ceremonies of each of the 36 winter and summer spectacles have been visually attractive, impressive, symbolic, and essentially serious. One might take issue with this, but what is irrefutable is the escalating length and elaborateness of this afternoon-long ceremony. There can be no Olympic Games without Opening and Closing Ceremonies: It says so on page 33 of Olympic Charter '90. What this booklet does *not* say is that the Olympic Games are unthinkable without these two richly-tapestried, bookend events—in the opinion of the Olympic hierarchy. My friend Geoffrey Dyson (1914-1981) strongly disagreed and told me once, on the eve of the 1972 Olympic Games,

> the Opening Ceremonies are fawning, fake, pseudo pomp-and-circumstance. Tell me, John, exactly when will the Opening Ceremonies take place so that I can be sure *not* to be there.[18]

This, from one of Britain's greatest athletic coaches, a man who loved almost everything about the Games and the Movement.[19]

Big is the name for the Olympic Games Opening Ceremonies, and millions of dollars were spent on them by Canada's OCO and Seoul's SLOOC in 1988. Calgary, Alberta, on 13 February 1988, was very special, "joy-filled . . . on a high note," as their vision of the Winter Opening Ceremonies began. Several hours later, following pronouncements, historic multimedia displays, the Stampede Show Band, Albertan Indian peoples on horseback, colorful, inflated dinosaur balloons, the parade of athletes from 57 nations, the Torch ceremonies, athletes' oaths, churchbells, sirens, came another hour of fantasmagoria.[20] But if Calgary was big, then Seoul was enormous, stupendous, a national enterprise of a once oppressed people that Christopher Brasher of the *London Sunday Observer* called "a pageant which reflects their dignity and their desire to live in peace and harmony."[21] Bigger is not necessarily better, though, and it is my hope that "folks" in Albertville and Barcelona unwrap to the world opening ceremonies that are exquisite—and smaller.

The Cultural Olympics in Calgary ran 5 weeks, involved 2,200 artists from 18 different art disciplines in more than 600 performances and exhibitions, and cost nearly $13 million, $3 million of which went for the Native People's Museum and its programs. Performing groups included the Alberta Ballet Company, National Ballet of Canada, the Joffrey Ballet, the Toronto Symphony, Québec Esprít Orchestra, Juilliard String Quartet, Calgary Philharmonic Orchestra, National Arts Center Orchestra; plus visual arts (including a week of films, posters, stamps, billboards, and photography) crafts, a book fair, and "on February 19, a sell-out National Poetry final."[22]

Calgary was big; Seoul was far bigger, and its culture and arts festival was so huge that a listing of the 6-week, SLOOC, blockbuster events filled a 50-page booklet, the *Seoul Olympic Arts Festival 1988*, 17 August to 5 October. The Seoul Metropolitan Opera performed as did the UNESCO International Theatre, the Comédie Français of Paris, and Kabuki dancers from Japan. Czechoslovakia's Crazy Mimes Theatre, the European Master Orchestra, national choruses from USA, West Germany, Canada, Brazil, and Japan, and 10 Korean groups devoted themselves to entertainment. Greece's magnificant chanteuse Nana Mouskouri led singers from America, France, Italy, England, Germany, Hungary, and Japan. Folk artists from two dozen countries joined Korean artists of every single specialization, including "calligraphic renditions of ideographics as well as ink paintings."[23]

The full cultural and educational program for the double 1992 Olympics has been outlined by the organizers, and Norway's new minister of culture, Åse Kleveland, discussed the Lillehammer arts program of 1994.[24] Well-funded by their respective governments, by international businesses, and by the IOC, Olympic aficionados will be able to enjoy some of the world's best art, music, dance, and cultural amenities. The Baron de Coubertin created the whole idea, and he would enjoy these cultural Olympics of the 1990s, provided he could look above and through the perpetually surrounding vulgarities.

A Plethora of Olympian Decorations and Recognitions

It is impossible that any organization or government could make more awards than does the International Olympic Committee and its far-flung affiliates. The overwhelming majority of people involved are volunteers and by definition serve without salary. Occasional reinforcement with a precious and tasteful gift presented by Samaranch himself is frequently nothing short of memorable for hundreds of pride-filled recipients. From Day One of his presidency, Samaranch believed in the need for and binding power of formal recognition of work well done, and in strengthening it with an Olympic "glue"—of a fine piece of art, a plaque, scroll, trophy, prize, cup, or gold, silver, or bronze "order."

And in turn, Mr. Samaranch, since 1980, has accepted hundreds of gifts from every corner, from some extremely interesting and admiring people, and from grateful organizations, sporting and governmental. From 1981 through 1987, there is hardly an issue of the *Olympic Review* in which one or two pages are not devoted to a description and photograph of formal gift exchanges. In December 1987 the prestigious (and all the awards are "prestigious") Olympic Order was presented to International Canoeing Federation president Sergio Orsi and to educator-journalist Marcel Pasche, for their lifelong professional skills and devotion to the Olympic cause. At the same meeting, IOC member Kéba Mbaye proudly presented his son Hrahima, who in turn donated a statue, *Olympafrica,* to his host.[25]

That scene or something similar was repeated time and again in the next 3 years. *L'Equipe* of Paris was for 40 years the best sport newspaper in the world, and on 25 January 1988, "visibly moved, the founder . . . of the newspaper, Mr. Jacques Goddet, received the award (the Olympic Cup) from the hands of the IOC president."[26] Wolf Lyberg was awarded the Olympic Order for 50 years of voluntary work for the Swedish and the International Olympic committees. So was Coca-Cola's chairman, Roberto C. Goizuela, for his company's 60 years of patronage. In 1988 Samaranch was in Prague for the Second Sport-For-All Congress and to receive another academic degree, Doctor Honoris Causa from Prague University for "his extraordinary personal contribution." That summer of '88, the head of the Spanish government, Felipe Gonzáles, presented Samaranch a sport medal for having served his country so admirably. A few weeks later, Samaranch was in London to award Katarina Witt the Olympic Order and to participate in an award ceremony recognizing Lord Luke's 60 years of service to the British Olympic Association. Gift-giving was in the air, and no sooner had Samaranch presented longtime IOC member, H.S.H. Prince Ranier of Monaco with the Gold Olympic Order than the prince donated to the IOC Museum a sculpture titled *The Baton of Friendship.*[27]

The Olympic Cup was awarded by the IOC in 1988 "to the whole population of Australia on its 200th anniversary" and individual Olympic Orders were given to 17 deserving supporters of the Movement. In Seoul at the IOC's 94th Session, President Samaranch awarded posthumous Olympic Orders to Turkey's Turgot Atakol and Canada's Roger Rousseau, and an additional 14 men and women (including my dear American friend and founder of the U.S. Olympic Academy, Harold Friermood). The Grand Duke of Luxembourg reciprocated with a gift to Samaranch "for your accomplishments in the past two Olympiads." Last, at least in 1988, three Koreans were awarded Olympic Orders for work well done, and in return, Wan-Kyo Cho, president of Seoul National University, crowned Samaranch with still another honorary doctorate, this one in political science.[28]

It was the same through 1989 and 1990; the IOC (in the person of President Samaranch) was never too busy to confer an award or to receive a gift. And there were scores of gifts, such as Jordan's highest decoration—the Grand Sash of the Jordanian Order of Volunteers of Istiqual. Awards included the IOC's Sports Medicine trophy, the Olympic Cup for Milan's *Gazette Dello Sport*, the Simon Bolivar Order to IOC executive board member, Flor Isava Fonseca, the awarding of the Golden Podium trophy, and more Olympic Orders presented by the peripatetic Samaranch at the Romanian Olympic Committee's 75th birthday.[29] And, notably, after receiving two more honorary doctorates in Quebec City and Tokyo, Samaranch received the "Seoul Peace Prize and a cash award of $300,000" from the Korean government, and then the First Order of the Sacred Treasure from the Japanese government. He kept both prizes but donated the money to the new Olympic Museum in Lausanne.[30] It does not matter, for all of President Samaranch's awards will probably eventually reside in the new facility.

The Special World of Olympic Art Awards

It would be crass to attempt an accurate cash evaluation of the IOC's art treasures. The Olympic Villa in Ouchy by Lake Geneva is a veritable trove of donated and commissioned works. The grounds around Olympic House at Vidy, the Olympic Park, and the Olympic Museum are filled with works of art, not to mention the world's largest collection of Olympic books. The Olympic Movement, Samaranch has said, "endeavours, in spite of difficulties, to be a promoter of culture."[31] One of Samaranch's cultural passions is stamp collecting, and the IOC's official organ, the *Olympic Review* is replete with such articles as "Pointillist Stamps"; "Stamp Support for Sport"; "Philately"; "Olymphilex"; "Sportphilex '90"; "Pre-Olympic Stamp Issue";[32] and the most important item, "Samaranch Donates His Nearly Priceless Stamp Collection to the Olympic Museum." His collection of 45 years—72 albums, 5,076 pages, 62,000 stamps with 15,200 blocks of four—belongs to posterity. So it should be, he said:

> Today I am giving something I love very much. These 9 years in Lausanne have been the happiest times of my life. I hope that this gift will serve as an example to many others.[33]

Among the myriad of art objects in the IOC's possession are these:

From Moscow to Los Angeles by Annick de Fornel

Olympic Symbol by Jordi Alumà

Hurdlers by Dero

A Winter Scene with Skaters and Bird Traps by Jacob Gummer

Goddesses and Athletes by Josep Clará

Floating in Marble by Joan Miró

The Seabird, the Artist, and the Skater by Roger Ames[34]

Olympic Suite by Rosa Serra

The American Athletes by Auguste Rodin

El Paseo de Colón by Pablo Picasso[35]

I cannot refrain from mentioning my own favorites, paintings by LeRoy Neiman and Hans Erni, an American and a Swiss. Their paintings would be accepted by any of the world's museums of modern art. Neiman's themes are frequently sport, "the limits of human capacities," and his mediums are painting, sculpture, book design and illustration, etching, lithographs, monotypes, and computer graphics.[36] Hans Erni's breathtaking, slashingly color-filled paintings of human figures and athletes-in-action are also favorites of Samaranch and his administrative colleagues. A new book, *Hans Erni Olympart*, by the Swiss IOC member, Raymond Gafner, is a hymn of praise to the artist as well as a statement of the sport and art symbiosis.[37]

Olympic Museums, Centers, and Libraries

For generations, the preservation of Olympic documents was in the hands of amateurs and well-meaning preservationists. That changed in the 1990s, and hundreds, possibly thousands of scholars, have taken advantage of the historical materials in the Lausanne, Switzerland, repositories. It is not that way everywhere in the Olympic world of historical scholarship.

An increasing number of African countries have small museums, centers, and libraries that celebrate the universality of the Olympic Movement and display their own athletes' participation in the Olympic Games since liberation in the 1960s. They join similar institutions all around the world, but the Château de Vidy does not have the exact number. Olympic headquarters is aware of the London, Canada-based Centre for Olympic Studies, on the campus of Western Ontario University, only because in February 1991, its director, Robert K. Barney, traveled to Switzerland to *inform* them of the Centre's existence. Helsinki, Finland and Oslo, Norway have sport and Olympic museums. The Olympic library and national academy in Budapest is a gem, as is Nadia Lekarska's 50-year collection of Olympic memorabilia in Sofia. Frankfurt, Germany has an invaluable NOC library and archives of Olympic Games history, and yet it pales in comparison to Frau Liselott Diem's library, named after her husband. The Carl Diem Institute is an Olympic archive of the highest order. The Wingate Institute at Natanya, Israel has a huge library with several hundred volumes on the Olympic Games.

A visit to Colorado Springs and the United States Olympic headquarters and training center can be stimulating, because 400 to 500 athletes occupy the facility on any given day. The library is impressive, but more important to me are the huge subterranean archives of the USOC, lovingly and skillfully collated by Mr. C. Robert Paul. In Paris, Dr. Jean Durry has gathered together these past 25 years in his Musée du Sport an attractive Olympic Games art and literature collection, not all of it French. The British Olympic Association Library and Archives in London preserves the 100-year history of the Olympics, revealing among many things, how indifferent and cool the English were to "joining" the Olympic Movement in its first decade, 1894 to 1903. Judge Conrado Durántez has collected Olympic documents for more than 30 years and his Olympic Academy in Madrid is a model. My own personal Olympic library of 700 books serves me well but is inadequate for some kinds of research, compelling me to travel to the Olympic museums and libraries in Athens and Olympia, Greece, and Lausanne, Switzerland. The IOC museum, library, and archives are unrivaled, and all serious scholars of the Olympic Movement must go there to study. I did just that in 1959 and 1960, when I wrote my doctoral dissertation on Pierre de Coubertin, and have returned to Lausanne a baker's-dozen times in the past 30 years.

The new Olympic Museum will be ready in 1994,[38] just in time to celebrate the 100th year of existence of the IOC. The city of Paris, the French National Olympic Committee, and the IOC have completed plans for an international celebration, a *Congrès Du Centenaire*, 23 to 26 June 1994. The entire Olympic Tripartite will be there for *Le XIIᵉ Congrès Olympique*, the whole historic meeting in the able hands of Nelson Paillou.[39] Playing a vital role at the centennial gathering will be the grandnephew of Pierre de Coubertin, Monsieur Geoffroy de Navacelle, Président du Comité International Pierre de Coubertin, an organization of several score members around the globe dedicated to "make known, make understood the significant ideas of Pierre de Coubertin's work in its immense diversity."[40] Navacelle's summer home, the ancestral home of the Coubertin family in Mirville, Normandy, contains a treasure of art and literature. The potpourri of Olympic art and archives is literally everywhere in the world and has yet to be catalogued.

On 1 March 1990, a wet evening in Lausanne, citizens of that lovely city must have wondered why so many of its distinguished members were headed for the Fondation De L'Hermitage. Several hundred guests enjoyed the marvelous, stunning collection of Greek athletic art, "Le Corps et L'Esprit." This collaboration of the modern Hellenes and the Swiss occupied the entire Lausanne mansion and was a perfect way to celebrate both Greek antique glory and the 75th birthday of the International Olympic Committee.[41]

One of the more specialized units of the IOC, the Court of Arbitration, was created in 1983 "to settle disputes among athletes" and answer any of their legal questions. IOC member Judge Kéba Mbaye is director. The court has a 15-page brochure, *Court of Arbitration for Sport* (1985). The IOC pays the bills, but the members of the court "are completely independent from the IOC in the exercise of their duties."[42]

The Olympic octopus is much larger and more complicated than what one might glean from reading this chapter. All of this, and more, is the organization's way of striving "to see the diverse realities of the Olympic Movement better and more accurately reflected."[43]

Something must come of all these efforts. If the IOC's good fortune continues, then there will be money available for these Olympic auxiliary enterprises. Scholarly and public interest in the Olympic Games and all that touches them is 10 times greater in the 1990s than it was at midcentury. All of it should be collated into a booklet on "Olympic Museums, Collections, Libraries, Centers, Art, and Cultural Collections." There is a need. How many know that the good people in Shropshire, England (in collaboration with the British Olympic Association) have created a fine museum, memorializing the names of Dr. William Penny Brooks, and their 1890 visitor, the 27-year-old Baron de Coubertin? Every NOC and all sport federations should be sent a questionnaire (by the IOC) asking for details of all extant scholarly, historic, literary, and artistic memorabilia in their possession. These same NOCs and federations should be encouraged to enrich their holdings of Olympic art and historic materials. Collectors of Olympic materials around the world should be invited to donate some or all of their artifacts to the Olympic Museum and Library.[44] There are 200,000 former Olympians out there who should all be encouraged to share their medals, trophies, books, diaries, photo albums, and mementos with the appropriate sporting or Olympic association. They, their sports, their NOCs, their countries, and the world Olympic community would be richer for such thoughtfulness and generosity.[45]

Notes

1. Coubertin, letter to the BOA, undated, but "received by the BOA in 1930." Library of Institut Fur Sportgeschichte, Koln, Germany; reproduced in author's essay, "Coubertin's Overarching Views of Ten Olympic Games 1896-1936," *Olympic Message, 15*, September 1986, 64-65.

2. Coubertin's letter and that of Wheeler are in the Stanford University Archives, *President Wilbur Papers*, box 27, folder 4.

3. Coubertin, quoted in Geoffroy de Navacelle, *Pierre de Coubertin. sa vie par l'image* (Zurich: Weidmann, 1979), 35.

4. Andrea Peterson, "The Olympic Art Competitions From 1912 to 1948," *Proceedings HISPA XI Congress 1985*, 239-241.

5. Herman Andreas, letter to author, 16 January 1990.

6. "Showplace for Treasure," *Newsweek*, 10 August 1959, 59.

7. Ibid.

8. Robert Shaplen, "Amateur Avery Brundage," *New Yorker, 36*, 23 July 1960, 71.

9. Allene Talney, "The Avery Brundage Collection," *Vogue, 136*, 15 September 1960, 161.

10. Edith Weigle, "The Man Who Has Everything," *Chicago Tribune*, 30 July 1961, Magazine section, 21.

11. Brundage, quoted in Harry J. Seldis, "Avery Brundage: Olympian Patron of Art," *Los Angeles Times*, 11 September 1966, West Magazine section, 52, 54.

12. In an enviable dispassionate, even-handed manner, historian Allen Guttmann wrote the definitive biography to date, *The Games Must Go On: Avery Brundage and the Olympic Movement* (New York: Columbia University Press, 1984).

13. René-Yvon Lefebvre d'Argencé, *Chinese Ceramics in the Avery Brundage Collection* (San Francisco: The de Young Museum Society, 1967), and *d'Argencé's Chinese Jades in the Avery Brundage Collection* (San Francisco: The de Young Museum Society, 1972).

14. Samaranch, on 22 February 1982, at the celebration of "Lausanne, Ville Olympique;" *Olympic Message, 2*, September 1982, 14.

15. Samaranch, in Shirley's interview, *Los Angeles Times*, 2 February 1983, part 3, 10.

16. Jesse Abramson, "Olympic Games End . . . ," *New York Herald Tribune*, 9 December 1956, section 3, 3. For me, Abramson was the greatest descriptive, narrative sport journalist in American history. Also Harold O. Zimman, *Amateur Athlete, 28*, January 1957, 7. The original letter has found its proper place in the Melbourne Olympic Museum.

17. Andre Laguerre, "Down a Road Called Liberty," *Sports Illustrated, 5*, 17 December 1956, 19.

18. Dyson, conversation with author, inside the Olympic Village, Munich, Germany, 25 August 1972.

19. Dyson lectured all over the world, including the International Olympic Academy in 1962 and 1979, convinced to the end that when done right, "sport can be an active and civilizing force in the world." Born penniless in South London and indifferently educated, he became one of the world's greatest coaches. His obituary in the *London Times*, 6 February

1981, 16, was a quarter-page in length and began, "Mr. Geoffrey Dyson, OBE, pioneer in athletics coaching techniques. . ."

20. Michael Janofsky's "An Emotional Opening in Calgary" is typical of essays describing the ceremony. *New York Times*, 14 February 1988, sec. 5, 1-2.

21. Chris Brasher, "Glory in the Land of Morning Calm," *London Sunday Observer*, 18 September 1988, 20.

22. *Official Report: XVth Olympic Winter Games* (Calgary: OCO, 1988), 281-283; also Rosaleen Gray, "Olympic Arts Festival," *Olympic Message, 19*, December 1987, 38-44.

23. *Seoul Olympic Arts Festival 1988* (Seoul: SLOOC, 1988), n.p.

24. "The Olympic Arts Festival," *Magazine of the Organizing Committee for the XVIth Olympic Winter Games 1992*, COJO, October 1990), 48; also "Actions Carried Out by the COJO"; also "Sport, Échange, Culture," *Jeunesse Du Monde En Savoie 1992*, COJO, 1990; also "Start of Barcelona's Cultural Olympiad," *Olympic Review, 263-264*, September-October 1989, 462; and *Olimpída Cultural Barcelona '92* (10-page pamphlet). Norway's beginning effort is discussed in *Newsflash 3*, December 1990, 8-9. The French, by contrast, have their Albertville cultural celebration fully in place. See Olivier Schmitt's essay in *Magazine of the Organizing Committee of the XVIth Olympic Winter Games of Albertville and Savoie*, February 1991, 54-55.

25. *Olympic Review, 243-244*, January 1988, 22.

26. *Olympic Review, 246*, April 1988, 152.

27. For more information see *Olympic Review*, volumes 247-251.

28. See Olympic Review; volumes 245, 253, 254.

29. See Olympic Review; volumes 274 and 278.

30. *Korea Herald*, 25 September 1990, 7; *Olympic Review, 277*, November 1990, 480-488; *Japan Times*, 15 September 1990, 18.

31. Juan Antonio Samaranch, "Sport, Culture, and the Arts," *Olympic Message, 26*, April 1990, 13.

32. See Olympic Review; volumes 245 through 278.

33. Samaranch donated his stamp collection on 5 December 1989; *Olympic Review, 267*, January 1990, 11. For a history of Olympic stamps, see J.M. Vidal, *Barcelona Olimpica, III* (15), 1990, 70-71.

34. Ames's beautiful figures seem "frozen in the solitude of their transparency;" *Olympic Review, 254*, December 1988, 686-687.

35. There are many more pictures and descriptions of art objects given to the IOC in *Olympic Review*, December 1980 through August 1990.

36. Vladimir Markov, *Olympic Review, 260*, June 1989, 271-274.

37. "Hans Erni's New Olympic Feat," *Olympic Review, 278,* December 1990, 550-551.

38. Mr. Samaranch's comments in *Olympic Review, 263-264,* September-October 1989, 453. Details on the new museum are found in *Olympic Review, 277,* November 1990, 502.

39. Nelson Paillou, "Congrès Du Centenaire," *Olympic Magazine Tribune ACNO, 1,* May 1990, 55-56; also "The IOC Centenary Paris 1994," *Sport Europe. AENOC Official Magazine, 3,* 1990, 46-49.

40. Brochure, Pierre de Coubertin International Committee.

41. *Le Corps et L'Esprit* (Lausanne: Fondation De L'Hermitage, 1990). *L'Oeil. L'Art Sous Toutes Ses Formes* (Lausanne: Revue D'Art Mansuelle), No. 414, March 1990. "Mind and Body," *Olympic Review, 266,* December 1989, 564-565; François Daulte, "Le Corps et L'Esprit," *Olympic Message, 26,* April 1990, 15; "Mind and Body," *Olympic Review, 270,* April 1990, 185-187.

42. See a description of the court in *Olympic Review, 277,* November 1990, 503; *Court of Arbitration for Sport,* 1985, p. 3; Gilbert Schwaar, "Report on the Court of Arbitration for Sport," *Olympic Review, 259,* May 1989, 202.

43. Samaranch's 29 August 1989 address, *Olympic Review, 263-264,* September-October 1989, 434.

44. My own will directs that my collection of 700 books on the Olympic Games and the Olympic Movement is to be placed in the Lausanne library. In 1987, the IOC sent a letter encouraging all NOCs to set up their own Olympic and sports museums. Benin, in Africa, immediately opened such a center on 12 March 1988. I have no data on the response elsewhere; *Olympic Review, 247,* June 1988, 239.

45. At the time of publication, Anita DeFrantz pointed out that in addition to the Avery Brundage collection mentioned on page 184, the Amateur Athletic Foundation of Los Angeles' Paul Ziffren Sports Resource Center also houses one of the best Olympic library collections in the United States. The AAF's collection includes thousands of Olympic publications, including every official report since 1896; hundreds of video volumes; 5,000 photographs; dozens of oral histories; dozens of original posters; medals and other artifacts; a microfilm version of the Brundage Collection; and thousands of personal papers.

C·H·A·P·T·E·R·17

The Centennial Year 1996

Coalition and arbitration have been Atlanta traditions for several generations. [In] this island of civility where whites and blacks have learned to get along, a great Olympic Games might come of it.

Bert Roughton, Jr., *journalist, Atlanta Constitution*

The Hellenic Olympic Committee, Greece's 1996 Olympic Organizing Committee, most of the people, and the country's postal service were so sure that they would be awarded the Olympic Games of 1996 that, between 6 May 1988 and 13 July 1990, 10 stamps were issued anticipating the 100th anniversary celebration in Athens.[1] In September 1990, the IOC chose not to go to Greece and startled many with its decision for Atlanta. Olympic shock waves were felt throughout that special world, no less than in Greece. In far away London, one despondent letter to the *Times*'s editor decried the injustice of money winning so clearly "over any form of sincerity."[2] Even in the winning city, a Greek-American attorney could not avoid sarcasm when asked if Atlanta was the right city for the '96 Games. "Imagine," he said, "an international organization honoring the birthday of Martin Luther

King, Jr., but instead of Atlanta as the site for the celebration, they decided to hold it in Oslo, Norway."[3]

Athens and Greece had and have so very much "magic" going for them that it is no wonder their organizing committee of the bid to host the 1996 Olympic Games got swept away with some of their own rhetoric. No city is more historic, none more beautiful than Athens. The weather is warm and, for many, idyllic. Several hours' drive to the south is the mother site of western sport, Olympia, and location of the ancient Olympic Games. And Athens today has some of Europe's finest modern stadia. Understandably not dwelling on a half-dozen formidable handicaps to holding a 1996 Games in that city, several Greek spokesmen went too far in trumpeting their ancient greatness. Just before his selection for IOC membership, Lambis Nicolaou, leader of the Hellenic Olympic Committee, announced with pride that "Greece believes that she has every right to claim the honor of staging the Games of 1996." That same year (1986), Prime Minister Andreas Papandreou spoke to all the world, but indirectly to the IOC: "I believe that Greece is entitled to have this honor." A Greek journalist, speaking for most of his fellows, said, "Everywhere it is recognized that the Greek candidature has had precedence over all the others." Tzannis Tzannetakis, deputy prime minister and culture minister, reminded all of a well-known history—Greece had hosted the first modern Olympic Games, so "now, we are morally and historically entitled to stage them again."[4] It was a mesmeric meld of contemporary national pride, justifiable confidence in their sporting facilities, euphoria of past glories, and a touch of arrogance.

The Greeks are an emotional people, and so was their organizing committee. Far less so were the southern lawyers and business people from Atlanta. Their leader, William "Billy" Porter Payne, as early as June 1990, admitted, "Very simply, there was absolutely and unequivocally no genius involved in our effort"[5]—just monumental hard work, graciousness, modesty, and the coordination of 10,000 details. Hardly stalling the blizzard of essays written on 19 and 20 September 1990, congratulating Atlanta for its "glorious Olympic feat," were European murmurings such as the Bonn, Germany *Die Welt*: "Atlanta's victory assures that an insane Coca-Cola Olympic Games will become a reality."[6] Such unrestrained bitterness was common for weeks following the IOC vote. There were equal numbers of essays and articles that stated categorically that in every single way that mattered, except historically and sentimentally, the American city was superior to Athens. Straddling both the forward look of the Atlanta organizers and the nearly perpetual backward gaze of the Greeks to past glories was F.D. Vardamis, the spouse of a former member of the diplomatic staff of the American Embassy in Athens, who wrote, "Savor the Olympic ideal, Atlanta—my head is with you, but my heart was for Athens."[7] I share the sentiment of the *Washington Post*'s Tom Boswell that "Atlanta's enthusiasm was as craftily orchestrated as it was genuine."[8] *Le Figaro* wrote that in everything technical and financial, Atlanta is superior to Athens, and, the editorial continued, the American city has sufficient savoir faire to deserve the victory.[9] John Powers of the *Boston Globe* was ambiguous regarding his personal feelings but accurate in writing that Atlanta was chosen "because the Lords of the Rings [IOC] wanted to look ahead to the 21st century instead of back at the 19th."[10]

Atlanta Rallies in Clearing Stumbling Blocks

Following Atlanta's immediate "explosion of exuberance and joy" and weeks of euphoria, the leadership set about the grim task of looking for $600 million to build stadia, an Olympic Village, a natatorium, a velodrome, and other necessary, extremely expensive infrastructure. A hundred Atlantan special-interest groups descended on Billy Payne, asking for and sometimes demanding "a piece of the pie"—monies that were nonexistent. Payne tried to keep calm and revealed "the plan":

> Obey the IOC instructions, but never, never, never become intimidated by the process. Whatever happens along the way, we will remain Atlantans, Georgians, and Americans." Interviewer Steve Woodward concluded that for Billy Payne and his committee, "gently cultivating friendships became pivotal.[11]

Writing from the *Atlanta Constitution*'s city desk, Bert Roughton, Jr., was assigned on a near-permanent basis to cover the 1996 Olympic Games. The event was of historic importance to nearly everyone, so Roughton accompanied Billy Payne to Lausanne and to an IOC executive board meeting in Lillehammer, Norway, in December 1990. (His articles appeared in the Metro section of the *Constitution* from September 1990 through March 1991.) Fierce opposition from the black community in Summer Hill centered on Billy Payne's statement that all the money had to be spent on Olympic Games preparation and not on urban redevelopment. His words fell on deaf ears; one lady even shouted, "We don't want no Olympic stadium in our backyard." In downtown Atlanta, Mayor Maynard Jackson marshaled his city hall forces *against* Billy Payne's Atlanta Organizing Committee (AOC), and the Governor's Office formed its own ad hoc Olympic monitoring group. All through November and December 1990, there was no progress in the organization of an IOC-approved Atlanta Committee for the Olympic Games (ACOG). Roughton's headlines were discouraging: "Will the World See Atlanta's Inner City Blight?"; "Corruption and Black Market Already a Possibility"; "Fight Vowed over '96 Stadium"; "Differences Remain Between the City and AOC"; "Activists Shout 'We Will Not Be Fooled Anymore'"; and on 10 December 1990, "Olympic Hurdles Appear Higher."[12]

These early and serious Atlanta squabbles displeased USOC and IOC officers. A single, approved committee had to be in place by 18 March, and shortly thereafter, the grand-design plan by the ACOG had to be submitted to the IOC executive board for approval.[13] Billy Payne flew to Lillehammer and discussed Atlanta's "thorny questions" with IOC moguls. Samaranch said little, as was his way, whereas Vice President Richard Pound spoke a great deal—which was his way. "We must have a committee the next time we meet," he said. All of this is old stuff, par for the course, and occurs at all Olympic Games. He went on:

> There's always this amazing dance. . . . When you've got a mega-project like this, a certain amount of this is inevitable. We're not alarmed. We must, however, deal with a single organizing committee.[14]

The clash of egos, the concern for all the people of Atlanta, and the special resolve to help the underrepresented and poor—all began to coincide (somewhat) with those committed to hosting the Olympic Games' 100th birthday celebration in 1996. Finally, on 29 January 1991, the *Atlanta Constitution*'s front page headline read, "Handshake Seals a Game Deal." Mayor Jackson's people struck an agreement with Billy Payne, who emerged as chief executive officer (CEO) of ACOG. Former USOC president and IOC executive board member, Bob Helmick, was there and appeared pleased, although the astute journalist Bert Roughton noticed that

> the glow masked the tension and uncertainty that surrounded the agreement almost until the moment it was signed. The mayor signed an agreement that vests in ACOG vast authority with practically no direct control by the city.[15]

Atlantans could not shake the concept of the Olympic Games as a "social tool," as Roughton put it in a 3 February 1991 essay. All that money can help the poor, he wrote. Another Atlanta writer noted that city folks were optimistic about the future despite an economic depression, and the reason was . . . the Olympic Games. There were poor everywhere in the city, but *Fortune* magazine 11 March 1991 chose to concentrate on a different strata of society (as they always do) and wrote that "for upper-middle managers, the world's most luxurious lifestyles are in . . . Atlanta."[16] The most perplexing problem of an Olympic host city is always the same: Who will benefit directly and significantly from the several billions of new dollars? And so it began—preparation for the world's largest nonbelligerent human gathering, the Summer Olympic Games of 1996. The ACOG staff started small—6 senior executives and 200 employees. "After Barcelona, ACOG will grow to as many as 3,000 paid staff members and more than 70,000 volunteers."[17] Very close to Games time, the staff will get smaller and smaller and eventually disappear. John Bevilaqua, a former Los Angeles Olympic Games official, called this phenomenon the *meteor complex*: "A meteor is flaming its brightest at the moment before it goes out. That's what it's like to work with an Olympics."[18]

Only in the narrow sense of size is the comparison a good one: "The Olympic Games of 1996, if they are held in Atlanta, Georgia, will be equal to 20 Super Bowls [occurring] simultaneously."[19] Despite such an ominous image, the city forged ahead and won the IOC's vote for the Centennial Celebration of the modern Olympic Games. In late January 1990, the Atlanta delegates presented to the IOC executive board their city's bid "brochure," a 15-pound, five-volume master plan for 1996. All the other cities—Athens, Toronto, Manchester, Melbourne, and Belgrade had already delivered their own versions of community greatness and Olympic Games organizational capabilities. For all of them, including Athens, these plans were visionary, idealistic, and years away from realization, if they could be realized at all. It was the IOC's job to pick the city that could most closely approach the chimerical written documents. Media, transportation, hotels, facilities, and big money are all very important, and we have them, was Billy Payne's opening remark to the 11 visiting, poker-faced, IOC jury. But Atlanta is more than that, he continued:

It's about the united people of Atlanta, rich and poor, black and white, taking the once-in-a-lifetime opportunity to truly make a difference in world peace and friendship.[20]

Purse and passion combined beautifully in Billy's presentation. If the IOC listeners were especially taken with his speech, they were not talking. After all, the final vote would not be until mid-September in Tokyo, a full 7-1/2 months away. Off came the wraps on the Atlanta grand design. Opening and Closing Ceremonies, venues for 26 Olympic events, cultural and media support systems, all of them set for the Olympic Stadium, Georgia Dome, World Congress Center, the Omni, Atlanta University, Fulton County Stadium, Natatorium, Georgia Tech Coliseum, Civic Center, Blackburn Park, Stone Mountain, canoeing on the Ocoee River, yachting in Savannah's harbor, and the biggest and best Olympic Village ever built.[21] Several billion dollars would be needed, and Payne admitted that that was a challenge still needing a solution.

The five black, leather-bound volumes, 600 pages, describe Atlanta as a very modern city with great expectations, in a region with 60 million people and rapid and easy railroad "Marta" train, bus, and plane travel to the city. Fully aware that North America already had hosted four Winter and Summer Games in 15 years, Billy Payne's people emphasized (and underscored in the huge multivolume document) the uniqueness of the American South, so different, "a region set apart" from all other areas on the continent.

"Nous voulons les Jeux—We want the Games" shouted freshly scrubbed, handsome groups of white, Asian-American, and black children to IOC members on their Atlanta inspection tours. The visitors came away loaded with literature, received very special VIP treatment, and saw numberless smiling faces . . . from the smallest child to the mayor of Atlanta and the governor of Georgia. There was plenty of "ammunition" to strengthen their claim to a piece of Olympic history. The media section of the Atlanta Olympic Bid Book was 56 pages of handsomely packaged statistics celebrating Atlanta's reputation as the media capital of the world, not unimportant with IOC pragmatists. For those IOC members of an altruistic bent, there is, William O. Johnson wrote, Atlanta's reputation as "the putative [supposed] capital of the American civil-rights movement." The city's famous black leaders, Maynard Jackson and Andrew Young, played this theme for all it was worth. And none of the other competing cities could touch Atlanta in high-tech, in airport grandeur, and in the number of luxury and first-class hotels.[22]

Technology, warmth, very big money, cultural diversity, and a "city capable of propelling the Olympic Movement toward the 21st century with fresh momentum" describe only some of Atlanta's attributes, stated another handsome brochure, *Atlanta 1996*. Like every Olympic Games organizing committee, ACOG has very big plans for its birthday celebration in 1996. One of them is the USOC-supported "First Century Project—The History of the Modern Olympics 1896-1996," a 25-volume set of books celebrating 100 years of Olympic history. The first volume was planned for June 1992, with a new volume following at intervals of 7 weeks, thus completing distribution as the Atlanta Olympic Games opens its gates to the world. Director of the $15 million enterprise is Charles Gary Allison, Hollywood motion picture producer, editor, and coordinator for World Sport Research and Publications.[23]

There seems to be no end to the projects planned by the Atlanta '96 organizers:

"Dance of Life," a reenactment of Christopher Columbus's historic voyage 500 years ago (a four-year project, 1992-1996)

Thematic festivals, 1992-1996

Pre-Olympic international yachting regatta in Savannah harbor

Laser shows at Stone Mountain

Olympic Day celebrations for all Georgia's children

Special Olympic celebrations at the family amusement park, Six Flags, White Water Theme Park, and at nearby Grand Ol' Opry, Kennedy Space Center, and "the incomparable charms of the Magic Kingdom, Epcot Center, and the Disney/MGM/Disney World."[24]

Most of these locations are in contiguous states and indicate a growing cooperation between Atlanta, GA, and exciting educational and recreational centers, all contributing to the 1996 celebration.

The monies for these projects and the $2 to $3 billion more for the "greatest Olympic Games ever," must and will be found, announced governor-elect Zell Miller in early 1991. "Failure to fund this would send the wrong signal from the state honored to host the 1996 Olympics," he warned.[25]

Payne Gears Atlanta for Celebration of Pride

The handsome but restrictive ACOG headquarters on the 35th floor of Atlanta's IBM Building was quietly busy during my day-long visit in March 1991. "As soon as we hire several key vice presidents, administrative officers, and specialists, we'll be moving to larger quarters," revealed media relations chief, Robert M. Brennan. "Billy Payne is a brilliant, creative guy, a near genius, with unvarnished motives. He and the team want to put on a very great Olympic Games in '96," said the soft-spoken Brennan. One of Payne's vice presidents, the cool and cultured Ginger T. Watkins, nearly got emotional as she spoke of the future of her city:

> We believe a successful Olympic Games can occur only by blending super high-tech specialization with the highest, purest kind of old-fashioned visionary humanism, idealism, and a singular dedication to the upliftment of humanity. And we're building the team that can do it. And our leader, Billy Payne, is perfect for the task.

Over lunch, ACOG photographic specialist and retired 59-year-old IBM executive, Norm Drews, usually not prone to hyperbole, admitted that "Billy Payne is a potential powerhouse for good in this Atlanta community." Physical education director at Emory University, Dr. Clyde Partin, echoed Drews's comment and added, "Some of our European friends were wholly misled in calling these the 'Coca-Cola Olympics.' Absolutely no one, not a single person presently on the ACOG team, is in this thing for the money." Later, at dinner, Professor Joseph Krasevec of Georgia State University revealed his sense of satisfaction that "one of ACOG's goals over the next 5 years is to educate every child in Atlanta, in Georgia, and maybe over a much larger geography in . . . what the Olympic Games are all about—historical, philosophical, and humane perceptions—in languages and images that the children will understand."[26] There it was—an impressive, synchronous chorus of ACOG voices all in agreement that Atlanta's Games celebrating the 100th anniversary of the Olympics on the eve of the 21st century would be a very great occasion—but only, they all said (in different ways), if three ingredients were present:

1. Hard work, dedication, and unabiding loyalty to Atlanta's living, and consecration to those who had gone before . . . in America's "Renaissance City"
2. The constant application of 21st-century high-tech, state-of-the-art techniques, skills, and physical structures
3. Strict adherence to the undying spirit of humanism of the Games' founder, Pierre de Coubertin

I had to discover if there was a discordant voice somewhere, so I kept my appointment with Bert Roughton, Jr., at the *Atlanta Constitution*. He was on a 6-year assignment to cover the political, social, and economic implications of these Olympian goings-on. He was cordial, insightful, and honest. He did believe, having spent a great deal of time with Billy Payne, that ACOG was devoted to putting on a great Olympic Games consecrated to the upliftment of all Atlanta's people—and in that close order of importance. The January 1991 contract between Mayor Maynard Jackson's city hall and Payne's ACOG had ended to a large degree (though not wholly) the acrimony between the two camps.

Roughton was convinced that despite being rookies at hosting an Olympic Games (but then, everyone is), the downtown city hall group and the ACOG team are so talented that this "new, powerful coalition" is already working well and should work even better. "Coalition and arbitration have been Atlanta traditions for several generations," said Roughton, and in "this island of civility where whites and blacks have learned to get along, a great Olympic Games might come of it."

A concerned journalist, Roughton looked for legal clarity regarding ACOG's status as either private or public, not an unimportant distinction in responsible journalism where access to *all* the information is essential. He concluded with several observations, which, if accommodated by the high-level leadership hired during 1991, will complete a team worthy of the city and reflective of the host nation, thanks to the IOC which gave Billy Payne and his Atlanta "Dream Team" permission to organize the 100-year Olympic Games.

> Billy Payne and all his people are 'fast learners.' A Payne-Young-Jackson coalition will be formidable. The lovely essence of Atlanta's tradition combined with its super 21st-century thrust is reflected in the ACOG dualism. The collective mind of the committee, like Payne himself, works in an evolutionary rather than visionary manner. They complete each short-term project with amazing facility and go on and on again to finish each task.[27]

The IOC jealously guards its singular responsibility of selecting future Olympic Games sites. Their collective vision of the future, imperfect as it is for them and for all of us, saw in Atlanta, Georgia, USA a greater potential for combining supertechnology with traditional, even old-fashioned civility, than in the other five cities. If there is anything that marks the IOC today, it is this hermaphroditic blend of the very old and the very new. Take, for example, one of the modern members of the IOC, who should reach her full potential in the next century, Anita DeFrantz. She is the quintessentially modern IOC person and, yet, listen to her "other side" in an official preelection visit to Atlanta:

> When you're asking an IOC member for their vote, what you're asking is for us to give you the only thing we have of value. I'm giving you my only child, and I get to come back 6 years later for Commencement.[28]

The *Economist* exaggerated when it said, "Sentiment no longer counts for much among Olympic administrators."[29] In truth, pure sentiment and rock-hard business acumen in nearly equal amounts are attributes of today's IOC. Andrew Young marched with Martin Luther King, Jr.; he was mayor of Atlanta; he served as ambassador to the United Nations and, from the beginning, was a key member of the Atlanta Committee for the Olympic Games. He vehemently denied the charge that Coca-Cola bought the 1996 Games and underscored this with the old-fashioned Southern saying, "That dog won't hunt."[30] The old but always very new scenario of devoting 6 years of individual and collective lives to organize an Olympic Games is well under way, and, short of international cataclysm, will take place in the summer of 1996, exactly 132 years after General Sherman's army burned Atlanta to the ground.

Notes

1. "Stamps Didn't Help Olympic Bid," *Linn's Stamp News*, 8 October 1990, 2.
2. Clive Cheesmom, "Money Dictates IOC Decision," letter to the editor, *London Times*, 27 September 1990, 36.
3. William B. Marianes, quoted in Bill Rankin, "Atlanta Greeks Still Carry a Torch for Athens," *Atlanta Constitution*, 30 September 1990, D6.
4. Nicolaou, in *Hellenic Olympic Committee*, February 1986, 6; Papandreou, in *90th Anniversary of the First Modern Olympic Games* (Athens: HOC, 1986); Sporides, in *Hellenic Olympic Committee*, April 1987, 28; Tzannetakis, in *Athenian*, September 1990, 7.
5. Billy Payne in *Proceedings USOC XIV 1990*. A flattering biography is Thomas Boswell's "Man Behind the Scenes," *Washington Post*, 19 September 1990, F1, F3; and Randy Harvey's rollicking Payne biography in *Los Angeles Times*, 20 September 1990, c11. Harvey got serious in one paragraph of his article from Tokyo and the IOC meeting:

   The Greeks were so rude to reporters during the news conference that the chairman of the Bid Committee, Spyros Metaxas, held another impromptu news conference outside the room later to apologize.

6. "Die Spiele 1996 finden in Atlanta statt: Der Traum eines. Verrückten wurde wahr. Drohen in den USA die Coca-Cola Spiele?" *Die Welt*, 19 September 1990, 10.
7. F.D. Vardamis, in the *Chicago Tribune*, 17 November 1990, 13.
8. Boswell, "Man Behind the Scenes," F1. Greece's minister of culture and former motion picture actress, Melina Mercouri, lamented, "Coca-Cola won over the Parthenon." Her quote in Randy Harvey's essay,

"Atlanta Selected to Host Olympic Games in 1996," *Los Angeles Times*, 19 September 1990, A16. The *Japan Times* of 20 September 1990, 22, called the "unfair Atlanta victory the Coca-Cola Olympics."

9. "Atlanta Olympique: La Puissance Américaine" *Le Figaro*, 19 September 1990, 16.

10. John Powers, "Atlanta vs. Athens: No Contest," *Boston Globe*, 23 September 1990, 50. Chris Brasher called the Greek delegation in Tokyo "arrogant and disorganized." See *London Sunday Observer*, 23 September 1990, 21. Olympic expert and *London Times* chief sports correspondent, David Miller, pointed out that Atlanta lawyers Billy Payne and Charlie Battle alone flew more miles in quest of IOC votes than all other bidding city committees combined (19 December 1990, 32).

11. Billy Payne, quoted in Steve Woodward, "Bunts and Singles," *Olympian, 17*, January 1991, 18.

12. From 20 September 1990 through 28 January 1991, a period of 121 days, over 50 articles appeared in the *Atlanta Constitution*—lead articles on page 1, in the Metro section, and editorials. Several of the more important articles are in September 30; November 6, 17, 19, 29; December 1, 5, 10, 11, 12, 17, 25, 31; January 1.

13. "USOC, Atlanta Join Forces for 1996 Plans," *Olympian, 17*, January 1991, 51.

14. Bert Roughton, Jr., "Payne in Norway Without ACOG Pact," *Atlanta Constitution*, 10 December 1990, D4. (Roughton was in Lillehammer with Payne).

15. Bert Roughton, Jr., "Atlanta Seals a Game Deal," *Atlanta Constitution*, 29 January 1991, A1, A6.

16. Shawn Tully, "Where People Live Best," *Fortune, 123*, 11 March 1991, 44-45. Roughton's comment on "Olympics as Social Tool" is in the *Atlanta Constitution*, 3 February 1991, E1. Also Henry Unger, "Poll: Atlantans Not Depressed by Recession," *Atlanta Constitution*, 15 February 1991, 1, A18.

17. Bert Roughton, Jr., "Olympic Workout: Don't Stop Till You Drop," *Atlanta Constitution*, 22 February 1991, C5.

18. John Bevilaqua's quote, ibid.

19. *Atlanta Constitution*, 20 February 1990, A1.

20. Bert Roughton, Jr., "Eager Atlanta Group Unveils Soaring Dream for Olympics," *Atlanta Constitution*, 1 February 1990, A12. Also "The Visit," *Atlanta Constitution*, 16 February 1989, D1, D9.

21. Ibid.

22. William O. Johnson, "The Push Is On," *Sports Illustrated, 73*, 27 August 1990, 43.

23. Information packets on the "First Century Project" may be obtained from Dr. Chas. G. Allison, 1300 N. Alexandria, Los Angeles, CA 90027.

24. Information brochure, *Atlanta 1996*.

25. Gov. Miller, quoted in Jeanne Cummings, "Preparing for '96 Olympics," *Atlanta Constitution*, 9 January 1991, 1.

26. Brennan, Watkins, Drews, Partin, and Krasevec, interviews with author, in Atlanta, 5-6 March 1991.

27. Bert Roughton, Jr., interview with author, Atlanta, 6 March 1991.

28. DeFrantz, quoted in Karen Rosen and Bert Roughton, Jr., "City's Bid for Games Stirs IOC Visitor," *Atlanta Constitution*, 7 April 1990, C8.

29. "Greece—Home Again for the Olympics?" *Economist, 316*, 15 September 1990, 65.

30. Andrew Young's no-nonsense colloquialism quoted in "The Olympics Go Better with Coke," *Economist, 316*, 22 September 1990, 24. Under different circumstances, Mr. Young might have said that the allegations of Coca-Cola complicity are utterly without foundation in fact.

C·H·A·P·T·E·R·18

The 21st-Century Olympic Games: Nothing Is Forever

Balance is everything to the future of the Olympic Movement. Commerce must be balanced by philanthropy, fluffy if important pageantry by every effort to get most of the world's great male and female athletes to the Olympic stadia.

John A. Lucas

Flor Isava Fonseca of the IOC's executive board agreed with the second half of this chapter title, and wrote me, "You are right, nothing, including the Olympic Games, are forever."[1] The Games, as transitory as are all other human institutions, are only worth supporting into the next century if Olympic leadership at every level accept John Locke's pronouncement that "the great business of all is virtue and wisdom." The Olympic Games of the future can become much better only if the IOC is made up of better men and women; if the 168 national Olympic committees have international and humane agendas that balance their admirable desire to send honest athletes in search of gold, silver, and bronze; if the several score sport federations moderate their natural parochialism with a touch of altruism and team spirit. No one is asking for Olympic Games in perpetuity. Rather, many of us look at these Olympic Games as an arena of intense competition,[2] one capable of being a genuinely good human experience—a Mount Everest of sport and culture. But it can only happen if these Olympic Games emerge better than those of the past. Aberrant human conduct, we are told by philosopher Morton White, is "by far . . . culturally and experientially determined";[3] therefore, the Olympic elite, in the stadia and in their administrative headquarters, can learn to build a better world for themselves during the 1990s and beyond. Good regional games evolve into strong continent-wide sport festivals, and both contribute immeasurably to global Olympic Games. But as the great journalist of the 1930s—Dorothy Thompson—said in her "Ten Articles of Faith," the human animal cannot improve only through materialistic concepts of history or by biological interpretations. "Man is Body, Mind and Spirit, with needs, desires and aspirations in all three elements of his nature."[4] These are, of course, classical values, and they need to be reborn into the 21st century. The Olympic Games, well done, can contribute to such a renaissance. We need to look backward in order to make suggestions for future change; my 40 years of doing so having emboldened me to suggest a revised Olympic agenda. By no means are these proposals a criticism of Samaranch's first 10 years in office. Just the opposite. His nearly unmatched leadership skill, extremely well chronicled in *From Moscow to Lausanne: Juan Antonio Samaranch Ten Years as IOC President*,[5] should reassure all that Olympic stewardship in the post-Samaranch era will be even more progressive and humane. But again, a rosier Olympic future is possible only if there is appropriate modification and change.

21 OBSERVATIONS FOR THE 21st-CENTURY OLYMPIC MOVEMENT

1. Avoid overextension; the Olympic agenda is already full to overflowing. The Olympic Tripartite must not become enmeshed in trying to solve humanity's perpetual agonies of hunger, disease, political and social injustice, and global racism and sexism.

2. Balance is everything to the future of the Olympic Movement. Commerce must be balanced by philanthropy, fluffy if important pageantry by every effort to get most of the world's great male and female athletes to the Olympic stadia.

3. Quality athletic performance from top to bottom is even more important than getting athletes from all 168 nations to the summer Olympic Games. I respectfully direct this recommendation to the IOC executive board: No athlete who is not among the top 100 performers in the world should be allowed to participate in a summer Olympic Games event.

4. May the Olympic leadership never (consciously or unwittingly) aspire to be among the Fortune 500. Olympic income is accumulated to be immediately directed toward Olympic "family" constituent members, nowhere else and for no other purpose.

5. It is my hope that sometime between the end of the 1996 Olympic Games and the beginning of the year 2001, the IOC will have accumulated enough money and invested it so wisely that it can then devote all of its considerable energy and intellect to other even more important enterprises.

6. For the collective good of all aspiring athletes, I should like to see in the next 6 years a new Olympic Charter rule that "No athlete may participate in more than two Olympic Games." I believe that this restriction would be no restriction at all, but rather a form of liberation, an emancipation from the specter of athletic gladiator to someone even more interesting.

7. There are too many medal-award ceremonies on any given day of the Olympic Games, too many interruptions in the flow of the all-important competitions. A single 45-minute ceremony in the "main" arena, dignified and symbolically beautiful, would more appropriately honor the winners.

8. The democratic momentum, already an established fact within the Movement—in the Olympic Tripartite—should be increased. More athletes need to be involved, and the magnetism of Mr. Samaranch and, hopefully, his successors should allow for expansion rather than restriction of the democratic process.[6]

9. I urge that a subcommittee of the IOC be "struck" and charged with writing a contingency plan for a "Permanent Site for the Winter and Summer Olympic Games." The IOC presently sits in the catbird seat, with dozens of cities desirous of hosting the Games. But it may not always be so in the 21st century.

10. Clearly, athletes on steroids will never know how good they really can be. I find unacceptable the *Toronto Star* editorial which broadly hinted that athletes should be free to do whatever they wish to themselves with needles or pills: "Let them all have heart attacks at $30,000 a race."[7] The best that sport federations, national Olympic committees, and the IOC can do is everlastingly remind

the athletes that their every action is a personal account of who and what they are and how they wish to be remembered. Over the next generation, most athletes' drug problems will be markedly reduced. I have *that* much faith in most of these young men and women, all over the world.

11. I hope for, I predict, and I urge that an evolutionary change of attitude regarding women's physical abilities and intellectual talents be encouraged in those countries of the world that have found such considerations unthinkable. As this change happens, the Olympic Tripartite's subtle but persistent efforts will result in a gradual worldwide increase in the number of women Olympians and female sport administrators.

12. I cannot emphasize enough the need for (a) an Olympic speakers' bureau on each of the six continents, and (b) the expansion of educational national Olympic academies, eventually to every country in the world. Speakers and academies should emphasize the need for ethics, internationalism, mutual respect, and as UNESCO called it, the "new culture" which affirms the primacy of the person over technology.[8]

13. Although it asks a great deal more of the Olympic leadership than of the larger world's leadership, I suggest that they always take the "moral high ground" on every difficult issue, never compromise, act with everlasting integrity, and avoid wrong answers and (even worse) "cheap answers."[9] Olympic leadership must itself be led by the dictum of Abraham Lincoln that we must "cultivate the moral world within us as assiduously and prodigiously as we have cultivated the physical world around us, that we may endure."[10]

14. In every way possible, the Olympic Games leadership must do a much better job of celebrating the honest triumph of the individual athlete. Doing this consistently will reduce ultranationalistic posturing and put the emphasis, the triumph, where it belongs—on the athlete.

15. I reaffirm a suggestion that originated long before my time: The IOC must divest the Olympic Games of those sports that are utterly antithetical to the democratic and pacific nature of the Movement. I leave it to the common sense and integral strength of the Programme Committee and the IOC to be wise enough to create a different Olympic Games agenda for the 21st century, one cleansed of those sports that are identified so strongly with the very rich or the military, and of those sports that, sirenlike, lead to confrontation, animosity, and subjective miscalculation.

16. Mundane as it may seem, the Olympic community must come to a clearer perception of its "reason for being," eliminate the motto *Citius, Altius, Fortius*, and substitute the Coubertin-Talbot exhortation: The important thing in the Olympic Games is not winning, but taking part. The essential thing in life is not conquering, but fighting well. To fight well means, of course, to embrace, to be consumed simultaneously by the spirits of competitive aggressiveness and of fair play. His Royal Highness, the Grand Duke of Luxembourg wrote that "fair play is the deliberate and constant refusal of victory at any price."[11]

17. All those connected with the Olympic Movement, inside and outside the sport venue, must cultivate an earnest optimism. The Olympic Games are not immortal and will some day "fade away." But for those like myself who believe they presently serve a high-minded purpose and can become much better, rational optimism will help *make* them better. When the highly successful Summer Olympic Games of 1956 were held in Australia (over the American Thanksgiving holiday, November-December), the *Melbourne Age* editor wrote, "There can be no perfect Games until there are perfect people, but we have watched a sincere attempt to achieve this human ideal."[12]

18. An independent committee of Olympic Games experts should be "struck" and after 3 years of intense study before, during, and after an Olympic festival, should write an "Evaluation Report" and widely distribute it within the Olympic community, especially to future Olympic Games organizers.[13]

19. Rather than limiting their zealousness and expertise to their particular sport, international sport federation administrators should broaden their technical, intellectual, ideological, and altruistic horizons. Such a new embracing of sport and personal philosophy will free them from grim parochialism. I like the comments of George E. Killian, president of the Federation Internationale de Basketball (FIBA):

> My goals are to make basketball the premier Olympic Games sport of the 21st century and through this great and democratic sport to make a contribution to the highest aims of the international Olympic movement.[14]

20. The International Olympic Committee will be exactly 100 years old in June 1994, and there will be a giant celebration in Paris and an international Olympic Congress. I suggest that not a single session, meeting, or presentation at this week-long celebration be devoted to Olympic business, Olympic marketing, Olympic entrepreneurship, media negotiations, or TOP-ISL-contracts and profits. Leave these

mundane though necessary Olympic topics for gatherings before or after this all-important recognition of the brilliant, if erratic, Baron Pierre de Coubertin.

21. With all the passion that I can muster, I urge all IOC members to adorn themselves in a Joseph's-coat of wisdom and, in 1993 or 1997, select a new president even wiser than Juan Antonio Samaranch. And while I'm at it, they (the IOC) should exercise a little more intelligence and elevate within the movement Mr. Samaranch's silent secretary, the efficient, loyal, and intelligent Annie Inchauspé.[15]

No amount of money can buy *true* loyalty. The Olympic Movement has the means to add to its cadre the very best technically trained people, but it must do so circumspectly with an eye for those who believe its philosophy and trust the direction in which the Movement is headed. The need for technical skill and personal constancy will be especially critical when Mr. Samaranch relinquishes his leadership. The Olympic Tripartite must focus on several extremely critical problems . . . and solve them *before* the century's end. To expand the Olympic Movement's interests and responsibilities in an exponential manner would be a serious error, for, as *Fortune* magazine said (and it ought to know), "If you try to be ready for everything, you could end up not being good at anything."[16] Loyalty, technical skill, and supportive influence for the sport federations, national Olympic committees, and the IOC must be actively solicited in an even more skillful manner than at present. Loyal, nonconformist thinkers are needed to balance out the wisdom and traditional conservatism of, let us say, IOC's Princess Royal, who told David Miller how important the forces of loyalty and old-fashioned sportsmanship are. "What I do best," she said, is "being a mediator and not a professional fence-sitter."[17]

Olympic boycotts are probably a thing of the past. Nations have concluded that the only effect of such actions is the injury they do to themselves and their own athletes. I was present at all three boycotted Olympic Games, and there seemed to be no reduction in their drama World and Olympic records were still broken, and there were the usual near-capacity crowds in the stadia. The Africans, Americans, Soviets, and Cubans learned to their chagrin that the Summer Olympic Games 1976 through 1988 got along quite well without them. None of them reckoned with what researcher Derick Hulme called the "IOC's fierce independence and that of its many NOCs [plus] the steadfast independence of the administrative apparatus of the Olympic Movement."[18]

The Olympic leadership is utterly without visible political power, and yet these past few years under Samaranch's leadership, it has gained significant influence, restrained and private. Eternal vigilance is and must continue to be the hallmark of the whole Olympic Movement if it is to make a real difference in helping the world avoid brutal frontal assault or volatile international conflicts. This same worldwide Olympic leadership must see the whole tapestry of life—politics and a great deal more—in order to play the role of a poor person's Sophocles who, Matthew Arnold said, "saw life steadily, and saw it whole." There are far too many people in the modern Olympic Movement who are unwilling to or incapable of imagining such global vision. They all must be invited to leave the Olympic Movement and be replaced by better equipped people. Olympic strategic thinkers and planners are needed, those men and women with focus and flexibility[19] who will lead the Movement and the Games into newer and better realms.

I have abiding faith in the *idea* of a near-perfect Olympic Games as a festival of elite sport, as a peace-filled gathering of the human race in a grand union of the beginning and end of life "through the endurance of affection, of trust, of friendship, and of love." The convergence of the Olympic laurel with Olympic gold need not be traumatic, but rather wholly natural. After all, idealism and pragmatism are not necessarily antithetical, just different. I've said throughout this book that balance is the key, the path to Olympian harmony and progress. But this course of prudence, of Grecian sophrosyne, does not appeal to everyone. The ebb and flow of Olympic history reveals inadequacies, problems created, said television journalist John Chancellor, "by drift and inattention." I have attempted to avoid such vacillation and substitute instead "work and dedication."[20] History tells us that 1000 A.D. was a special year, one in which millions of people believed they were "living on the brink of Apocalypse."[21] Such fears are less universal today. Instead, hard work, alertness, and the comingling of rationality and nonrationality will move us all smoothly past the millennium just as they will infuse the whole Olympic Movement with new life and purpose. If we do our duty to those we love, we need not worry. Sophocles's Antigone tells the man who has condemned her to death (her uncle and king), "It's not my nature to join in hating, but in loving."[22] Culture, science, and sport are part of "an artful tapestry" and, when sincere men and women sit at the loom, they make a small contribution to one and all, which is in reality a kind of immortality. Then we can allow ourselves to say that we have lived life according to our convictions and our hearts. It is what I have tried to do in this book.

Notes

1. Flor Isava Fonseca, letter to author, February 1991.

2. For an elaboration of this theme, see "Editors Preface" in Emilie Buckward and Ruth Roston, *This Sporting Life* (Minneapolis: Milkweed Editions, 1987). War is the number one arena of competition, according to the pair.

3. Morton Hunt, *The Compassionate Beast: What Science Is Discovering About the Humane Side of Humankind* (New York: Morrow, 1990), 62.

4. Dorothy Thompson, quoted in Peter Kirth, *American Cassandra: The Life of Dorothy Thompson* (Boston: Little, Brown, 1990), 330.

5. Marie-Hélène Roukhadzé, Ed., *From Moscow to Lausanne: Juan Antonio Samaranch Ten Years as IOC President* (Lausanne: CIO, 1990).

6. Longtime loyal member of the international Olympic family, Richard W. Palmer (secretary-general of the British Olympic Association) told me that "nothing is more important than balance and representative democracy within the Tripartite" (Palmer, interview with author, in Tokyo, 14 September 1990). Historian Uriel Simri in Israel wrote that "the 8-year term of the IOC president represents an open-door for too much power. Reduce it to 4" (Simri, letter to author, 23 September 1989). Michael T. Harrigan, author of the very important United States Amateur Sports Act of 1978, told me that his greatest complaint against the IOC is "their frequent indecisiveness, arbitrariness, ambivalence, and timidity in the implementation of their own rules" (Harrigan, conversation with author, 8 January 1990).

7. Two essays worth reading are Edward Grayson, "An IOC Decision That Should Be Challenged," *London Times*, 16 February 1991, 26, and David Miller, "A Sport on a Tightrope of Credibility," *London Times*, 11 January 1991, 33.

8. *The World by the Year 2000* (Paris: UNESCO, 1987), 12. Also Gilbert Allardyce, "Toward World History: American Historians and the Coming of the World History Course," *Journal of World History, 1*, Spring 1990, 23-76.

9. Hanna H. Gray (president, University of Chicago) in R.W. Kidder, ed., *An Agenda for the 21st Century* (Cambridge, MA: MIT Press, 1987), 64.

10. Abraham Lincoln, quoted by George Will in Cameron Barr's essay "George Will Weighs In," *Christian Science Monitor*, 21 February 1991, 12.

11. "H.R.H. the Grand Duke of Luxembourg, Doyen of the IOC," *Olympic Review, 277*, November 1990, 510.

12. The Age quotation is reproduced in Andre Laguerre, "Down a Road Called Liberty," *Sports Illustrated, 5*, 17 December 1956, 19.

13. The Seoul Olympic Organizing Committee (SLOOC), with authority from the IOC, formed such a committee; an evaluation report was written and was given to (among others) the Barcelona '92 organizing committee. I was on the review committee and had the unenviable task of writing an essay on "the ambiance inside the Olympic stadia and in the city of Seoul."

14. George E. Killian, letter to author, 10 January 1991.

15. In a letter to me, 26 February 1991, Ms. Inchauspé, winner of the *Chevalier du Mérite* from the French ministry of youth and sports, shared something of her background, her skills, and her unbounded devotion to the principles undergirding the Movement that she served as Mr. Samaranch's only private secretary during his long tenure:

> My feet have hardly touched ground since the IOC Session in Tokyo . . . as I accompany the President on his innumerable trips . . . I was born in the southwest of France where I followed my studies before travelling to England and Spain in order to gain linguistic experience. From there I came to Switzerland to complete my studies in Lausanne . . . My hobbies include running, as you well know*, tennis, cycling and badminton. I enjoy my life in Switzerland where I particularly appreciate the peacefulness and beauty of the country.

> [* I had intercepted her in the lobby of Tokyo's Takanawa Hotel in the early morning as she was about to run into the teeth of an early developing typhoon. A few moments later, IOC's Anita DeFrantz also departed for a "quiet" run.]

16. *Fortune, 123*, 31 December 1990, 77.

17. David Miller, "A Princess Loyal to the Olympic Ideal," *London Times*, 18 October 1989, 54.

18. Derick L. Hulme, Jr., "The Viability of International Sport as a Political Weapon: The 1980 U.S. Olympic Boycott," unpublished PhD dissertation, Fletcher School of Law and Diplomacy, Tufts University, 1988, 334, 346.

19. The phrase *focus and flexibility* is not mine, but comes from Ronald Henkoff's essay, "How to Plan for 1995," *Fortune, 122*, 31 December 1990, 70.

20. John Chancellor, *Peril and Promise: A Commentary on America* (New York: Harper & Row, 1990), 131.

21. Richard Erdoes's subtitle of his *A.D. 1000* is "Living on the Brink of Apocalypse" (New York: Harper & Row, 1988).

22. *Sophocles: Antigone*, Andrew Brown, Ed., Trans. (Wiltshire, England: Aris & Phillips, Ltd., 1987), 65.

Photo Credits

Chapter 1 Pierre de Coubertin. Photo courtesy of Robert K. Barney.

Chapter 2 The 1967 Olympic torch ceremony at Olympia, Greece, site of the ancient games. Photo courtesy of George Dales.

Chapter 3 Czechoslovakia's Emil Zatopek, right, leads France's Alain Mimoun (607) and Germany's Herbert Schade, left, into the home stretch of the 5,000-meter run in the 1952 Olympic Games. Photo courtesy of *Track and Field News*, Mountain View, CA.

Chapter 4 Bob Beamon of the United States sets the 1968 Olympic long jump record of 29 feet, 2-1/4 inches. Beamon's record held until the USA's Mike Powell leaped 29 feet, 4-1/2 inches in 1991. Photo by the Adidas News Bureau.

Chapter 5 Athletes gather during the opening ceremonies of the 1988 Winter Olympic Games in Calgary, Canada. Photo by A. Riethausen, courtesy of the International Olympic Committee.

Chapter 6 1976 Olympic champion Shun Fujimoto exhibits grace and strength on the still rings. Photo by John A. Lucas.

Chapter 7 Television has helped to increase the popularity and financial status of the Olympic Games. Photo courtesy of the National Broadcasting Company, Inc.

Chapter 8 International Olympic Commitee president Juan Antonio Samaranch awards speedskater Jens-Uwe Mey of West Germany the gold medal for his performance in the 500-meter race at the 1988 Winter Games. Photo by A. Riethausen, courtesy of the International Olympic Committee.

Chapter 9 The laurel wreath symbolizes Olympic success and victory. Photo courtesy of George Dales.

Chapter 10 The use of performance enhancing drugs by athletes was a highly publicized issue during the 1988 Summer Games in Seoul, Korea. Illustration courtesy of the Bulgarian Olympic Committee.

Chapter 11 Horace Ashenfelter of the USA clears a hurdle during his gold-medal winning performance in the 1952 Olympic steeplechase. Photo courtesy of The Pennsylvania State University.

Chapter 12 Gold-medal winning sprinter Florence Griffith-Joyner combined incredible speed and strength with trend-setting running suits and a flashy image in becoming one of the best-known female Olympians of all time. Photo by A. Riethausen, courtesy of the International Olympic Committee.

Chapter 13   International Olympic Committee president Juan Antonio Sama-ranch and his wife, Maria Teresa Salisachs-Rowe Samaranch. Photo courtesy of the International Olympic Committee.

Chapter 14   Barcelona organizers were unsuccessful in their attempts to play host to the Summer Games in 1924, 1936, and 1972. But renewed efforts paid off when the 1992 Summer Games were awarded to the Spanish city. Photo courtesy of the Comité Olimpico Organizador de Barcelona '92.

Chapter 15   Dr. Carl Diem of Germany was one of the founders of the International Olympic Academy. Photo courtesy of Liselotte Diem.

Chapter 16   Hans Erni's Olympic art represents the essence of sport art. Illustration courtesy of Hans Erni.

Chapter 17   The citizens of Atlanta, USA, celebrate capturing the opportunity to play host to the Olympic's Centennial celebration in 1996. Photo courtesy of the Atlanta Committee for the Olympic Games.

Chapter 18   The face of the Olympic Games will continue to change as we head into the 21st century. Photo courtesy of Robert K. Barney.

Index

Numbers in italics indicate the subject is mentioned in a footnote on that page.